THE LONG EMBRACE

THE LONG EMBRACE

Contemporary Poets
on the Long Poems
of Philip Levine

edited by

Christopher Buckley

Lynx House Press

Spokane, Washington

Acknowledgments

Christopher Buckley's "Philip Levine's 'Belief'" first appeared in *South Florida Poetry Review*, 1991, and in *Appreciations: Selected Reviews, Views & Interviews 1975-2000*, Mille Grazie Press, 2001.

Peter Everwine's "On 'Silent in America'" reprinted by permission of the Literary Estate of Peter Everwine, with thanks to Bill Broder.

Richard Jackson's essay, "Philip Levine and the Extensive Poem: 'Jewish Graveyards, Italy'" is a revised version of an essay that appeared in *The AWP Chronicle*, 2013.

Mark Jarman's essay "'Letters for the Dead': What It Is Without You" first appeared in *Miramar No 4*, 2016.

Paul Mariani's "The Song Old Rooms Sing: A Poem With No Ending" first appeared in an early version in *The American Journal of Poetry*, May 2018.

FIRST EDITION

Cover Photo: Frances Levine.
Book Design: Christine Holbert.

LYNX HOUSE PRESS books are distributed by the University of Washington Press, 4333 Brooklyn Avenue NE, Seattle, WA 98195-9570.

LIBRARY OF CONGRESS CATALOGING-IN-PUBLICATION DATA

Cataloging-In-Publication Data is available from the Library of Congress.

ISBN: 978-0-89924-171-5.

I hold it and bend to the names
and say them as slowly as I can.
Full majestic, vanished names
that fill my mouth and go out
into the densely yellowed air
of this great valley and dissolve
as even the sea dissolves beating
on a stone shore or as love does
when the beloved turns to stone
or dust or water . . .

—Philip Levine

Contents

Preface

THIS PROJECT BEGAN more than ten years ago. Many contemporary poets were eager to contribute to it, knowing the importance of Philip Levine's poetry, and especially acknowledging that his was a singular achievement when it came to the writing of the long poem.

I had known Philip Levine as mentor and friend for over thirty-five years. As a young poet and teacher I was blessed to share an office with Phil for the two years I taught at Fresno State University. Years subsequent, teaching at various universities, Phil visited to give readings, most often and very generously for much less than the going rate. In 1989 at Bread Loaf, we began working on a volume in the University of Michigan Press' *Under Discussion* series, *On the Poetry of Philip Levine, Stranger to Nothing* (1991). I'd been a fan since the first book of his I read, *They Feed They Lion,* in the early 1970s at San Diego State University; my first teacher, Glover Davis, a former student of Phil's in the '60s at Fresno State, had ordered it for our workshop.

I soon became a collector of his books, and was thrilled when Phil gave me a copy of *On the Edge*—the Second Press paperback reprint of his first letterpress book from Kim Merker's Stonewall Press in Iowa—when he was in San Diego for a reading and workshop. The poem I found most compelling in *On the Edge* was the long poem "Sierra Kid," a *tour de force* syllabic poem. I ordered *Not This Pig* from the bookstore and received a copy of the original Wesleyan edition in which "Silent in America" captured my imagination and admiration. As the years went by I began to discover, with almost every book, another amazing and unique long poem, from "New Season" and "No One Remembers" to "Letters for the Dead" and "A Poem with no Ending." I was at the Dodge Festival in New Jersey in 1996 when Phil read all of "A Walk with Tom Jefferson" for his reading under the big tent and it held the audience spellbound. I still have my copy of *Poetry* from September 1990 with the first appearance of "Burned," Phil's approximately six-hundred-twenty-line poem contained in *What Work Is.* It is one of Levine's most realistic and yet luminous poems, and in twenty sections Levine examines his life and the industrial lives of others in Dantesque overlays. It is actual, experiential as well as archetypal: "I have to go back into the forge room / at Chevy where Lonnie still calls / out his commands to Sweet Pea and Packy / and stare into the fire . . ."—for Levine knew

1

that you must descend into hell and confront and recover the shades before you ascend into the light. It is a brilliant physical poem of detail and vignette that leads to a final metaphysical acceptance.

Several more important long poems followed. Levine was a master at the sustained form, in many strategies. I had engaged an impressive list of contemporary poets, each writing on a significant long poem. The proposal was accepted by a major university press, and Phil agreed to support the book despite the fact that the original poems could not, for the obvious reasons of exorbitant permission fees, be reprinted with the essays. But then for reasons never discovered, the editor at the press kept not sending the contract she had promised. Each month I emailed asking where the contract was and each time was told it would be sent that week? This went on for months, and I never received an explanation.

After so much time, Phil changed his mind about the project—mainly, I think, from our inability to reprint the poems—and I had to withdraw the book; something like eight months has gone by waiting for the contract? Shortly thereafter, Phil would be appointed Poet Laureate of the U.S.—a really substantial opportunity for that press and for readers of poetry bungled for reasons unknown.

Years now after Phil's passing, it is still a compelling fact that he is the contemporary master of the long poem, that his mix of voice, and detailed grit of daily working life—combined with his compassion for the dignity of the individual and his secular metaphysical perception and imagination—are unequaled. I have been fortunate that the majority of the original contributors have agreed to write for this volume—fortunate as well to have added poets new to the project. This then is a tribute, an appreciation and testament to his exceptional vision and invention in the writing of the contemporary long poem—no one to equal him in the last sixty years.

The *Michigan Quarterly Review*, in its summer 1997 issue published a wonderful essay by Phil, "Two Journeys." It can also be found in *So Ask*. Very modestly, Phil offers his view as to what his life's work has accomplished, an achievement that is especially, we feel, exemplified in his long poems:

> But the art I have pursued for better or worse for over fifty years is poetry, and I have found it an enterprise worthy of a human life, and I haven't the least notion if anything I have written will in the hearts of others outlive me. Why, you might well ask, with that knowledge do I call it an enterprise

worthy of a human life? Because I have been part of something far larger than myself; I have been part of the attempt to verbalize as precisely as possible what it has meant to live through the great depression, the horrors of World War II, the fiasco of anticommunism, the long, painful failed struggle for racial justice, and wind up in old age in a country gone to ruin through the greed of capitalism with a technology that can take us to the moon while our streets are stained by the lives of the poor and the homeless, the present world of Microsoft, unfettered pollution, the epidemic of murderous drugs. . . . I have been part of the generation of Adrienne Rich, John Ashbery, Galway Kinnell, W.S. Merwin, Robert Creeley, Anthony Hecht, Denise Levertov, Etheridge Knight, Sylvia Plath, Allen Ginsberg, Gary Snyder: we have done our best to capture the century in verse. We have told America, and the rest of the world should it care to listen, what it's been like living through this age. We have been useful.

Our hope for this book then is that the appreciations expand and illuminate a reader's appreciation of Philip Levine's long poems. We trust that a reader will be inspired to return to the poems in the individual volumes, or in the *New Selected Poems,* and we hope in a *Collected Poems* soon to come.

—*Christopher Buckley*

3

Introduction

A POPULAR ON-LINE ENCYCLOPEDIA offers a definition of the Long Poem that sounds very much like a tautology: "The Long Poem is a literary genre including all poetry of considerable length." Given the range and variety of examples in the late 20th century and early 21st, this umbrella definition is serviceable. While the genre can be traced deep into literary history—Homer's *Iliad and Odyssey, Beowulf,* Milton's *Paradise Lost,* Wordsworth's *Prelude*—in more recent times we have Whitman's *Song of Myself* (1855), Pound's *Cantos,* and William Carlos Williams' *Paterson,* and in some sense Berryman's *Dream Songs.* However beyond the deep past and the Romantic traditional book-length association with the genre, we begin to see the range and hybrid parameters of the long poem emerge in the modern, in the work of T.S. Eliot, most notably "The Waste Land," "The Love Song of J. Alfred Prufrock," and "Four Quartets"— all examples with various strategies and speakers and with which readers of poetry and literature are long familiar.

In the past, a poet was often judged by a major long poem, a tradition that manifested itself in epic, narrative, and mythological, modes. In the second half of the 20th century, we see fewer long poems, especially book-length poems. There have been a number of poetic "sequences" in contemporary poetry, Galway Kinnells' *The Book of Nightmares,* for example; but given the predominant lyric mode of the last fifty or sixty years, the long poem has been less in evidence and certainly has not been as celebrated. When the long poem does surface, it is difficult to attach a discrete definition to it; it is a hybrid in form—not necessarily narrative, rarely or if ever epic—and it can be four pages, fourteen, or forty. Ginsberg's "Howl" comes immediately to mind, and a good bit of Kenneth Patchen. One characteristic of a contemporary long poem is that it is driven by thematic ambition, one that takes up a substantial concept or cause, one whose drama and incident call a great deal of social, political, and even metaphysical order into question; it can often be a rant, and has, in most instances, both bulk and gravitas.

Practically, for contemporary poetry, a poem is a "long poem" when its length develops and expands the theme and structure of the poem. *The New Princeton Encyclopedia of Poetry & Poetics,* edited by Alex Preminger and T. V. F. Brogan, 1993, is helpful in defining the thematic focus of the modern Long Poem:

Ezra Pound's 1909 definition of the epic as "the speech of a nation through the mouth of one man" points as well to the central tension which animates the 20th century long poem. Typically, the modern long poem attempts to identify and synthesize the various voices and details of a culture or "tribe," but, unlike the traditional epic, finds itself, "in a society no longer unified by a single, generally accepted code of values . . . justifying its argument by the direct appeal of the author's own experiences and emotions" (*Bernstein). Such an appeal brings about both an inevitable foregrounding of the poet as "hero" and an almost ritual acknowledgment of limitation that follows when the desire to speak for a culture stands revealed as a drive toward self-portraiture as well. This tension also generates the technical innovations for which these poems are noted; if no single narrative exists to explain a culture, then it follows that such discontinuous yet accumulative forms as cantos, letters, catalogs, songs, notes, passages, dreams, or journal entries might be useful in tracking a repeatedly engaged, non-guaranteed movement toward an explanatory tale. Individual cantos or letters themselves often become strikingly tentative arrangements of the shifting, resistant materials of a culture.

It is in light of this appraisal from the Princeton Encyclopedia especially that the long poems of Philip Levine can be seen in the forefront of contemporary poetry. Philip Levine was winner of the Pulitzer Prize in Poetry, two National Book Awards, two Guggenheim Fellowships, three NEA grants, The Lenore Marshall Poetry Prize, The National Book Critics Circle Award, The Ruth Lily Prize, and the Wallace Stevens Award among many prestigious honors in poetry. In 2006 he was elected a chancellor of the Academy of American Poets, and in 2011 was appointed Poet Laureate of the United States.

This collection of essays focuses then not only on the fact that Levine is one of our foremost poets of the last sixty years, but moreover that he is a master and foremost practitioner of the long poem in our time. No recent poet has written as many exceptional long poems as Levine, and in doing so, developed a range to the personal voice that testifies in support of a culture and the individuals who have built that culture. Levine invented as many original strategies for the long poem as his subjects demanded, and they reinforce visions with a

*Michael Andre Bernstein. *The Tale of the Tribe: Ezra Pound and the Modern Verse Epic.* Princeton University Press, 1980.

variety of approaches that indict the political, personal, and cultural, saying freshly and uniquely—narratively, deductively, lyrically, paratactically—what it has been like to exist as a working, thinking human being in the 20th and early 21st centuries. Philip Levine died in 2015.

One of the major features of this book is that the appreciations are all written by poets who are significant voices in contemporary American poetry and who follow in the tradition that Randall Jarrell called for regarding critical response to poetry needing to be written by practicing poets. Senior poets such as Peter Everwine and Paul Mariani have contributed to this project, as have many "mid-career" poets (quickly becoming senior) such as Dorianne Laux, Mark Jarman, Kelly Cherry, David St. John, Kate Daniels, Kathy Fagan, and more.

While editing *On The Poetry of Philip Levine: Stranger to Nothing* (1991), several poets commented to me that there was a need for clear critical prose on poetry written by poets that addressed the work itself instead of promoting the theoretical discourse of an academic industry. While these essays are of course analytical, they are not theory-driven. They address how and why a Levine long poem realizes its vision, how the virtues of the strategies—relative to themes, vision, and humanity—are achieved. Our poets / writers speak to where exactly they see the poem in the development of Levine's career and style, his themes and vision. For example, with *Sweet Will* (1985) there is a pronounced shift in tone and thematic development away from earlier work, subsequent books shifting from a fierce witnessing to often more multi-dimensional visionary or metaphysical resolution. The rhythms are often more reflective and pensive; there is more final recovery. All of our poets know the work and most knew Levine; and so there is often the bonus, as a way into the essay, of memoir-like reflections, which amplify the accessibility for a reader as well as the insight into composition, function, and thematic directions.

As early as his first book, *On the Edge* (1963) we have "Sierra Kid," a long narrative lyric that is a *tour de force* of syllabic strategies embracing one of Levine's main themes—the dignity and struggle of the individual—as well as environmental concerns adumbrating a political movement that would not surface for a decade or more. Not long after, in *Not This Pig*, (1968) Levine gives us "Silent in America," a major long poem which not only again showcases his formal syllabic mastery, but a poem that speaks with wit and realism, in the language of the tribe called for by William Carlos Williams, in support of the dispossessed. Here, we find his attachment to and development from Whitman, especially with the epigraph "Vivas for those who have failed." This is an eight-page poem in which Levine characteristically stands shoulder to shoulder with the disenfranchised, lost in the suburbs, "drifters in the drifting crowd" who would arrive "late / and tired, beyond the false lights / of Pasadena / where the living are silent / in America."

From that point on Levine's voice and vision continued to develop and mature with a new approach for each new poem in each new book. A compelling list of major long poems emerged over the decades, not least among them "Letters for the Dead"; the autobiographical "1933"; the unique paratactic structure of "A Poem With No Ending"; the heightened urban elegy of "A Walk With Tom Jefferson"; the apocalyptic vision of "Burned"; and the inventive sonnet sequence of "Naming." There are over twenty-five significant long poems in his eighteen full-length collections of poetry. *The Long Embrace* offers critical appreciations of twenty-one of Levine's major long poems as well as their important contribution to American poetry.

Our title derives from Richard Jackson's essay—"The Long Embrace: Philip Levine's Longer Poems"—which he wrote for *On The Poetry of Philip Levine: Stranger to Nothing* in the University of Michigan Press' *Under Discussion* series. The term "Long Poem" is used in a contemporary and serviceable sense as opposed to an historical / traditional usage, much the way an editor of a current literary journal or press might use it. "Long Poem" then is used as it has been for the last sixty years—designating not only poems whose de facto length exceeds the one to two page lyric, but those poems whose avowed ambition in theme and strategy functions far beyond a sustained lyric moment, beyond the witnessing of a single dramatic event or meditation on a particular memory, irrespective of the fact that the poems may run four to five pages, or more.

Thus, not included are poems that, while they might extend for a few pages, remain with a single strategy and narrative, travel in one direction only. The shorter of the long poems included are those that work inclusively, symphonically via theme, variation, and recapitulation. The Long Poem movement / strategy—especially in the hand of master like Levine—makes several moves, includes many disparate events, uniting a variety of experiences into a singular vision. A hallmark earlier example is "New Season" with its poignant time and emotional shifts; or strikingly the poem "Burned" uniting the workers of the automobile industry in Detroit to a Dantean and Wordsworthian undercarriage of meaning to make a whole, to witness the industrial "burning" of America and the individual.

What the poems in this collection testify to is that especially and significantly in his long poems, no poet of the last sixty years has written with the gravity, scope, inventiveness, tenacity, and brilliance of Philip Levine.

—Christopher Buckley

PETER EVERWINE

On "Silent in America"

PRELUDE: "MY POETS" APPEARED in Phil's first book, *On the Edge,* in 1963. It is one of the few poems from the book he included in his *Selected Poems.* The poem's setting is on "the eve of Thanksgiving," but he begins the poem by listing four un-named poet-friends who are not writing (I am one of them)— in other words, we are "silent" (my word, not Phil's) while the nation "calls for its soul / calls for its blood and belly, / and we, we number the five / fingers of our fists and try / anything to stay alive / without poems." It is only at the conclusion of the poem that Phil—for surely the speaker can be no one else—introduces an unseen William Blake "as a dark child" who cries out that the nation went dreamless until " 'I came with 27 words / and a hand . . . to make you America.'" The poem is both a testimony to Phil's great belief in the transformative power and obligation of the poet and the frustration in not finding in the nation "something to love / and to celebrate." It reminds me of W. C. Williams: "It is difficult / to get the news from poems / yet men die miserably every day / for the lack / of what is found there." The subject was clearly in Phil's mind and I see "My Poets" as a significant step toward "Silent in America", which he will publish in his second book, *Not This Pig,* in 1968.

• • •

It must have been 1961 when Phil flew from Fresno, CA to Iowa City to attend the festivities associated with the publication of *Midland,* an anthology of Iowa Workshop poets. The celebration lasted several days. At one of the last evenings—and here I have to rely on second-hand reports, since I was not present at the time—some members of an Iowa athletic team crashed the party and matters got ugly. Drawn by friends into the melee, Phil was pushed to the floor and kicked. By the time I reached the hospital, his broken jaw was being tightly wired, and it was in that condition that he returned to Fresno.

"Silent in America"

Like many modern long poems, "Silent in America" is divided into sections or scenes, VIII in this case. The technique is cinematic, allowing a variety of separate but coherent scenes to develop the dramatic movement of the poem. Perhaps more important, Phil decided on using syllabic lines, in general, largely composed of 7, 5 or 3 syllables in various combinations. No one, I think, can really "hear" syllabic lines in English—hence the often general belief that Phil was writing prose broken into lines. But the syllabic line is of great value to a poet. It provides a rigorous discipline and variety for his composition, and by using odd syllables he frees himself from the duple and triple rhythms that dominate verse in English.

During his year at Stanford (1957-1958), studying with Yvor Winters, Phil had been exposed to the virtues of using syllabics ("My Poets", for example, is written completely in 7 syllable lines). They provided him with two enduring principles of language: First, do not write in "the language of princes"; second, a hope that no one would ever read one of his poems and say, "Wow! What a vocabulary!" Words were to be transparent, a clarity through which the importance of the poem could be reached; if anything, to disappear rather than draw attention to themselves. Syllabics provided Phil with a "voice" and a rhythm of speech that allowed his work to reach its distinctive status in American poetry.

The Poem by Sections

Sections I & II

The first two sections present a contrast. Section I is a social gathering after Phil's return to Fresno. People "mouth / to each other, and the wind / answers them. . . . The poet, his jaw locked, goes "unnoticed among men" and, unspeaking, "discovers a foreignness / that is native." That is, one discovers the banality of social communication, of language as we spend it freely and to little use beyond chit-chat. We live among others like strangers, trailing our lives as approximations. Section II becomes more intimate and in a natural setting: the poet alone at evening, an almond tree, sprinklers sweeping into dark and light. The stanzas are quatrains, more lyrical, using varied rhymes, but the first line is in 7 syllables. The poet desperately wants to speak, his "jaws ache for release. . . . For words, or for what lies beyond words The eternal metaphysical enigmas end the section: the need "to remember / who I am / what I am, and / why I am here."

Sections III & IV

Section III, written in stanzas of 5 and 7 syllables, takes place in a medical office. Dr. Leo examines the "white-on-black / map of my throat." The starkness of the examination is set apart from the previous need for speech, a reduction to physical terms, an objective matter of healing that has little bearing on the great necessity for speech that has been at the center of this poem. The Dr. "is an existentialist / with no faith in facts." Section IV seems to be a reaction not only to the medical exam but to all the frustrations encountered in the previous sections The poet returns to being "Fresno's / dumb bard, America's last / hope. . . . It is an angry turn, bitter and self-accusatory: "I am everything / that is dishonest, / everything under the sun." We seem to be left in a baffled hopelessness.

Section V

I have not commented sufficiently on Phil's variety and shifts in stanzaic forms while using syllabic lines, but lengthy quotes would be necessary. Now, in a six-line stanza, the poem seems to reach—almost reach—an equilibrium. The poet rises by the natural rhythm of the sun. he assumes his name, stands "in the clouded presence of / the things I observe." Natural and materialistic laws are in operation, and yet "I have not found peace. . . . "What is it that moves / when it's still, and strikes me dumb / when it speaks / of being alive." Beyond physics, beyond language, what?

Section VI

This section contains the weakest, least-nuanced writing in the whole poem. We descend into a nightmare: a demon, little Bobby, who is an incarnation of inexhaustible appetite and infantile gratification, pursues and seemingly overwhelms the poet.

Is it a recap of the Iowa experience? A commentary on our capacity for the monstrous? A follow up to the belief we are only animals unless guided by something like a sense of spiritual or a common decency and humanity, something beyond the coiled snakes of the primitive brain? Perhaps only the next section makes clearer the reason for including this scene.

Section VII

This section is among the most beautiful, eloquent and heartbreaking poetry that Phil ever wrote. I don't see how anyone with an ear cannot hear Phil's syllabics move into the great swell and under-current of a soliloquy fit for The

Globe Theatre, even though "The great night is half / over and the stage is dark. . . . It is the first section in which Phil clearly addresses a public outside of himself, and in which he announces his desire to speak for those who will become the future subjects of his poetry: the common laborers of Detroit, the ugly, "the used and the unused / those who had courage / and those who quit—" The previous section of the poem makes better sense now, since the poem reaches for community rather than the self. But it is heartbreaking to hear him say "surely I have failed." And to know that each life remains "private and sealed."

Section VIII

In the conclusion of the poem, Henri Coullete, "the bad Baudelaire" of "My Poets" sits with Phil in a bar. Archimbault is a secret agent from Henri's first book, *The War of the Secret Agents.* Among other things, the poem is about betrayals, the failure of innocence, ambiguities, even codes—those most esoteric and private systems of language. If "Archimbault is near", then so is his world and one that Phil knows. It is at this point that Phil declares "Let me have / the courage to live / as fictions live, proud, careless / unwilling to die." We are invited to walk with the poets "beyond the false lights / of Pasadena / where the living are silent / in America." It is a fade-out into what seems like an elegy.

GLOVER DAVIS

On "Silent in America"

PHILIP LEVINE'S LONG POEM, "Silent in America," deals with the problem of poetic identity in a social and political context sometimes either indifferent or somewhat hostile to the value of this great literary genre. The poet who desires to assert himself authentically within the American context, Levine suggests, must be a witness and a speaker, despite the inevitable failure to be heard. Hence the epigraph to the poem quotes Whitman: "Vivas for those who have failed." To succeed in our capitalist society has too often involved the amassing of wealth and the accompanying power at the expense of aesthetic and spiritual values. The poet who would express these values with language and speech encounters difficulties peculiar to our endangered democracy. And this long poem in eight sections, each section with its own lyrical integrity, insists on the importance of those whose voices often might be ignored. This theme of the dignity of the common man which threads through American poetry, beginning most notably with Whitman, is taken up in the contemporary late twentieth century context by Philip Levine.

Levine's personal and aesthetic concerns were made relevant in the classrooms at Fresno State College where those of us who took his classes listened to this charismatic and inspired teacher of poetry. Embedded in his lessons regarding the literary construction of poems were ethical and moral teachings. He repeatedly enjoined us: "One must never lie." And "what we say should seem real and true." In such an atmosphere, it's unsurprising that some of us decided we would also be poets. Until that time I didn't much like the poems we had studied in high school including Longfellow, Whittier etc., though I always wanted to be a writer, having written sports stories for *The Santa Cruz Sentinel*. So when I arrived at Fresno State, I had not focused on poetry. But Levine gave us an example and a vision of something worthy of our best energies. He demanded excellence from us, and he got it from students like me who had barely achieved entrance into this state college. A number of us began to write with energy and dedication and published our poems in important journals. As a result of Phil's rigor and encouragement, we were awarded writing fellowships to the University of Iowa's Writer's Workshop, where I began studying in the Fall of 1964.

At Iowa I took a course in typography from Harry Duncan, the much-admired owner of the Cummington Press. Harry had designed and produced some very important books, books by Robert Lowell, William Carlos Williams, Wallace Stevens and others. He taught us how the design of a book could enhance the effects of its poems. Wanting to do something to demonstrate my gratitude for Philip Levine's teaching and help, I made the production of a booklet of "Silent In America" my typography project. Written sometime in the early 1960's, one or two sections had been published in *The North American Review*, but this whole long poem had not been published anywhere in its entirety. (Phil would go on to include it in his second book *Not This Pig*, published in 1968.)

And so I set about memorizing the California job case so that my hand could go to the requisite letter without looking. This was something like typing. I did this over fifty years ago and I am not sure what typeface I used but it must have been a classical typeface with sharp, clear lines and no flowers fluting out of capitals. I think I used Hosho, an excellent, handmade Japanese paper. I must use memory here because I no longer have a single copy of this booklet which I naively lent to students in my first year of teaching. I gave half of my copies to Levine and sold another quarter of them to the bookstore to pay for the Hosho.

As I proceeded with this project, I could almost feel the letters deeply pressed into the page and loved what I learned about this kind of craftsmanship. Even more significant for me as a student poet was what I learned as well from Phil's skillful employment of syllabic meters in this poem.

Levine had studied with Yvor Winters at Stanford, and Winters at that time was encouraging his students to use syllabic meter, a meter in which only syllables are counted. In syllabic meter, no stresses would be counted as they are in accentual meter, no metrical accents counted as they are in accentual syllabics. At the time I was setting "Silent in America" into letterpress, Phil was still early in his career, having published his first book in 1963.

Levine would soon begin his transition to free verse with enumeration, phrasal repetitions and anaphora—which would give us some of his most powerful poems such as "They Feed They Lion," "The Poem Circling Hamtramck, Michigan All Night in Search of You," "To Cipriano, in the Wind" and others. But from the beginning he understood the latent possibilities of formal, poetic composition and might have agreed at that time with William Butler Yeats who claimed, "In measurement began our might."

And so he begins "Silent in America" with a seven syllable line, the classical line for syllabics:

Since I no longer speak I
go unnoticed among men;
greeted occasionally
with a stiff wave, I am seen
aslant as one sees a pane

of clear glass, reflecting both
what lies before and behind
in a dazzle of splendid
approximations. They mouth
to each other, and the wind
answers them . . .

His syllabic compositions, though they may not resonate as deeply in memory as accentuals or accentual syllabics, give the poem a sense of visual order. His choice of syllabic compositions also gave him something to work against and at times engender materials which would not otherwise have entered the poem. The syllabic count and the shape and stationing of lines changes from section to section to section and this not only provides variety but allows for slightly different qualities of feeling. In Section I, for example, there is more narrative, embedded in long, six-line stanzas with rhymes, some of which are only slant or partial. And this first section with its long stanzas each enjambing into the following stanza is very close to stichic composition.

Then in Section II, Levine composes syllabic quatrains; the rhymes are more assertive. The effect, by way of contrast, is almost lyrical. Levine gives us the following:

Sometimes on especially
Warm evenings I
take a card chair out under
the almond tree
and catching the last light, speak
to myself without
words. I try to catch what is
behind my throat,
without words, all that exists
behind and before.

In Section I, Levine begins with one of the major themes of the poem, the difficulty of being heard and even being clearly seen as a poet. There is in this section and in other sections the sense of isolation and the need to empathet-ically connect with other human beings: the poet resides "in the far corners of rooms," his tongue "captive," accompanied by "One woman / hearing me grunt for breath, sits / by my side in a green dress, / her hands cupped in the valley / of her life. She would receive / my sympathy and in my / eyes sees— God knows what she sees / in my eyes. Let them have / all they find under the sky."

In Section II, the focus shifts to the poet's almost desperate effort to speak "words that will say anything." Ceaselessly trying to "catch what is behind my throat," the poet finally forces himself "to remember / who I am, what I am, and / why I am here." The poet's search for why the words won't come leads him to the wry scene depicted in Section III, the shortest section, where Dr. Leo, pointing at the x-ray image of the poet's throat, dismisses him: "Look here, Philip, no damage." The poet must give up trying to find answers in the doctor's office, a man he deems "is an existentialist / with no faith in facts."

Section IV announces a shift in the tone of the poem. Here is the strongest echo of Whitman, the clearest statement of the poet's realization of his own place in American poetry: "I am Fresno's / dumb bard, America's last / hope, sheep in sheep's clothing. . . ." It's significant that Levine uses the word "bard," which connects him to a long and rich tradition of poets who compose epics, poems that embody the values and heroic traditions of the culture. This sense of having found a significant place is strengthened in Section V: "I rise, dress / assume my name . . . The poet declares, "I have not found peace, / but I have found I am where / I am by / being only there, / by standing / in the cloud-ed presence of / the things I observe." Despite the difficulty of speaking and being heard, the poet stands and witnesses what he is given to see. He declares the specificity of the places, situations, and people in his lived experience. His task is to be present, to witness, however unclearly, "the clouded presence" of what he observes.

Section VI seems to deal with the destructive distractions of sexuality, his "squat demon / my little Bobby, jumping up / and down, demanding wom-en". In an intensely personal examination of the divided self, Phil finds his voice in his desire to escape the demands of the flesh: "Knowing he would master me, / I turned to you: "Levine," / I called softly, and called you / again and again, and it was I who / given unto Bobby, screamed NO." In this section, Phil extends his vision of the kind of artist / poet he aspires to be: he must work out of the spiritual / intellectual self, the man "Levine" who is greater than the sum of his parts, more than his sexual self at its most base. Nevertheless, the power of his "little Bobby" is intense, and his rejection of being given over to it is expressed in a primal scream.

In Section VII, Levine further elaborates his poetic intention to move beyond the confines of the self. His is a far-ranging vision. Here, he states clearly the purpose of his poetic work: to give voice to the voiceless and powerless—"For a black man whose / name I have forgotten . . ." "for that great stunned Pole / who laughed when he called me Jew / Boy, for the ugly / who had no chance." Again echoing the broad inclusiveness of Whitman, Levine asserts that for all of these, including Rousek and Ficklin (foremen in the Detroit factories where he worked) "who ate their own shit / in their own rage," "I had presumed to speak / in measure." He realizes that in spite of his energy, "all my care for / those I cannot touch / runs on my breath like a sigh; / surely I have failed." Levine closes this penultimate section with the realization that despite the connection he feels to his fellow man, isolation is inevitable, even from his own wife and children: ". . . each has his life / private and sealed."

In Section VIII, Levine ends this long poem with a warily triumphant tone. He recounts a meeting with Henri Colette in an L.A. bar, referencing Colette's poem in which he describes a figure named Archimbault—who may have been a pseudonym for a real person, an amateur who headed a group of amateur spies sent by British intelligence sent to France during World War II to screen real spies. Most of them were caught and executed by the Germans, except Archimbault, who may have betrayed them. Archimbault and all of his complexities as depicted by Collette may serve as a metaphor for the poet in a contemporary context. The poet functions unseen as a spy in his own culture, one who infiltrates, observes, and reports. Not even understanding exactly why he is touched by "the mad ones / imagined / and real . . ." Levine reasserts his determination: "Let me have / the courage to live / as fictions live, proud, careless, / unwilling to die."

Levine's strategic use of the long poem form here places "Silent in America" squarely within American long poems with an epic scope—Whitman's work as well as Ginsberg's *Howl* come to mind as striking examples. The long poem form is necessary for "Silent in America"; no other form would as successfully contain the large themes and broad inclusiveness implied in the title itself. Levine's division into sections gives each section of the poem the kind of energy and contained lyricism of a fresh start even though the various sections advance familiar Whitman-like themes. The cumulative effect of varied forms from section to section is a kind of contrapuntal composition of acclamation, "Vivas," for not only those marginalized who have failed but also the poet in all his efforts to perform his highest function even while facing inevitable failure.

Levine closes the poem with an invitation to the reader: "Come with us tonight . . . beyond the false lights / of Pasadena / where the living are silent /

in America." Finally, the poet is a guide to that space where truth replaces the "false lights." So in the end, Phillip Levine will join those who are truly alive, most of whom are silent in America in their powerlessness. He speaks for all of them, for all of us in this poem—ultimately stating his intention to keep going, to keep searching for the words. Finally, "Silent in America" becomes an ironic title, a title for a poem in which the poet has asserted his voice at length, in which the poet has determined to break the silence of both the poet / bard and the powerless.

DEREK MCKOWN

All That We Learn We Learn Too Late

"I've Been Where It Hurts," the Kid

IN THE SPRING OF 1957, Philip Levine received a Stanford Writing Fellowship; he was to study with the marvelously notorious poet, Yvor Winters. That summer, having left behind his wife and sons at his mother-in-law's in Colorado, he set out for the San Francisco Peninsula to find a place to live. Along the way, he came down with the flu, hallucinating in his fever "flying cats and dark birds who disappeared in the shadows," creatures who began to speak to him. By the next night, leaving the Great Basin of Nevada behind, he drove up and into yet another mountain range. As he recounts in *The Bread of Time*, "Never before had I seen such dramatic landscapes." These were the Sierra Nevada Mountains. In 1963, Levine begins another journey with the publication by Kim Merker's Stone Wall Press of his first book, *On the Edge*. It is in this book we find the long poem, "Sierra Kid."

But is "Sierra Kid" a "long poem," or just longish, lengthy? The long poem as a form, though the only type of poem we routinely identify by dimension, would seem to resist ready genre qualifications. The Canadian poet and scholar Smaro Kamboureli refers to the long poem as "the genre that is not a genre." If I exclude from consideration as obvious the historical epics and poems of book-length duration (many built over a lifetime of work), can I then ask if it enough to say that the defining feature of a long poem is its length in comparison to a "shorter" self-contained poem? By this measure, at one-hundred-forty-four lines, "Sierra Kid" certainly qualifies. But those long poems I grew up studying and learning from, those encyclopedic and visionary collagist "epics" to emerge from that modernist urge to make it new, all held, in the words of another Canadian poet and critic, Sharon Thesen, "a certain kind of ambition, whether conceptual or expressive." So, a long poem's length and *scope*—perhaps both structurally and thematically—must exceed those of shorter lyrics and narratives. "Sierra Kid" combines an "epic" scope with intimacy of voice. There is something filmic, performative, theatrical, even ritualistic in how the poem opens up within and outside itself. But, while "Sierra Kid" tells the story of a single and solitary character located in a familiar mythopoetic American West, it is not simply a miniature writ large. The story the speaker and titular character, the Kid, tells is both his and ours, his voice both personal and darkly prophetic, the poem conscious of both the past and the present.

"Sierra Kid" comprises five subtitled sections—chapters, after a fashion: it is a serial poem, paratactic much in the way film montage works. As such, it foregrounds Levine's attention to language and narrative process. Having been encouraged by Winters to read the English poet, Elizabeth Daryush (1887-1977), it is written in sinuous and musical syllabics. Counting syllables had become fairly popular in the late 1950s and early 1960s, particularly with many English poets experimenting in the form, among them Levine's friend (and former Winters student), Thom Gunn. In a late interview published in *Poetry London* in 2016, Levine stated that syllabics had given him "a sense of structure, even rhyme, and at the same time sound so much like speech." In this earliest work of Levine's, we of course do not yet see or hear his mature lineation, the balanced yet propulsive trimeter or tetrameter line that breaks across thought and syntax, but we do feel his rhythmic inclination in the subtle music of his rhymes (full, slant, and visual) and the patterns of lineate organization. In the same interview, he observes that with metrical poetry, he always thought in terms of stanza, but found with syllabics, "I'd get a sense more like a paragraph, how it would proceed down the page." In "Sierra Kid," the five titled "chapters" containing these syllabic "paragraphs"—each with its own syllabic scheme—create both rhythmic movement and narrative enlargement, a sense of individuation and historical dilation. This structure, particularly suited to the long poem, in which the subtitled sections are each singularized by their syllabic schemes and paratactically integral to a serialized whole, also supports Levine's thematic thrust and scope: that we, man or woman, are inescapably caught, fight though we may against it, in History's narrative, and the story is of our struggle for freedom and dignity in the face of control and exploitation.

He Becomes Sierra Kid

"Sierra Kid" begins, like many such sagas do, with a trek away from civilization and into the wilderness; in this case, Philip Levine sends a young man—the proverbial greenhorn—into the foothills, forests, and high meadows of the Sierra Nevada mountains. Levine leaves us to imagine his motivations—is he driven away from or toward something? But once the 1st-person speaker, the Kid, tramps past formerly famous, now dilapidated gold mines, he tells us that having "left the road // I left myself behind; / Talked to no one, thought / Of nothing." He seeks to shed his civilizationnurtured ego; if he is to enter the Edenic wilderness, return to Paradise, he must do so an innocent. Without the seeming impediments of a priori knowledge, driven upward, purpose is reduced to seeking and leaving behind:

> Without direction, compass, path,
> Without a way of coming down,
> Until I stopped somewhere
> And gave the place a name.
>
> I called the forests mine;

To follow the Kid as we do, we too find ourselves alone in the wilderness, surveying our new domain, the irony of which has yet to unfold. The impulse to leave behind social control, the accoutrements of progress, drives the Kid, and we recognize this trait (as Levine's mid-20th century audience would have) in the context of the mythic American Western—he is the mountain man, *Jerimiah Johnson,* but also the more ancient seeker of wisdom, of the godhead. Additionally, the reader of today, having read another forty-five years of Levine, should also recognize a nascent anti-authoritarianism, what Levine himself described as his "anarchist" political beliefs. In *Don't Ask,* Levine writes, "I don't believe in the validity of governments, laws, charters, all that hides us from our essential oneness. 'We are put on earth a little space,' Blake wrote, 'That we may learn to bear the beams of love.'" And the young Levine, whether by design or superb poetic instinct, chose to enact this drama, this human ritual, in the long poem, itself a form with anti-authoritarian qualities.

He Faces His Second Winter in the Sierra

The Kid is a sort of novice—or novitiate—in this second chapter, in body and mind. He has survived more than a year in the wilderness, but what initially felt his to possess, now absorbs him.

> A hard brown bug, maybe a beetle,
> Packing a ball of sparrow shit—
> What shall I call it?
> Shit beetle? Why's it pushing here
> At this great height in the thin air
> With its ridiculous waddle
> Up the hard side of Hard Luck Hill?

And the furred thing that frightened me—
Bobcat, coyote, wild dog—
Flat eyes in winter bush, stiff tail,
Holding his ground, a rotted log.
Grass snakes that wouldn't die,
And night hawks hanging on the rim
Of what was mine. . . .

Adamic naming has begun to fail him, and he must share dangerous dominion with the other living creatures. Here is that Blake-ian sense of oneness that flowed from Levine's anarchist beliefs.

. . . I know them now;
They have absorbed a mind
Which must endure the freezing snow
They endure and, freezing, find
A clear sustaining stream.

The Kid must struggle to survive like the other animals, but Levine cleverly flips his and our perspective: "They have absorbed a mind." While Levine personifies Nature in the familiar Romantic mode, our storyteller, the Kid, observes his assimilation by and into Nature as if from outside himself—the individual story is absorbed in dilating layers of history. Within the drama and ritual of Levine's narrative process, the Kid is now positioned to face a challenge to his newfound knowledge.

He Learns to Lose

In this third chapter, we make another of those paratactic leaps: an unknown amount of time has passed, and we're introduced to a new character. We know that the Kid is our speaker, but the episode is told with clenched detachment; as Levine skillfully pares back narrative details, we sense that the Kid is holding something back.

She was afraid
Of everything,
The little Digger girl.
Pah Utes had killed
Her older brother
Who may have been her lover

> The way she cried
> Over his ring—
>
> The heavy brass
> On the heavy hand.
> She carried it for weeks
> Clenched in her fist
> As if it might
> Keep out the loneliness
> Or the plain fact
> That he was gone.

The Kid focuses our attention upon the brass ring the Digger girl carried (a brother and sister mining up there in the mountains?), physical evidence of the heavy loss she suffered. Is this what draws him to her, that now she too is alone? Do they recognize something essentially familiar in each other? Some time passes, her grief perhaps abating, she gets about the business of preparing for the coming winter. The Kid notes with telling dispassion, "We slept together / But did not speak."

When the girl disappears mid-winter, the Kid is left "To face alone—/ The slow gray dark / Moving along / The dark tipped grass / Between the numbed pines." The loss of her company, however silent, shifts how he meets his world: the landscape divergent and foreboding, he benumbed. For four months they had shared the night together, a shelter he hadn't known he needed. It is no longer enough to have the mind of winter. We must also "learn to bear the beams of love."

Civilization Comes to Sierra Kid

Whether we read the subtitled sections of "Sierra Kid" as novelistic chapters, or filmic scenes, or acts in a play, they do by this point in the long poem register as the sequential actions in a grand performative ritual—we know this story: a fall is going to come. In "Sierra Kid," the State, or History, is inexorable.

> They levelled Tater Hill
> And I was sick.
> First sun, and the chain saws
> Coming on; blue haze,
> Dull blue exhaust
> Rising, dust rising, and the smell.

Wilderness despoiled, the animals flee from the machines of progress, and the Kid is left "exposed." After six weeks, he returns to survey the ruins: "There, there, an A&P, / And not a tree / For miles, and mammoth hills of goods." There is, of course, a fertile ground to examine here from an ecocritical perspective, but I can't help but hear the desperate anger of a Romantic's heart. Sierra Kid walks among "[f]at men in uniforms" and "men in aprons"; in the face of their fear, he declares, "I am Lincoln, / Aaron Burr, / The aging son of Appleseed. // I am American. . . ." Those civilized men see a madman. His last thoughts before they shoot him down are those of a hapless victim staring upon the grinding gears of capitalist greed: "Oh God, what have I seen / That was not sold!" The Kid's despair brings to mind Wordsworth's 1802 sonnet, "The World Is Too Much With Us." Wordsworth admonishes his modern, industrial society that "we lay waste our powers" by a devotion to "getting and spending," thus losing a vital connection to Nature and its restorative force. Perhaps "Sierra Kid" nods back to Wordsworth, who in that sonnet declared he'd rather be "[a] Pagan suckled in a creed outworn," than a materialistic modern man. I wonder also if Levine's vein of fatalism doesn't also reach back to Wordsworth: "The world is too much with us; late and soon." A more nuanced reading of this first line might include that we—human civilization—have made up too much of the world, have granted ourselves too great an importance, not just presently, but always, in the past, and forlornly, in the future. The Kid cannot escape his story, any more than we could our own, Levine shows us, any more than we can escape history.

Mad, Dying, Sierra Kid Enters the Capital

In the final chapter, the Kid's final act is one of defiance, and possibly of transcendence. The Kid's first words reverberate within each of us and across the whole of civilized time: "What have I changed?" He had removed himself from society, entered the wilderness, looked to regain innocence, receive the wisdom of the godhead, live in one mind with the natural world. But he learned the individual is not solitary: to be human is to need another, even though we must experience the loss of that other. He has learned, witnessing the miners, the loggers, the builders, and the mercantilists who followed him, that he has failed, and perhaps inevitably so; but he doesn't give up.

As he limps across the "civic lawns," gut-shot and bleeding, his flesh burning with fever, he wonders what others might learn from his example.

> Who will they find?
> A man with no eyes in his head?
> Or just a mind

24

Calm and alone?
Or just a mouth, silent, dead,
The lips half gone?

Will they presume
That someone once was half alive
And that the air
Was massive where
The sickening pyracanthas thrive
Staining his tomb?

The Sierra Kid contemplates his place in History, what role he has played in that story told by forces, he now realizes, far more powerful that he could account. Will those who find him, and those who come later, see in him someone who resisted those forces, sought to escape the horrors of human progress, who stubbornly believed and struggled to create a different, if not better, life? Or will they, the social animal more deadly that any he lived with in the wild mountains, see merely a corrupt and rotting corpse? What is the monument to his struggle? The answer to this question is not easy, for Levine, or for us. For now, at the end of this epic, the Kid casts a final gesture of defiance.

I came to touch
The great heart of a dying state.
Here is the wound!
It makes no sound.
All that we learn we learn too late,
And it's not much.

The Sierra Kid is, of course, that "great heart of a dying state." He is "the wound." He is that desire to escape the systemic subjugation and exploitation of each other and the natural world that has accompanied civilization. He is imagination and faith in the possibilities of humankind. Near death, the Kid ends his story in fleeting despair, in silence.

But what of Levine, the author of *Not This Pig, They Feed They Lion, 1933, The Names of the Lost, 7 Years from Somewhere, What Work Is*, the memorialist of all those he described as having been "born in the wrong year and in the wrong place"? The poet Robert Hedin notes in his essay "In Search of a New World: The Anarchist Dream in the Poetry of Philip Levine":

Indeed, the underlying irony in all of Levine's work is the pronouncement that the past is both inescapable and uncorrectable. Rather than achieving their new world hopes, his characters continually find themselves ushered back into a reality that subverts all dreams of perfectibility.

But he *does* chronicle those lives (and who are just as much our lives); he honors their struggle, and this feeds our own struggle. In *Don't Ask,* Levine writes: "I don't believe in victory in my lifetime. I'm not sure I believe in victory at all, but I do believe in the struggle and preserving the names and natures of those who fought, for their sake, for my sake, and for those who come after." And one of those first names is Sierra Kid. In this, one of the first of many long poems over his own decades-long stubborn struggle to articulate the necessity and value of human freedom and dignity, he creates a template, an epic story, for his fierce convictions.

GARY YOUNG

On *Pili's Wall*

PILI'S WALL IS AN OUTLIER among Philip Levine's many books. It marks a departure from Levine's earlier, more formal verse, toward a new poetic voice whose diction is looser, more extravagant, and simultaneously, more relaxed. Published in 1971 by Unicorn Press, *Pili's Wall* utilizes tropes Levine discovered in Spanish surrealism, and it explores a new landscape, leaving the acrid smoke of Detroit for the red soil of Spain, with its heat, dust, and bloody history.

Although "Pili's Wall" appeared in Levine's *Selected Poems,* this poem in ten parts was not included in *Red Dust,* also published in 1971 by Kayak Press, nor did it appear in *They Feed They Lion,* published by Atheneum in 1972. It is an orphan, and significant insofar as Levine sought to privilege this poem as a stand-alone book. A volume of ten individual poems, even poems integrated or thematically connected, would not be enough to sustain a whole book, but the ten sections of "Pili's Wall" are dynamic, and the poem builds in structural complexity as the sections resonate and interact, one with another. The first edition is noteworthy for several reasons. It is clearly an object of high aesthetic ideals—the typesetting, printing, and binding were all done by hand. But what stands out most are the photographs that grace the cover of the book and accompany the poem's many sections. These are black and white photos taken of a stone wall in Spain, with childish drawings incised upon the wall's plaster surface. Some of the images clearly represent a child, others represent some creature or other, but all of them are abstracted, monochromatic visages, dreamlike in their power and simplicity. The photos work in counterpoint with the sections of the poem, and contribute to the overall structure and strategy of the book.

It is impossible not to see the first edition of *Pili's Wall* as an artist's book, a collaboration between poet and visual artist. The structure of the long poem allows for a kind of symphonic development of theme, variation, and resolution, and there is a tension built up between the text and the images that only a long poem can afford. The illustrations in *Pili's Wall* cannot be disentangled from the poem, and though the poem stands admirably on its own in

Levine's *Selected Poems,* the missing images leave a palpable void. The book has a charming, even sentimental dedication:

> For the stone masons & plasterers, the wind,
> the sun, the rain, & my Pili, the
> Spanish girlchild, all of you who
> made this wall
>
> & for Fran, who found it

Levine spent seminal years in Spain with his family, and I suspect his wife Fran took the photos, and one presumes she had an influence on the poem's creation.

As a long poem, "Pili's Wall" is an eloquent bridge between Levine's lyrical earlier poems and his subsequent longer, more narrative verse. The pivot is a rarity in Levine's work—a feminine voice. Pili is a girl, not a woman, but her femininity pushes against the assertive masculine voice so prevalent in Levine's poetry. It modifies and ameliorates the dominant musculature of Levine's poetic utterance. Part child, part tutelary spirit, Pili guides Levine into a world of magic, and vatic utterance. Her presence is both spectral and literally etched in stone. The images on the page are stately representations of a literal wall, but they also mirror the sections of the poem that fit together like the very stones that give a wall its integrity and strength.

"Pili's Wall" is filled with a series of questions, some answered, others not, and the first section begins, "Why me?" This can be read as an existential complaint, an exaltation of being, or perhaps it's meant to be both. Levine then launches into a litany of particulars:

> . . . From this small hill
> the river flows in March.
> The soil gives grudgingly
> grass, thyme, poppies,
> thistles, cactus,
> an olive grove climbing
> the far hill, a row
> of cedars shading the river.

He ends this first section with another question: "What more?"

In Section II, Pili tells us,

> I am the one
> you never drew

the small sister
jumping rope
just within the circle
of the cypress

This small sister is not the only thing ignored. A lost dog and a shepherd are also banished from the wall, as are

seven jackdaws
soundless, until the sky
darkened
and there was
no place

The wall, peopled by a child's hand, vanishes as light is drawn out of the sky. Like the reflections in Plato's cave, these doodles and drawings stand in for the real world, which returns with dawn. The wall is a star map that spins like the narrative voices in the poem, none of which are fixed.

Section III continues the existential interrogation:

Why am I here?
cries the gorse

Take these needles
crowding to your blood

these dense yellow mouths.

Later in this section, the moon carries on a harsh interrogation, presumably in darkness:

What can a child know,
says the moon

Look at her bones,
unbroken, and her teeth

The moon curses the child:

May she sleep with stones
may she waken round a stone[,]

but a gull "far from the sea and drunk / on the sweet grass" turns to the girl for succor, crying, "Help me, help me may she help me . . ."

The lapidary structure of the sections allows the narrative voice to shift over the course of the poem, first from Pili, "the small sister/jumping rope", then to the gorse crying out, "Take me, take me // the mother of spines/here under the olives". A major transition occurs in Section IV, when we can almost hear the voice of the wall itself, speaking in a child's voice:

> Here is a face for you
> who will not show
> your face.
> I cut a smile
> and give it to you, the rain
> gives you tears.

The last admonition to the beings that populate the wall is

> Spit your teeth
> in the face
> of creation.

The poem's length and sequencing allows for the development of a kind of parallel, shadow poem that works in tandem with the operative narration. By this point, it's as if the shadows on Plato's cave have turned out to be real after all.

The aggressive and violent voice in Section IV abruptly shifts in Section V. Pili, the child, speaks in a hushed, protective voice, perhaps to the poet himself, saying,

> This is my hand
> reaching to you . . .
>
> You're bigger than me
> so put your hand
> on my shoulder.

The pair walks through "the green tunnel/of the spring . . . my hand/ in yours."

The following section provides for further variation, a shift, or a merging of consciousness. It begins, "This is me. // As I am. // There is no child/

inside me. I // am a child." Pili the girl child, and the child scratched into the stone wall have become a single entity,

> . . . unfolding
> like a tree
> turning and
> turning
>
> like a hand
> in water or a widow
> lost on the road.

These binary voices continue in Section VII, when the wall speaks, addressing the child who's created the imaginative beings etched into the wall's surface, as well as to the child who lives upon the stained, scarred surface.

> A blood bean
> leaps at the foot of the wall
>
> and I am with my face
> turned in.

The poem then shifts in both tone and syntactical structure, and mirrors the cadence and the aggrieved anger of a poem written during this same period, "They Feed They Lion."

Here are lines from Section VII of "Pili's Wall":

> Out of lime
> out of thatch, straw, stones
>
> out of the years
> of peeling and crying
>
> Out of saying No
> No to the barn swallow, No
>
> to the hurled stone
> No to the air

out of you can't
to the crying grain, you won't

to the lost river
of blackening ivy

out of blind
out of deaf . . ."

Compare these lines with "They Feed They Lion," which begins:

Out of burlap sacks, out of bearing butter,
Out of black bean and wet slate bread,
Out of the acids of rage, the candor of tar,
Out of creosote, gasoline, drive shafts, wooden dollies,
They Lion grow.

"They Feed They Lion" is the more achieved poem of the two: politically astute, stylistically assured, taut, pared down to essentials, and burning with rage. It is a masterful poem, whereas "Pili's Wall" embodies so many voices and points of view, that it loses focus at times to the point of confusion. "Pili's Wall" relies more on the aggregate of voices and images to complete its vision—like a wall of stones handset without mortar—and it is hard to imagine "They Feed They Lion" without the prelude of "Pili's Wall."

After the darkness, and the "black sun" that dominates so much of the poem, section eight begins with "A simple dawn", and returns to an essential lyric vision. No questions are required of this particular morning; all is still and quiet:

In side the stalls
the pigs snuffle awake . . .
and the world starts.

From the far hill
of olives the wall is white
and perfect in the new sun.

The reader can be excused for being lulled by this bucolic scene, but at the end of the section, we are reminded that

> no one can hear
> the lost shoe
> screaming in the weeds.

The final two sections of the poem reach apotheosis for the child, who identifies completely with the wall and the figures scratched upon its surface:

> Today I am
> the wall, but once
> I was seed
> huddling between the grains
> of stones, drawing a tongue
> of salt into my blood, a fist
> tightening into
> a turnip

This radical identification is answered in the poem's final section, with the child reclaiming her human identity, replete with her place in a larger, familial world:

> Today I am Pili.
> Palm Sunday, and I wait
> in the cool morning
>
> for my sisters, each one
> in white to come
> from the beaded door.
>
> . . . I seem
> to be this girl, this Pili, waiting
> for children
> with particular names
>
> to gather before the chipped wall
> and descend along
> the goat trail . . .
>
> where the pigs won't run
> and a long dense shadow sleeps
> at the roots.

"Pili's Wall" vacillates between a fulsome, detailed description of the Spanish landscape, and a startling, often sinister surrealism. In poems such as "The Children's Crusade" from *They Feed They Lion,* the children are craven, merciless, caught up like the adults in a culture of violence, war, and moral corruption. "Pili's Wall" gives us Pili, specter, sibyl, symbol, who speaks in a multitude of voices until she arrives at last as a real little girl—Pili—intact, indivisible, and whole. "Pili's Wall", a long poem structured paratactically, and expanded past the scope of a typical lyric, allows Levine to create a poem of dreamy, marmoreal intensity. Levine's mastery of the long poem form, which came to fruition in "Pili's Wall", freed him to explore complex historical, personal, and political subjects in his later long poems. Levine's ability to adapt the form—to vary its length, its tone, and its structure—allowed him to s support the voices and visions that constituted his world, and mark his mature work.

CHRISTOPHER HOWELL

"The Angels of Detroit"—Levine's Angels

"And Jacob said to the angel, I will not let go thy hand, except thou bless me"
Genesis 32/26

IT IS AXIOMATIC THAT POEMS worthy of the name are not "about" their topics but about their results, what we typically refer to as their subjects. But sometimes the two are so closely aligned that topic has its own resonance, over and above its service as vehicle for the poem's metaphorical progress and being. This is manifestly true of Philip Levine's "angel" poems, of which there are at least a dozen. His angels are not celestial in the ordinary sense, but are the earth-bound haunters of the undersides of cities. They keep watch and sometimes inhabit butchers, steel workers, hookers, janitors, bums, and all the lost and downtrodden whose lives are constant struggle for emotional clarity and relief from toil that brutalizes their inner lives. In fact, angels seem often the manifestations of these inner lives, full of feeling but without leverage against the mortal forces ranged against them: and then these angels themselves are mortal in the sense that God has left them, seemingly, to simply carry on.

They are reminiscent of the angels in the Wim Wenders film *Wings of Desire*, wherein angels are mostly invisible witnesses to the joys, deceptions, brutalities, accidents, and sufferings of humanity. They witness it all, utterly incapable of intervening without casting off their angelic nature and so themselves becoming subject to the whims, fortunes, and mishaps of the mortal world. Among other things, the film proposes that love cannot exist without death; which begs the question: if true, how could a loving immortal being exist?

In Levine's angel poems he insists, explicitly, that an essential aspect of angelic nature *must* be mortality, with all its attendant suffering, temporal servitude, and joy, the defiant embrace of which is what rescues life, and the very notion of angels, from pointlessness. Also common to Levine's angel poems is a biographical drift, the sense of essential lessons learned and relearned in the crucible of the individual's experience of self and the world. The true long poem in this group, the seven section, one-hundred-thirty line "The Angels of

Detroit," is also the best example of this Levinian angel and of the developmental narrative that accompanies its appearance.

The traditional roles of angels as messengers, mediators, and protectors are referenced, but with the difference that God is missing and his angels as abandoned and untethered as the rest of us. The poem tightens the tension between angels as we have known them, culturally, and the city (the world) of purgatorial labor, survival of which requires, as a form of honor, a tug of war between suffering and sweetness. Section One begins:

> I could hear them in fever
> hovering in the closet or
> falling from the mirror. I
> could see them in the first dream
> of my dead.

With no narrative framing, other than "fever," "closet," and "first dreams," we infer that the speaker's point of view, through memory, is that of a child, in the delirium of sickness, watching its mother—another kind of angel—iron clothes. "Perfume of scorched clothes," in the next line, gives us even the smell of it. Then:

> She spits back
> at the spitting iron, she slaps
> it with a round pink palm

The spitting on the iron to test its heat introduces the ageless familiarity with work and the hang-tough acceptance of its necessity that is a consistent feature of Levine's writing. And both the spitting and the slap also reference an objection to both the work and the circumstances that bring it back again and again. It is the mother figure both enduring and standing against tasks, against a life reduced to satisfaction of their endless demands. Then the angels "sigh / from the shadowy valleys / of my shirts," a perfect image of steam escaping into the air after an iron is lifted. It is like the sighing that must accompany all repetitive work: the angels, while they cannot do it for us, agree, in Levine's vision, to do it with us, or perhaps they become us in our doing of it, our suffering it.

The closing lines of section one tweak one's memory of the Twenty-Third Psalm—"Yea, though I walk through the valley of the shadow of my shirts"— it seems to say, introducing some comic irony into this room of sickness and labor. Both are emblematic of inescapable baseline human experience that is often comic, like a piano falling out a window, the mud puddle into which Oliver Hardy steps only to find it twelve feet deep.

This twelve-line introductory segment of the poem sets the tone, suggests that the angels we will meet are both literal and ephemeral, like time and experience, like pain and fear, work and its necessity.

Section two carries forward the notion of angels as clothing and clothing as a kind of armor:

> I wore angels.
> They saved me in the streets
> where the towers hung above
> suspended on breath, they
> saved me from the pale woman
> who smoothed the breasts
> of chickens or the red-armed
> one who sold bread in
> the shop of knives.

Angels and clothing offer a protective barrier against the consciousness of death (the pale woman) and general brutality (the shop of knives). Again there is a sense of childhood brought into challenging contact with the strangeness and danger of the world. The speaker "tried to cry and tried / to change." But the angels have sent him a "robed mother or a / promise in the dark hall," like a ritual enigma or a warning, those things often supplied to the young in place of actual help.

In stanza three the angels send "snow / to cover the steps, to crown / the teeth of garbage and bless / the deaths of old cars, snow / falling on our upturned faces / in the great church . . ." So the great church of the world is filled with garbage and death, the cold snow, like falling angels, being all that reclaims it, a kind of coming-of-age perception for the speaker, whose use of the third person plural provides a segue into teenage life in section three.

The segment opens:

> From Toledo by bus,
> from Flat Rock on syphoned gas,
> from the iron country on
> a dare. For one night.

In the next line we move directly to "Stash," a diminutive of the common Polish name "Stanislaw," helping to lend context:

> Stash says, nigger
> boy's crying in
> the shit house.
>
> All of us far from
> momma, and getting farther.

The angels met with in the memory of the speaker are not the angelic protectors and messengers of Augustine or the *Summa Theologica* of Aquinas. They are steam, they are clothing, they teach the speaker to syphon gas. They teach him the chill that can accompany ignorance laced with pity. Use of "nigger" is a difficult and polarizing word in this time of America's long overdue self-evaluation regarding systemic race-based inequities in our society. But Levine grew up in a working class city with rigidly defined ethnic neighborhoods and all of the predictable suspicions and prejudices. His context for the poem, and for his use of the term, was the 1940's, and in that context its use is essential, without it tension between the ignorance its use by the character represents and the character's pity for the boy's crying simply relaxes. But "in / the shit house" indicates clearly that this tension is central to Levine's purpose. If Detroit is the world internalized and cannot be escaped simply by fleeing to Toledo or Flat Rock, there is a sense in which to grow up in working class urban American is to be in the "shit house," crying "far from / momma, and getting farther." The America Levine invokes is a kind of pressure cooker, skewing everyone out of shape so that pity may often have been the only means to recognition of the basic humanity of everyone in the great stew of that culture.

Throughout, the way Levine manipulates tone and reference is masterful, particularly in a poem that seems so freewheeling. For instance, the great economy and tonal precision of the lines quoted above suggest the youth of the characters, the greater temporal context of the 1940's, the sadness of Stash's and presumably the speaker's ignorance, and the great distance to be traveled emotionally and intellectually from the events narrated and the moment of the poem's utterance. This flexing, referential latitude is a particular capacity of the long poem, is, indeed, one of its defining characteristics. It permits wide parabolas in a poem's development, the twining and recombining of motifs. It *fosters* significance, and is the source of our continuing conviction that long poems are almost always a good poet's signature works.

In the poem's fourth section we meet the Angel Bernard who, like the Angel Christophe in the poem "Angel Butcher" several pages on in the collection, is not so much a messenger as a kind of ritualized signal: In that poem the speaker says of Christophe:

> He asks
> me how I came to this place and
> this work, and I tell him how
> I began with animals, and
> he tells me how
> he began with animals. We
> talk about growing up and losing
> the strange things we never
> understood and settling.
>   I help
> him with his robe . . .

Like the butcher, Bernard, in clear counterpoint to Saint Bernard, is born of the legacy of nearly vanished industrial America. Bernard's brothers are not the Cistercian Brothers of the Rule of Saint Bernard who form part of the saint's legacy. They are, Levine tells us,

>   . . . factories and
> bowling teams, his mother is the
> power to blight, his father
> moves in all men like a threat,
> a closing of hands, an unkept
> promise of return.

The Angel Bernard is the speaker's confidant (or confessor, perhaps), keeper of all the lessons of despair passed on down the generations, a kind of sin eater:

> We talk
> for years; everything we
> say comes to nothing. We drink
> bad beer and never lie.

What Bernard has is directly contradicted by what he wants: passion, tenderness, the power to die "in the/chalice of God's tears." When he lies down to sleep, it turns out, he lies down not like the eponymous saint in a comfortable cold stream or on a bed of nails, but in a junkyard and "cries to sleep."

What has begun to emerge, at this point in the poem, is not a theology exactly, but an ethos built of the speaker's Blakean transit from innocence to experience, and it has an unwavering moral posture: the suffering and help-lessness of humankind must be, in the main, the result of the functioning of the mechanisms of power, and its minions, explicitly and persistently refusing to see the world in terms of the individual's experience and plight. All of the poem's characters and speakers reiterate this fact. The suffering is born, too, of the apparent absence of divine justice—though the angels are still here, left to carry on, in all their forms, alone.

And these forms, of both angels and of suffering humanity, somehow fused in Levine's vision, demand the aforementioned flexibility that only the long poem can provide. In this case, each intrinsically dramatic section reiterates and expands the range of the poem's treatment of both topic and subject without heavy reliance on either story line or the wide screen sweep of the classic narrative poem (à la Jeffers' "The Roan Stallion," for instance), the first objective of which is always story itself. The segmented expression of the long poem here preserves the lyric compression of each individual segment so that at no point is the poem required to explain itself. Its rhetoric is an experien-tial tableau.

In the world of this poem the cruelty of things, the lacrimae rerum, spares no one. Thus, a whole swift-moving little tragedy plays out in segment five, which has three stanzas and slightly shorter lines to jazz up the movement. This is appropriate since stanza one of the segment begins in a beat down jazz club with:

> Long Eddie on alto
> the yellows of his eyes
>
> brown on pot, the brown centers
> burned like washed gold.

Beautiful, crisp sounds form a background to the radically compressed narra-tive of the sixteen-year old boy, who may or may not be Long Eddie himself:

> so much sorrow in hatred
> so much tenderness
> he could taste coming up
> from the rich earth.

The "coming up" is somehow, both the earth-bound traditions coded into the music and a kind vomit choking off the promise, leading to

> Little clown. Caught all alone,
> arm in a mail-box.
> Never did nothing right. . . .

As in other segments of the poem the actual narration shifts fluidly from the poet as speaker to characterized speaker, which lends dramatic depth, preserves compression, and keeps standard narrative machinery at bay. It is telling that whether or not the poem's individual segments suggest the presence or possibility of angels, the characterized speakers mostly don't see or acknowledge them.

That ethos to which I referred is clearer still in the poem's sixth section where we get images of the collective speaker as a single sensibility worn down to surrender and beyond, something that occurs throughout *They Feed They Lion*:

> Unvisioned pale knot of
> West Virginia, mountain rock and
> black valley earth, ungloved
> yellow potato, dried tubers,
> yoked bean, frozen cedars
> of weariness, we gave up.

Again here Levine, by means a free indirect discourse, slips in and out of the dialect we are invited to associate with the beaten, down trodden, and used:

> Don't matter what rare breath
> puddles in fire on
> the foundry floor. The toilets
> overflow . . .

This proximal equating of the foundry with the toilet, forms an essential political trope in the poem and in much of Levine's writing, nailed down by rats, maggots, worms, whips and the final lines:

> among the angels
> we lie down.

The poem's concluding section takes us back to the individual as central character, introducing a "Red haired black skinned / Cuban woman" waiting for the inevitable date:

> . . . all night
> in the parking lot.

But in her inner life she is talking—"to no one—of home." Levine is very sensitive to the gestural value of timing, always, and this isolating placement of "of home" has a deep resonant echo of longing trailing it, which he turns back on immediately with, "Nothing lasts/forever—" again suggesting the thought originates simultaneously in both Levine and the woman, and we hear Detroit whispering in the background: "and it's the only thing that does.

The speaker here is an aspect or echo of the speaker in every phase of the poem's section by section development: the sick child in section one, the gas siphoning teenagers in three, the angel Bernard and the speaker who speaks into the junkyard enclave of that life, all of them. The implication is that the speaker is all of us, individually, and all of the lost angels by which we are surrounded unawares. The Cuban woman herself is a kind of angel, bearing witness, waiting. The poem closes with:

> She meets us, coatless, in magenta,
> an early flower late blooming
> in the fenced white wastes,
> bare arms open.

She may be seen also, in a way, as Detroit itself, patched together by angels who are part of the city (all cities), so it might as well be "home." And then there is the saving grace of that magenta dress, the woman like "An early flower late blooming/in the fenced white wastes, / bare arms open." Perhaps she is the last angel, the concluding phrase spinning the whole poem into a kind of Whitmanic invitation to hope. Hope, Philip Levine's poems with their clear view of the dark side of the human situation, are never without it. They show us that the better angels of our nature, if we have them, are kept alive not by wishfulness, but by strength of spirit.

The operative word here is "show," and in his long poems, in "The Angels of Detroit" particularly, dramatic and lyric elements combine over the expanse of lines to show us the range of human suffering and longing, and to offer us angels, whose nature is uncertain but somehow related to a developmental imperative their steadfast witnessing of which is yet another species of hope.

It is a little verse drama; but the long poem form has allowed Levine to side-step the usual machinery of the drama—the numbering of acts and scenes, the identifying of characters and speakers, the stage directions—which would have slowed the movement and given rise to questions regarding scene, plot, and spectacle. Though it gives us landscape, voice, characters, action, and much more, "The Angels of Detroit" is not spectacle; its province, its stage, is the inner life, the secret but shared dominion. It is a long poem with the force of an immense lyric, a result only the long poem form can supply.

MARK JARMAN

"Letters for the Dead":
What It Is Without You

LETTERS FOR THE DEAD," of all of Philip Levine's long poems, contains in its title the germ of its length. The dead are so numerous, that any communications with them via letter would have to result in an uncountable number of letters. That the poem is actually limited to ten sections suggests that the definition of "the dead" is limited to a more discrete number, one that would not be overwhelming for a living mortal, even one so prolific and gifted as the poet Levine. And yet there is also the play on words in the title of "letters" as members of the alphabet and implicitly words themselves. The title implies, then, that these are letters arranged into words for the dead. Still, those letters and words could proceed in infinite variations. So, who are "the dead"? The book in which the poem appears, Levine's 1973 collection *1933*, focuses mainly on the death of the poet's father in 1933. The dead in this case would be pretty clear. To consider the poem exactly in the context of the volume, as it ought to be, would identify him, the father, as the one addressed. But the poem in its very first section does not allow us to limit ourselves to that single individual. We may think of him, but not exclusively. The poet states that he has "tried to say/something to each of you/of what it is/without you," and with that the dead once again multiply into the numberless majority of those human beings who have died. Their numbers are brought under control because they have departed a world which, in Levine's fifth full-length collection of poetry, is recognizable and populated by the dead of industrial Detroit and rural Spain, two of Levine's primary landscapes. Spiritually, the dead are joined by the divinity who has absconded from these places long ago, leaving the poet to explain what it, life presumably, is like without him. The multiple dead addressed in this long poem include the dead God.

•••

The air darkened toward morning
the slag heap's yellow flame
paled against the sky

on the sill the old wren
slept till noon I wakened
read the paper

and thought of you one by one
and tried to hold your faces
in my eyes

tried to say
something to each of you
of what it is
without you

the winter sun
dipped below the stacks
the chilled tea whitened
in my cup

Levine in this poem, as throughout *1933,* is the non-narrative, imagist poet, influenced by Lorca, William Carlos Williams, and George Oppen. His style in "Letters for the Dead" tends toward minimalism, suppressing punctuation except when absolutely necessary for the sake of clarity, when a comma might appear or a dash. Stanza lengths are inconsistent, though frequently return to tercets, and the line lengths are only a few syllables long on the average, using spaces within the lines instead of punctuation for the sake of rhythm. The short lines are meant, however, to accommodate the image more than any storytelling velocity or continuity. Even with its ten sections, it seems inaccurate to call the poem a sequence or a series, since both terms imply some narrative. Every line and stanza of "Letters for the Dead" suggests that limited space of some narrow page or postcard, and yet the cataloguing of images, each revealing "what it is / without out," echoes Levine's other great master, Walt Whitman.

That said, the first of the ten sections of the poem unfolds as a setting in time and place, as the day begins in an infernal landscape of factory work, with a flaming heap of industrial waste outside the window, and the traditional voice of nature, the wren, usually a herald of the morning, preferring unconsciousness. The working speaker goes through his morning ritual, on this occasion as perhaps on all occasions trying to bring to mind the faces of his departed loved ones. One assumes that they are loved ones, for the world without them seems emphatically bleak, and even before the speaker rises to go to work, the sun has set below the factory chimneys, as if he has been in a revery all day long, his cup of tea a barometer of that suspended animation. But what is time when measured by working shifts? The natural sequence of morning, noon, and night has no meaning to a worker on the swing shift, for example. The very first line of the poem reminds us of the paradox of such a chronology. Toward morning in this world, the air does not lighten, it darkens. The speaker's morning may very well be when he wakes to work, and that may be as the sun is going down. His morning is not the natural morning. In a world "without you," time is measured by unnatural and artificial cycles.

Levine's militant defense of the human soul against this soul-killing regimen is, surely, one of the impulses of the poem. The first section gives us the speaker, preserving his sanity, by remembering those who are no longer living and, as the subsequent sections also reveal, remembering how they lived and the relics which recall them:

> The drug store fired your mother
> she dried and hardened
>
> the butcher never returned
> to beat his soft palms
> against the door
>
> his stiff coveralls hung in the closet
> your briefcase
> bulged with rusting tools
>
> your shoes aged
> the toes curling upward
> in a spasm
>
> your voice, your high voice
> of pear and honey
> shuddered once along the bare walls
>
> but someone ate the pear
> someone ate the honey
> —we still ate at the usual hours

and went off to the factories in the dark
with bloodless sandwiches
folded in wax paper
with tiny packages of sweets

no one felt your sleep
arriving
or heard the sudden intakes of fear

no one held your hands
to keep them still
or your face glowing like a clock's

at night the toilet ran
a window hummed in the wind
your final letter uncrumpled to the moon

when your father came home at last
drunk repentant eager to beg
there was no one to answer

the salt scarred on the table
untasted

The second section of the poem begins as a Whitmanesque catalogue of events and relics. Presumably the events—the mother losing her job and the butcher's abandonment—might not have occurred had the dead one been still alive. Certainly that anomalous briefcase of tools and those warped, unworn shoes would have had different ends had the dead remained to use and wear them. But the poem takes a surreal turn after these realistic details, and the transformation of the remembered voice into its metaphorical qualities—"pear and honey"—so that "someone" could consume them leads the poet back to a series of stark details which now alternate between the real and the surreal. Part of the propulsive energy of this long poem is Levine's own imagination. Minimalism and imagism tend to condensation, and the poet Levine of this era appears always to be reining in a powerful ability to narrate and associate. One reads the rest of section two fully aware that it could have been twice or three-times as long. The signature expression of this part of Levine's great ability to extend any poem is his use of negation.

Formally it makes sense to rely on negation in a poem addressed to the absent. Levine's insistence that "no one felt your sleep," "no one held your hands," "your final letter uncrumpled to the moon," "there was no one to answer," makes it clear that the effects of this absence are irremediable and inconsolable. But negation, as I've said, is also a signature of Levine's style, as much as affirmation is of Whitman's, and it usually serves to create the tone of anger that runs through Levine's poetry. Levine once said in an interview that he loves anger, and since so much of the anger of his poetry is occasioned by a sense of outrage at injustice, it is hard not to infer here that the absences of the dead also seem unjust to the poet. Losing your father at the age of five is certainly cause for a lifetime of grieving anger. But it is the injustice of death itself, including the death of God, which may be implied by the poem's angry negations. As the poet says in his characteristic fashion, at the end of "I Could Believe" in his book 7 Years from Somewhere: "except/for the dying I could/ believe." "Letters for the Dead" associates the loss of belief with the losses created by death. And yet Levine's naysaying can also be a form of yeasaying. To inform the dead of "what it is/without you" is to offer evidence of life, to affirm that life not only continues but is worthwhile.

> On south past Toledo
> the bus heading into the great oven
> into your first adventure
>
> a man is chewing
> a man is lying about love
> a frightened corporal loads
> and unloads a .45
>
> your face against the black glass
> unlined, forever young
>
> out of the miles
> of breathing fields suddenly
> a small white town
> locked against the night
> with one light burning
>
> then the cities
> the bus hot
> and filling with silent
> black men

no women anywhere
squad cars hunched on the corners
waiting for life
on past the dark barracks
rain yards
all-night car lots
the last bar winking

At Covington the pale Ohio
inches toward the sea
the bridge gathers its nerves
and you cross
holding your breath the whole way

the dawn of a new world
it grays
climbing the first hills
and up over the grinding ridges
turning slowly to stone
the roadside trees fighting

for light
later, slate waves
at Pensacola
you stood
and counted them
and turned for home

—The clock silent in the shrunken parlor
the cold plate waiting

Here the second person address identifies someone either currently living, in the absence of the dead, or it may be an evocation of how one of the dead—perhaps the father— lived, although the present tense creates an oddly disorienting immediacy. And of course there is the convention of American colloquial speech which substitutes second person for first person or third person neutral, "one." However it is meant, the bus is full of men heading for work, "no women anywhere," and yet you yourself are on "your first adventure," and the bus you are on heads south through Ohio, crossing the Ohio River into Kentucky, and ending with those "slate waves" of the Gulf of

Mexico in Pensacola, in the western corner of the Florida panhandle. As the journey continues, out of the city into the "breathing fields," and back into various cityscapes with "all-night car lots / the last bar winking," finally the Ohio River which "inches toward the sea" is crossed, while "you" hold "your breath the whole way" across the bridge, and into "the dawn of a new world." While this is a realistic depiction of travel by bus from the north to the south in the U.S., a sense of the symbolic also dawns, with "grinding ridges / turning slowly to stone" and "roadside trees fighting / for light." The character ends by standing on the beach in Florida, counting waves, then turning for home. But at home the clock has apparently stopped, the parlour has shrunk in a kind of withering, and the hot meal, "waiting for life" like those squad cars, has turned cold. You may turn for home, but you may in fact not be coming home, if we are to read this little narrative symbolically. The new world you have entered, with its gray dawn and numberless slate waves, may look a lot like the world you have left, but this is one you cannot leave and come home from. Death is your home address now

        She dyed her hair black
        circled her eyes with blue moons

        he drank beer and more beer
        till morning splotched his face
        his eyes puffed shut

        the doctors reworked her face
        the mirrors clouded

        so she lay with anyone
        turning toward the wall
        to cry

        outside the freezing church
        through half the night
        his lips soft and pink
        as a girl's
        he lay down in snow
        scratched at trees
        tore into his own arms

himself a child
he turned from his children
to shake his fist
in his own face

she married and unmarried
flushed and aborted
she wrote
The jar that stood so high
broke
and fell away
she showed the words to everyone

he whispered into the dead phone
I'm from Dearborn and I'm drunk

They were all we had
of you before the car
shuddered a moment
then faced the coming traffic
all we knew of you
before the siren's pulsing faded
and the white attendant
turned and lit a cigarette

This letter at first offers parallel portraits of a man and woman in what appears to be a dysfunctional marriage. The story of the marriage is implied by the juxtaposed images, rather than narrated. And yet these could be a series of portraits not of two people but of several people, all affected by the absence of the one addressed. Whatever, things do not look good, as she tries to change her appearance radically and indiscriminately takes lovers and he drinks himself into a stupor and ends up face down in the snow. That he "turned from his children" and that she "married and unmarried" implies to me that they are a couple who are breaking apart. Each is endowed with a certain eloquence, she with a scrap of cryptic poetry, he with a gift for blunt alliterative expression *("I'm from Dearborn and I'm drunk")*. Any story, however, that we might construct—and the imagist, nonnarrative mode always invites the reader's imaginative participation when characters, action, and story are implied— is complicated and even subverted by the final stanza of the section. These people are, in fact, "all we had / of you before" and "all we knew of you /

before" the accident that killed you. Once again, is it Levine's father that is addressed, or is the "you" multiple, addressing both the woman and the man or the women and the men portrayed in the previous seven stanzas. Critics have complained that there is little or no ambiguity in Levine's work, nothing for the imagination to nurture in his memoirs chopped into short lines. Such criticism comes from literal-minded readers who cannot fathom the complexities Levine creates with a few strokes. The dead, however many and whatever their identity, have left behind not only desolate lives but images from their own lives which seem desolate. If there is any consolation in these grievous portraits, it is in the vividness with which they are evoked: her eyes circled "with blue moons," his "puffed shut," her face "reworked," his lips "soft and pink/as a girl's" as he lies "down in the snow," and finally that "white attendant" who "turned and lit a cigarette" as the siren of the ambulance or police car fades. Identity itself is ambiguous, for the dead may include, as in James Joyce's famous story of that title, the living, too.

3 a.m.
Early April and the house chants
in the night winds
each window gives back
a face
the lie is retold in the heart
the old denials burn
down the hallways of the brain
the dead refuse to die

the air crackles with their angers
the young mother wakens suddenly
and flees her bed and her own children
running over the mountain ground
her old man choking on his lungs
demands to be heard
the aunt paces the closed room
the brother burned in Asia
howls like a tree

And the children die
the sacraments we waited for
go gray
little flat sacks of refuse

and no one can look
or look away

the father, enormous
bunched against the green wall
says
over and over
Can you believe we loved you

All night
the rain in the still river
off the loading docks in Wyandotte
locked wheels
blind eyes of cars
the scattered intestines of purses
a pale carp
warped on its side

they bump slowly underwater

Here we are back in the present tense, back to the illusion of narrative which is really a catalogue, of the young mother's behavior, the children's fates, the father's impotence, and the landscape's acceptance of death. That this section begins with the time, 3 A.M., ought to remind us of F. Scott Fitzgerald's recognition in *The Crack-Up:* "In the real dark night of the soul it is always three o'clock in the morning." This is, however, a pivotal section of the poem. Once again, though the images bespeak a world without divine involvement, the living even in pain are vividly alive, as is nature, with its winds in spring making the house chant, and the rain falling into the Detroit River at Wyandotte, one of the cities downriver from Detroit. The vigor with which life is lived, even as life accumulates more and more dishonesty about itself is recorded with unsparing starkness, as lies are repeated, "denials burn," and most importantly, "the dead refuse to die."

This section makes no pretense of addressing anyone, dead or alive. It simply records another space of time "without you." But a new landscape encroaches. The young mother in stanza three who runs "over the mountain ground" may be heralding the Spanish landscape which will haunt the sections to follow. At this time in his career, Levine is most alive, least angry, most reconciled with experience when he is situated in Spain. It is important to note, too, that in section three of the poem, with its references to Toledo and Pensacola, there is a kind of double vision with Spain. These are Spanish place names, too. Section 5 introduces the idea of sacraments ("the sacraments we waited for / go gray"), and the eye of the poet begins to turn toward an older landscape, no less beset by death, but still redeemed possibly by a pastoral tradition. Meanwhile the family members render their futility unto fates that are all too clear: the young mother running away as her husband chokes to death, the wounded brother howling in pain, the children dying, and the father—again an impotent figure—averring that *we loved you* over and over apparently without being heard. Anyone unaware that Levine is a poet who loves anger and invites it into his poems has to become aware in the middle of this long article of grief and grievance. The world "without you" is one hell of a place, where even purses may be disemboweled, and all the fish in the river, bumping against each other underwater, are dead. Still, "the dead refuse to die." They are spiritually present in this dispirited landscape

When will the grass be bread
when will the sea winds bring no salt
to raze the yellow shoots
the pear grind its sand
honey sting the tongue
when will the stars put out their eyes
our hands touch
and the onion laugh

Above Three Rocks
40 miles from here sheep gather
in the mountains
huddling together
in a cup of earth and stone
until the bud of light
flowers in the east

and the old Basque with a cane
comes to lead them down
the passes

The influence of Garcia Lorca's brand of elemental surrealism can be seen in the first stanza of this sixth section of the poem. Surrealism in any art is not only a mode of inventive juxtaposition, but of radical transformation, rooted in natural processes. How strange that grass might be bread, that the pear might grind sand, that honey might sting. And yet of course grass does become bread, there's a definite graininess to the skin of pears, and honey is produced by a stinging insect. As for the stars putting out their own eyes or the onion laughing, these potential actions are based respectively on metaphor (stars as eyes, the sun as the day's eye) and paradox (the onion produces tears not laughter). The last two images of the stanza bracket a simple emotive one, which has no surreal dimension, but expresses a longing for connection. Our hands might, once again, be the hands of the living and the dead. The poem receives part of its extensive reach by playing with time. When will these things occur, the stanza asks, as if they could never occur. It doesn't take long to recognize that they occur all the time.

Not only is the Spanish poet Lorca evoked in this section, but the Spanish landscape is as well, but again in a kind of optical illusion. The pastoral imagery of the second stanza, again with its elemental metaphors of mountains huddling in a cup and the sunrise budding and flowering, produces a Basque shepherd in one of those scenes as old as time. But "Three Rocks" is a community in the southwestern part California's Central Valley, near Fresno where the poet lived and worked. It is located at the base of the Coast Range. Basques from northern Spain settled throughout the American west, particularly in the south end of the Central Valley, known as the San Joaquin. In a poem where so much realistic detail, especially in narrative sections, turns symbolic, the "old Basque with a cane" who "comes to lead" the sheep "down/the passes," is our guide, too, our Virgil. Our destination is not the underworld, but as it has been throughout the poem, it is the world

> the dead have left to us
> The sea calmed
> the village darkened toward dawn
> I was there
> awake in a strange room
> my children
> breathing slowly in the warm air
>
> down the hall
> the workers bunched together
> three to a bed grunting
> in sleep
>
> beside me my wife
> in still another world

on the room
not a single light
the sea reflecting
nothing
one black wave untipped
with spray
slipping toward shore
to spread like oil
—and then no more
nothing moved
no wind
no voice

no sound of anything
not one drop riding down my face
to scald the earth

I am going to hazard a guess that the village where the poet awakes "in a strange room" is the one he identifies as Fuengirola, in the penultimate section of the poem, a place in southern Spain, on the Mediterranean. It is located in Andalusia, the region most closely associated with Garcia Lorca. In the poem's scheme, the Basque shepherd of section six has led us from Fresno to this village on the Costa del Sol and a landscape where Lorca himself is most prominent among the dead who refuse to die.

It is in section seven that the poet speaks in first person for the first time in the poem. He depicts himself surrounded by living beings, his family and strangers, all sleeping and even estranged from him in their sleep, but still present, in another dawn that darkens before the sunrise, like the dawn in the poem's first line. Has the poet awakened to another dark night of the soul, like the 3 A.M. which begins section five? The negations of the section's final two stanzas might be read as reflecting that isolation and abandonment created by the dead in dying. There is no light, the lightless sea is like a black wave of oil, nothing is moving, no one is speaking, and there is no sound of life, for even the sounds of breathing mentioned earlier have been negated. The poet is alone with his grief, as he has been throughout his life. However, he is in a new place, a foreign world, in which the simplest of things can seem transformed and given a new vitality. He sheds no tears, "not one drop." Here Levine's negation has to be read as affirmation. For this moment, and perhaps for only this moment, the griever is released from his grief. Temporary as such a release might be, it is not to be forgotten. The value of this vivid moment is reproduced in the next section of the poem, with images both stirring and troubling, consoling and mysterious, but all echoing the poem's earlier images of the dead and their desolate survivors, yet this time showing us a dramatic living intensity. In opposition to the enervating absences imbuing the earlier images, these radiate an invigorating sense of presence.

I ate an apple
the skin the sour white meat
the core
how I relished
the juice

Praise the apple

I struck my strange tall son
again and again
until my wife came begging
from our bed
and pulled me away

for 40 days
I dreamed my death like yours
at great speed
the bones shattering into meat
blood blurring the world
the spirit issuing outward
in a last breath

and came to land
weak and alive
the sunlight crossed my bed
I rose and fed the cat
the green worms fattened
on the vine
I looked in the corners
of things

high on my brother's left shoulder
I carved the old scar
again and again

my signature cut
almost to bone
even the brown silky hairs
and the mottlings from birth
will never hide it

Let the scars shine

south of Cadiz
I stopped the car and ran
in winter mist
to the black margin of the world
the wet rocks stared out unseeing
my tracks crumbled behind me

Bless our blind eyes

The potentialities of Section 6, e.g. "when will the grass be bread," are realized in that apple the poet bites into at the beginning of this section. Lyricism in the use of imperative refrains ("Praise the apple," "Let the scars shine," "Bless our blind eyes") and in the use of anaphora ("I ate," "I struck," "I rose," "I looked," "I carved," "I stopped") links the series of parallel actions, allowing a single, coherent personality to emerge. And though the first and last stanzas record images of praise, for the apple and for the freedom of running through a misty field in a foreign land, the other stanzas offer us more ambivalent portraits of a man who as father, husband, son and brother, continues to demonstrate what life is like "without you." The stanza about striking his son and being pulled back to bed by his wife is one of the most distressing in this poet's work, as much for the violence it depicts as for the recognition that his son is "strange." The dream of reliving the father's death, graphic and brutal in both image and sound, is given a symbolic aura by the Biblical preface, "for 40 days." Not only is the span of time mysteriously meaningful, but the acts of intensity, if not violence, seem to be part of a cyclical pattern. After the violent dream of father's death, the speaker experiences a kind of release and a return to life, though weak as if drained, and a return to simple domestic matters like feeding the cat and checking the tomato vines. Looking "in the corners / of things" might even suggest the sort of observation and meditation of the poet. But this respite ends with a recurrent memory of harming his brother, scarring him, and then affirming the value of such a record by commanding that the scars should be allowed to "shine."

The final stanza describing the poet running into the mist may be taken as a flight from himself. It occurs "south of Cadiz," another place in Andalusia, this one a famous port on the Atlantic side of the Iberian Peninsula. The discovery of Spain and Spanish history, particularly the history including the Spanish Civil War (during which Lorca was executed by the fascists), has been a central event in the development of Levine's poetry. It gave him a new direction and extended the range of his poetry. It allowed him a Keatsian access to negative capability and empathy. No wonder he blesses the blindness of himself and the landscape he runs through, those "wet rocks" that "stared out unseeing." Again the cycle of intensity and release is enacted, and the poet's responsibility to say "what it is / without you" is taken up once more in the penultimate section of the poem.

Early March
a clear and windy day
in the village of Fuengirola
near the new concrete housing project

the workers playing soccer
on their noon break

under the torn roof of rushes
he sat in shadow
legs crossed
a tiny man burned by sun
unshaven for days
a *campesino* I'd seen
many times coming home
his corduroys dusty

in the first dark
one special Sunday
bearing
a gleaming sea bass
gaffed and dripping
down the length of one leg

a small stiff man
now bowing forward to strike
his forehead against the earth

the left hand flung out
and opened to the sky
the right hand bunched
to his breast

hidden below the cries of play
the words I couldn't understand
the strikings of the earth
again and again
the shakings of the head
NO NO
the eyes riding in tears
seeing and unseeing
the mouth asking everybody and nobody
Why Why

until the trees blackened
the air chilled
the oil drums flared
a moment
and died
wind sound only
bamboo creaking through the cold night
and by morning he was gone

tending his patch of lettuce
combing the small field
of fine green onions
stooping all day
to the parched earth

Though Spain may be a place of wonder for the poet, it is also a country where lives go on in earnest, also in the presence of the dire and stressful absence of those who are dead. Though the curious and colorful peasant or campesino, sunburned and stubbly, in dusty corduroys, sporting a freshly caught sea bass makes a contrast under his "torn roof of rushes" with the "new concrete housing project" in the village of Fuengirola, his behavior on one particular day resonates strongly with the poem's other images of grief. His actions so captivate the poet that they are described in precise detail, even to the way his hands are held. The right hand "bunched/at his breast" suggests an act of contrition, and the words he utters, which the poet does not understand, masked by the cries of the workers playing soccer, seem to be translated by the way the "small stiff man" bows and strikes the earth with his forehead. Surely, according to the shaking of that head and the weeping eyes, he must be saying, "No" and "Why." Once the poet recognizes that he is seeing a public act of sorrow and remorse, a protest demonstration to the earth and to God, he paints the atmosphere and setting in ways that recall the scenes set in Detroit earlier in the poem: "the trees blackened/the air chilled/ the oil drums flared." Apparently the *campesino* mourns through the night. Once again the diurnal cycle comes into play, for in the morning the peasant is gone, the announcement of his absence rendering another ambiguity. Is he gone as the dead are gone? Or simply finished with his public exhibition? The final unpunctuated stanza simply by its grammar does not resolve the ambiguity of his departure. Is he gone, no longer to tend his bit of garden, or has he returned to it, to his small field of lettuce and green onions, where he stoops "all day / to the parched earth"? The formal style of the poem allows this mystery to achieve a power beyond its simple rendering. And the image of the man, striking his head against the earth in a Spanish village, becomes an archetypal figure of grief and grieving, casting its shadow across the poem and blending with all the others.

> No one comes home from school
> above the porch
> the light takes hold
>
> the papers bleed in a puddle
> all night the radio
> jives itself
>
> a photo torn in half
> dances in the grate
> like a cry for help
> your books on the shelf
> give up their words
> one by one
>
> your wedding band
> with its secret calligraphy of wear
> sleeps in a coffee can

a turnip forgotten
darkens
at the back of the drawer

the mice
settle in the walls
their fierce hearts ticking

Morning—
on the freeway
a white cap skips
and I slow for an instant
and pass

warm days—
the child you never saw
weeds the rhubarb
white grains collect above his lips
and flake away in the sudden wind

even the dead are growing old

Throughout the final section of the poem, small particulars—the porch, the newspapers in a puddle, the coffee can, and especially the freeway—strongly imply that the setting once again is America. Where in America, Detroit or Fresno, is not clear but it is only important that the poem, having established that the attitudes of human grief are universal, now returns to a native landscape. That said, the stanzas, as often before, exist in a paratactic, parallel relationship with each other, without a narrative to link them, so that many of the images could as well exist anywhere on the earth, wherever human beings experience loss and live in the penumbra of their dead. Images of absence and abandonment, almost exclusively domestic, unfold one after another. The relics of some former possessor lose touch with their meaning, the photo torn and incinerated, the books exfoliating their words, the wedding ring asleep in a coffee can. What has been taken from the natural world, like that turnip in the drawer, has been forgotten and will eventually spoil, and the mice, unhindered, seem to be the only living things in the place, wherever that place is; they settle in the walls as if they were making themselves comfortable, although the action of settling also suggests a kind of degradation, which their fierce, clock-like hearts may not be able to overcome.

The poem ends with two very brief narratives, neither set in the abandoned place the first seven stanzas of the section seems to depict. The first one is the image of the "white cap" skipping on the freeway, as the poet drives past, slowing—to observe it or to avoid it or both? The cap is another relic, once owned by someone, possibly denoting a trivial or tragic loss. It is morning when the poet drives past it, and whatever personal meaning the article of clothing has, now a piece of freeway flotsam, he keeps to himself. The second is not so much a narrative as an image of an event happening through time, on "warm days." A child, clearly the poet's child, works in a garden that recalls the *campesino's* small field in the previous section. Here, too, the identity of the "you" has a specificity it often lacks in previous sections. It could be that the child is a grandson of the father Levine lost when he was himself a child. He is weeding rhubarb, that tough, tart fruit of the poor, which has to be sweetened before it can be consumed, but which still bites through any amount of added sweetness. Those "white grains" that collect above the child's lips as he works and "flake away in the sudden wind" are tantalizing in their ambiguity. They could be specks of earth, sand, dust, or even the sugar which a stalk of raw rhubarb has to have if eaten right off the plant. A gust of wind blows them away. And the poem ends just as abruptly with a statement that combines relief and resignation. Time that has played such an important role in a poem that seems to have no overall chronological order is the antidote to eternity: "even the dead are growing old." If our dead haunt us in our temporal world, then they must grow old and die, too. New generations which never met and do not remember them will hardly note the passing and extinction of their memory. Though the dead surely know this, it is still important to give them this message.

KATE DANIELS

Learning from "1933":
A Modern Poetic Sequence

LONG AGO, WHEN I WAS FALLING IN LOVE with a man I sensed had great depth of feeling, but who often kept his conversations with me determinedly upbeat and maddeningly superficial, I interrupted his chatty conversation over lunch one day, to lean across the table, and say, "Tell me something real."

I could tell he was surprised. But then he pushed back from his plate, and took a deep breath. Looking straight into my eyes, he said, "OK. I think about death a lot."

I have often thought of that man over the years when reading certain of Philip Levine's poems. In particular, "1933"—one of Levine's most iconic poems which takes its title from the year of his father's death when the poet was only five—always brings back to mind my former lover, who also experienced the trauma of losing his father while still a boy . . .

* * *

I began reading Philip Levine in the late 1970s. He was a poet I admired from my first encounter with him on the page. I was immediately attracted both by his thematic content which resonated with my own background, and by the unique persona—feisty, working class, and occasionally profanely angry—that narrated his poems. Because my attraction to his work was mostly through my personal connection with its narrative content, I read almost exclusively for the stories that Levine's poems disclosed that I had not found elsewhere in American poetry. I read him breathlessly, almost lunging from narrative point to narrative point, amazed that the suppressed tales of the "unpoetic" lives of the underclass had been liberated at last into poetry. Reading him, I felt exultant and epic. As a consequence, the formal presentation of his poems was generally lost on me. It took me years to realize that Levine's lyric gift was as great as his narrative genius. But because I was so in love with his storylines, I privileged narrative over all, and impatiently rushed past the music that makes so many of his long narratives unforgettable in the ways that lyric language can permanently inscribe itself inside us, soldering together form and content.

As a young poet attempting to wrest poetry from the poetically unpromising exigencies of my working-class origins, I found that merely fulfilling the basis requirements of everyday life depleted both my physical and mental energies. Fitting the demanding work of poetry into this economy of scarcity was difficult to achieve, given poetry's absolute insistence on mental intensity and hyper focus. Poetry had been my friend and steady companion since childhood. I knew I could depend on it to sort and settle me. But for awhile at the beginning of my serious apprenticeship, perhaps as a practical response to the mental demands that poetry made on my taxed psyche, I developed a rigid syllabus for myself, and utilized a kind of tunnel vision about what specific poetic practices I believed I could learn from. I insisted on down to earth subject matter, plain-style diction, accessibility to ordinary readers—in other words, straightforward narrative poems that privileged storytelling over all. The story lines and the characters in Levine's poems fulfilled these requirements almost perfectly. At the same time, however, his narratives were always more than narrative. Even if I tended not to hear it in the early days, a lyric impulse internally enlivened all his poems with gorgeous linguistic displays that regularly lifted his hard working-sensible-shoes approach right off the page, relocating it in the atemporal, all-about-beauty realm of lyric utterance.

Of course, I see now that my rigid approach was what I thought constituted the most direct route to teaching myself how to write well in a narrative mode. I had chosen Levine to teach me how to do it because I loved the stories he told of proletarian lives, and the characters he created who often resembled people in my family of origin, and whom he treated with extraordinary respect, turning inside out the way the world tended to see people like them, conferring dignity. His poems were rarely straightforwardly "political," and yet they were radical in effect. I wanted to do something similar with my own stories. But I wanted to do it plainly, and directly. Why did Levine sometimes gussie it up with extraneous language? Couldn't he stick to straight and narrow of direct narrative? Couldn't he clear out the clutter? Couldn't he stick to the meat and potatoes? Why put fancy sauces on top of the good stuff?

"1933" the title piece of Levine's 1974 collection was a poem I admired from first reading. Right away, I connected it with a slightly earlier poem by James Tate, "The Lost Pilot," the title piece of Tate's first book in 1967. Both are elegies, addressing the archetypal and traumatic experience of father loss. While each poem begins with a startlingly assertive and visceral statement—

> Levine: My father entered the kingdom of roots
> Tate: Your face did not rot

—they take radically different paths and formal approaches after opening. While "The Lost Pilot," narrates clearly and directly its story of a father who was shot down in war, lost before the poet was born, "1933" unfolds elliptically in nine stanzas of irregular lengths with unpredictable indentions, no punctuation, and moves back and forth in time across settings and characters. "The Lost Pilot" utilizes straightforward and efficient storytelling that ends definitively with final closure that feels as permanent as death itself. "1933" can't seem to make up its mind whether it wants to go forward, or backward, to stay in real time, or enter the realm of alternative realities. It takes its time in the telling, and seems unconcerned with the brevity that poetry usually aims for. It is lush with imagery that sometimes veers into the surreal. Its narration is not chronological. It ends ambiguously:

> In the cities of the world
>   the streets darken with flies
>   all the dead fathers fall out of heaven
>   and begin again
>   the angel of creation is a sparrow in the roadway . . .
>
> Once in childhood the stars held still all night
>   the moon swelled like a plum but white and silken
>   the last train from Chicago howled through the ghetto
>   I came downstairs
>   my father was writing in a great black book
>   a pile of letters
>   a pile of checks
>   (he would pay his debts)
>   the moon would die
>   the stars jelly
>   the sea freeze
>   I would be a boy in worn shoes splashing through rain

To the narrative literalist I was at that age, "The Lost Pilot" was my idea of exactly what a narrative poem should be and do: accessible language that got right to the point, and was tidily organized and balanced on the page: nothing extraneous or fancy to detract (or distract) from the task at hand: to create a coherent character and to tell a story. "1933"—despite being written by my favorite narrative poet—was a more slippery character. Formally, "1933" is both tidy and untidy. In contrast to the soldier-straight tercets of Tate's poem which only took up a page and a half, "1933" surprised and unsettled me with the way it sprawled across four pages, and by how much of it entailed lyric imagery that I could not directly connect to the poem's storyline. Composed of nine stanzas that follow no regular pattern (and resist the attempt to identify one), the stanzas range from seven lines to seventeen. Syllable length of individual lines varies disconcertingly from two to fifteen. The poem is visually embellished throughout by indentions, but there is no punctuation to help with pacing. It seems determined to wrongfoot the reader by confounding the conventional narrative expectations of elegy. Whatever I might have thought I knew about poetic representations of bereavement and mourning, "1933" seemed to suggest that I was probably wrong. What I ultimately came to understand from studying Levine's approach in "1933" had to do with the way in which 20th century poetry re-imagined long narrative forms: not as continuous, scroll-like storylines of expressive exposition, but as what M.L. Rosenthal (in his eponymous study) called "the modern poetic sequence." Rosenthal defined this as a series of constellation-like segments or fragments that gained cohesive narrative power from being convened in the same text, and then being made dynamic by the reader's internal efforts to imaginatively connect them within the context of their own experience and associations. "1933" does that in ways that pushed forward the practice of elegy, and also added to our psychological understanding of the process of mourning.

In his comprehensive study, Rosenthal observed that while modern poetic sequences "spring from the same pressures on sensibility" that have always goaded poets into language, the sequence is revisionary and responsive to the particularities of contemporary life:

> [The modern poetic sequence] is a response to the lyrical possibilities of languages opened up by those pressures in times of cultural and psychological crisis, when all past certainties have many times been thrown chaotically into question. . . . [I]t fulfills the need for encompassment of disparate and often powerfully opposed tonalities and energies.

It is relevant, I think, that "1933" was written during the 1970s when trauma studies was first being researched and articulated. One of the main discoveries about the mental experience of trauma concerned its non-linearity, and its recursive dynamics in the psyche. It is not only emotionally devastating, but temporally catastrophic. Despite the poetic testimony of centuries, traumatic loss is rarely, if ever experienced as neat, tidy, and chronological. "The Lost Pilot" was perhaps one of the last poems that seemed to suggest that it could still be convincingly represented that way. In contrast, "1933" (written just a few years later) pushed us forward into a more sophisticated and contemporary arena of psychoanalytic awareness.

• • •

Early parental loss is considered to be one of the most significant traumas that a child can undergo. While any traumatic event disrupts a narrative in progress, the death of a parent almost always shakes a young child's life to the core, and tends to carry consequences into adult life. Lacking life experience, and linguistically unsophisticated, without therapeutic interventions and emotional support, children can fail to integrate traumatic loss in a way that allows them to reestablish their faith in the future, in life going forward. Long-term consequences can be permanent problems with depression, anxiety, substance abuse, and lowered self-esteem.

It was more than a decade after coming to know both Levine's and Tate's poems about the deaths of their fathers that I began to learn about trauma, and its influence on human development. I studied this just as new theories about narrative and narrativity were being articulated in scholarly criticism, and together, over time, these two streams of thought have come to influence my ultimate understanding of each poem. The straightforward narrative of "The Lost Pilot" that I loved so much as a young poet now strikes me as relentlessly one way, trapped in old modes of poetic representation, and uninflected by the kind of transformative, dynamic experience I look for in poetry. Although I still appreciate its sad and lovely music, I now read it as locked into its own sadness and overwhelming sense of irrevocable loss, and lacking in possibility for redemption or healing.

Conversely, "1933," which so frustrated me as a young poet with its deviation from "straight" narrative has grown in depth and acquired context over the years. Those "gussied up" extras of extravagant imagery that I objected to as a young poet? "I find the glacier and wash my face in the Arctic dust." "The old hen flies up in a spasm of gold." They now delight me with evidence of the irrepressible life force of the poet's imagination that overrode traumatic loss. Likewise, the poem's breakdown into fragmentary utterances which I once saw as eschewing narrative now testify to recovery from trauma, and demonstrate the efficacy of the modern poetic sequence as both replacement for and improvement upon the long poems of the past. Paradoxically, the poem's warped and discontinuous sense of time; its willingness to linger or lag on details or images that do not seem to move the narrative forward; its sliced up, out of context imagery; its broken utterances conjure a wholeness that—though ruptured by traumatic loss—once undoubtedly, authentically existed:

69

The hands that stroked my head
the voice in the dark asking
he drove the car all the way to the river
where the ships burned
he rang with keys and coins
he knew the animals and their names
touched the nose of the horse
and kicked the German dog away

Perhaps because what was lost—the father and the sense of security he lent to his son's life—has not been merely mourned, but has also been reclaimed and retained— processed—through writing, the poem suggests that a replacement for the lost father might be possible in the future: "I blink the cold winds in from the sea / walking with Teddy, my little one."

Even so, the traumatic taint of death, and the reality that traumatic change is a constant possibility in life insures that any walk the grown poet might take with a loved one can never be experienced completely free of trauma's heavy shadow. The passage that suggests redemption is possible completes itself warningly:

walking with Teddy, my little one
squeezing his hand I feel his death

In this, I see "1933" as moving beyond the keening and wailing that is generally the work of elegy. It plays on a larger stage than more conventional elegies, and is a masterwork in the poetic depiction of traumatic experience in early life; and the give and take, the imagistic "constellations" of the long poem strategy make this possible. Even if the worst happens, and "the stars jelly," "the sea freeze[s]" and "the moon . . . die[s]," the poem shows us that life can reinvent itself in the form of a newly fatherless son who will over time, with resiliency and support, and perhaps through the medium of poetry, evolve again into a living child, at ease in the world—something as ordinary and unselfconscious as what we see in the poem's final image: "a boy in worn shoes splashing through rain," caught up in the generative flow of human life, not death. From the interplay of these two binaries complicated by trauma, he will grow up to make a great poetry.

"1933," from *1933,* Philip Levine (Atheneum, 1974)
"The Lost Pilot," from *The Lost Pilot,* James Tate (Yale University Press, 1967)
The Modern Poetic Sequence, by M.L. Rosenthal and Sally Gall (Oxford University Press, 1983).

KEVIN CLARK

The Surprise of the Inevitable in
"No One Remembers" and "New Season"

MUCH IS RIGHTLY MADE OF Philip Levine's immersion in working class consciousness, especially the way he entered, rendered, and transformed the quotidian wounds and wisdom of blue-collar men and women. In his focus on the impoverished lives of proletarian Americans, I've always felt Levine was a kind of poet's cousin to Joe Hill, the songwriting union activist in the early 1900's. Both men recognized the foundational inequities inherent in a society in which figures of great wealth exert smothering control over people of less money, means, and education. But where Hill wrote songs to inspire collective resistance, Levine wrote poems intent on presenting the painfully circumscribed lives of the working poor. And where Hill imagined a better future, Levine usually offered only the hardscrabble present in the voice of a threnodic speaker who's both resigned to the necessity of such punishing work while unwilling to quit beneath its weight.

This impulse toward psychological naturalism is even more pronounced in Levine's longer poems. Though seeming fairly straightforward, his approach to the longer form is in fact deceptively complex. In the arc of modernism, starting primarily with Pound and Eliot but continuing with H.D., Stevens, Williams, Olson, and Zukofsky, long poems were often set off in enumerated sequences and, on a granular level, they could be quite intentionally fragmented. Sometimes taking sudden leaps in subject and voice, certain modernist long poems look dramatically disjointed in form. (Think of The Cantos or, say, "The Fire Sermon" section of "The Waste Land.") And in the tradition of much modernist verse, an equally challenging range of recondite allusions coincides with the magnitude of fragmentation. Readers might indeed benefit from encyclopedic knowledge of multiple cultures. But this was not to be Levine's style.

In *The Modern Poetic Sequence: The Genius of Modern Poetry*, M.L. Rosenthal and Sally M. Gall remind us that poetry is a matter of affect, and that tonality is the primary verse characteristic that influences affect. In other words, poetry is always first received as sensation, not idea—and the quality of sensation depends to a great degree on the poem's tone of voice. Rosenthal and Gall are particularly good at pointing out how tone, time, and attitude can shift to great effect in long poems. Certainly, a stable tone may adhere in short poems, but as poems grow longer the poet has much greater opportunity for a realistic psychological portrait that mimics real-time feeling. Just as most people experience emotions in flux—that is, just as emotions rise, fall, revert, undermine, split, pool, etc.—the lengthier poem may also experience ongoing emotional variation. Similarly, a long poem can change its point of view about a subject or event, while simultaneously flashing back and/or forward. Though Philip Levine's long poems under discussion here are not sequences, they seem always to foreground tonality at the same time they are quietly employing myriad modernist devices.

Because Levine wrote a reasonably accessible lyric-narrative that often romanticized workers in part because they worked without achieving just recompense, some critics have a mistaken tendency to find his oeuvre anti-modernist, thus thin on depth and originality. This dismissiveness can be particularly evident when the subject is his longer poetry. But in fact, his poetry—and especially his extended verse—is both formally inventive and emotionally resonant. Helen Vendler once infamously and erroneously asserted in *The Music of What Happens* (Harvard University Press, 1988), "I am not convinced that Levine's observations and reminiscences belong in lyric poems, since he seems so inept at what he thinks of as the obligatory hearts-and-flowers endings of 'poems.'" In applying the term "hearts-and-flowers," Vendler wants us to see Levine as a writer of melodrama rather than a serious poet who captures the daily agonies of working life.

But melodrama requires exaggeration, and, in their length and breadth, these poems do not exaggerate. It might in fact be the rarefied critic who lacks adequate experience and imagination to see the realism—and the innovations—in the poet's gritty flesh-and-soul depictions of physically exhausting labor. Vendler's assumption is as misguided as believing that Levine's men and women are too simple to be of interest. As Richard Tillinghast wrote in *The New York Times Book Review*, Levine's protagonist is never "a blue-collar caricature." Not only do Levine's people think and feel with existential depth and acuity, but his poems consistently demonstrate an inventiveness of form, particularly the longer poems.

In "No One Remembers" and "New Season," each roughly 100 lines and both from his landmark collection *The Names of the Lost* (Atheneum, 1978), Levine has ample room to veer suddenly from his concrete physical descriptions of place to employ singular metaphors and similes that appear in contrast so quickly and mysteriously as to seem surreal. For instance, in "No One Remembers" he enacts a signature Levine trope, saying he never saw his troubled uncle open his hands "like a prayer and die/into them the way a child / dies into a razor . . ." To "die" in these two ways—into one's hand and into a razor—is idiosyncratically effectively because both indicate a kind of giving up, the first into despair and the second into suicide. In the blend of the poem's mortal context and imagery, we sense the metaphor enacting its dread meaning. Similarly in "New Season" the speaker imagines visiting his elderly mother:

> Tonight, after dinner,
> after the long, halting call
> to my mother, I'll come out here
> to the yard rinsed in moonlight
> that blurs it all, She will not
> become the small openings
> in my brain again through which the wind
> rages, though she was the ocean
> that ebbed in my blood, the storm clouds
> that battered my lungs, though I hide
> in the crotch of the orange tree
> and weep where the future grows
> like a scar, she will not come again
> in the brilliant day.

Once more Levine has plenty of room to proffer his blend of existential context and image that suggests the way an adult son can individuate from a parent, even though the resulting freedom is marked by a harrowing understanding of the life to be lived. Thus, "the wind rages." In both cases, and in countless others throughout his work, the poet turns to unusual metaphors in order to enliven—indeed, recreate—the experience for the reader. His method grants immediacy to the scene, and we virtually experience the sensations his characters do.

In these longer poems Levine also repeatedly shifts time and place so rapidly that a reader has to constantly check on the speaker's positioning vis a vis other characters in the poem. Frequently, as in "No One Remembers' and "New Season," those characters include women who suffer along with the men in the family, sometimes victimized by the men themselves. We should always remember that the speaker of Levine's best poems is not merely a sympathetic outsider but a former laborer who has emerged directly from the same socio-economic milieu about which he writes, one that offers little succor, only the inevitable next day of work. Through that speaker, Levine finds ways to invest lost lives with great, if transient, sentiment and meaning. Forgotten lives are valorized. Though "No One Remembers" and "New Season" demonstrate the relentless pressure to do backbreaking work as well as the psychic damage that results from that pressure, both poems deliver various forms of surprise, which is the key requirement of all good literature. After all, we come to literature to find ourselves in a state of wonder—and to varying degrees close readers of these poems should be surprised from beginning to end of each.

Like many of Levine's poems, "No One Remembers" is a capacious exercise in stunning ironies. Depicting memories within memories, he stages at least five different time periods in the poem, which collectively enhance the speaker's simultaneous love and loathing for the older man. First, the speaker—later called *"Philip"* by his uncle—begins the poem in the morning at a cemetery:

> A soft wind
> off the stones of the dead.
> I pass by, stop the car
> and walk among none
> of my own, to say
> something useless
> for them, something
> that will calm me under
> the same old beaten sky
> something to let me
> go on with this day
> that began so badly
> alone in a motel 10 miles
> from where I was born.

We'll never exactly discover why the day began badly, though it's safe to assume the speaker finds his return to this environment dispiriting. Beginning with the next stanza, he (1) muses back in time when Uncle Joe would "come at him" in violent anger, (2) reflects on how it's one more tough morning in other working class locales, (3) considers how he will soon visit his aunt, Joe's wife, (4) recalls a time as a kid when Joe beat his wife, and (5) finishes with a memory from early childhood when Joe acted with contrasting kindness.

Asserting that the working life can contribute to the way caring people may transform into beasts, the poem is not a long version of the simple lyric narrative that Vendler would dismiss. That is to say, it's not traditionally formed; it's not a well-described event contextualized by a single epiphany. While we engage with its challenging metaphors, "No One Remembers" also demands we attend to its swift shifting, a trope that keeps readers captivated beyond the limits of a traditional lyric. Levine's velocity helps us to experience a consciousness in roiling contention with the inexorable forces of the brute world.

The onslaught of the implacable self-serving power of management— that is, an invincible dominance grinding the aspirations of ordinary human beings into weightless motes—engenders a range of emotions in its victims. Uninterrupted anger, violent desperation, climactic rage, ulcerous resentment, corrosive resignation . . . These are some of the more dramatic sensations I sense blowing through the typical Levine protagonist. His speakers channel these emotions into an articulate, rhythmic, melodic snarl. Though Levine's long poems are structurally ambitious, we remember his voice more than his inventiveness. In effect, Levine renders the gall of a politically unequipped, even impotent citizenry. I would guess that a critic like Vendler, who famously praises the intellectually dense constructions of poets such as Stevens and Jorie Graham, would find so much feeling suspect—and would fail to recognize Levine's artfulness in the face of his passions. She'd also fail to see the very complexities of those passions. Modernism (and postmodernism) has always favored experiment over the everyday poles of human emotion. (Which is why the coloratural voice of Dylan Thomas made him such an outlier). In the consensus opinion of many critics, a measured sadness may undergird form and point-of-view, but not much more. Rosenthal and Gall actually coin a term for the inability to move past previous assumptions: "critical recalcitrance."

"No One Remembers" depicts the intertwined compulsions of three people, all of whom are victimized by the larger market society, and one of whom— Uncle Joe—victimizes the other two. "New Season" also presents the complex crosscurrents of despondency, but where the harsh limitations of work in "No One Remembers" helped to push Uncle Joe to domestic abuse, those same limitations heighten the racist tendencies of the working classes. The opening of "New Season," which recounts how Levine's mother and her grandson work together in the garden, establishes the effect of even mild physical labor on the body and mind:

> My son and I go walking in the garden.
> It is April 12, Friday, 1974.
> Teddy points to the slender trunk
> of the plum and recalls the digging
> last fall through three feet

of hard pan and opens his palms
in the brute light of noon, the heels
glazed with callus, the long fingers
thicker than mine and studded with
silver rings. My mother is 70 today.

Nothing in these lines suggests the kind of raw heartbreak brought on by uncompromising labor. If anything they intimate how gardening requires the kind of effort that ultimately results in recognizing a job well done. It's a middle class preoccupation. Having "joined / each other in the in the fellowship / of the shovel," his son and his mother enjoy such work.

But Levine intends a contrast: Over time he juxtaposes the pleasurable efforts in the garden with the coarsening effect of long-term work. Soon, by depicting the lives of some local men, the speaker shoulders the mood from a middle class appreciation of gardeners to the violent catharsis of laborers:

Teddy talks
of the wars of the young, Larry V.
and Ricky's brother in the movies,
on Belmont, at McDonald's,
ready to fight for nothing hard,
redded or on air, 'low riders,
grease, what'd you say about my mama!"
Home late, one in the back seat,
his fingers broken, eyes welling
with pain, the eyes and jawbones
swollen and rough. 70 today, the woman
who took my hand and walked me
past the corridor of willows
to the dark pond where the one swan
drifted. I start to tell him
and stop, the story of my 15th spring.

And in that context of the harsh grind, he tells his adult son "the story of his 15th spring," a time of the racially charged three-day riot in Detroit during June of 1943, at the height of World War II. Jobs were tight and Detroit was flooded with people from all over the country looking for the work brought on by the war effort. False rumors among both blacks and whites abounded, exacerbating tensions. We learn of "the lie" that "a sailor had thrown a black baby / off the Belle Isle Bridge," a falsehood compelling a man named

Damato, who said "'he was / goin' downtown bury a hatchet / in a nigger's head.'" We learn that a subdued Damato came back a long time later, "his right arm / blooming in a great white bandage." Human motives are many, and they intersect. Like Uncle Joe in "No One Remembers," we can presume that Damato is aggravated by unremittingly difficult labor, and that his own racism is heightened by weariness and accompanying anger.

In its span, the poem has shifted in time from the present ("It is April 12, Friday, 1974") to the deeper past of the riots. Then immediately the speaker jumps seven years ahead, and, as the attention switches from victimizer to victim, the atmosphere changes. When the speaker was twenty-two, a black woman named Della Daubien told him how during the riots she was hidden from white gangs by three white girls "so the [white] gangs couldn't finder her . . ." Maltreated by the twin vices of bigotry and oppressive economics, Della's face "glows . . . in shame / and terror."

Because the poem is long enough to naturalize the reader, we come as close as literature can bring us to inhabiting the full range of the psyche under duress. I read Levine for his presentation of the human heart as for his structural originality; or better yet, I am swept up in his passion due to his ingenuity. By the deeply moving end of "New Seasons," Levine is so far into his troubled reverie that Damato and Della—and even his son—have fallen out of his focus. Again, due to the poem's length, over time the poet has the ability to change attitude and even subject. His mother, who as a younger woman presumably experienced the full range of working-class hardship, has turned 70. The overbearing emotions of a past scarred by physical drudgery and seemingly unstoppable traumas funnel into a wondrously dark harmony of closing images:

> My cat Nellie,
> 15 now, follows me, safe
> in the dark from mockingbird
> and jay, her fur frost tipped
> in the pure air, and together we hear
> the wounding of the rose, the willow
> on fire—to the dark pond
> where the one swan drifted, the woman
> is 70 now—the willow is burning,
> the rhododendrons shrivel
> like paper under water, all
> the small secret mouths are feeding
> on the green heart of the plum.

I've always felt this ending is a remarkable convergence of opposing impulses. On one hand we have the willow, the rhododendrons, and the primal rose distressed not simply by time but by human tragedy. On the other hand, aren't the last two lines a dramatic image calling up—if not hope—then adamant endurance? The foundational emotion of this gut-reliant poet is the rage to *continue*.

Poetry is ultimately the art of affect. If we're lucky, we don't realize we're being influenced by literary device. Rather, in his lengthier verse, the gestalt of the poet's many poetic devices comes together in our immediate experience of the poem. Among the very best of all overtly political American poets, Philip Levine appeals to our sense of justice by first targeting our passions before our more cerebral appetites. Velocitous, metaphorically ingenious, complex in voice, his many (virtually invisible) devices help us to enter the lives of the working-class wounded—and to make us know not only their labyrinthine pain but their dogged stamina.

KATHY FAGAN

On "Ask the Roses"

Nel mezzo del cammin di nostra vita

ASK THE ROSES" IS THE TWENTY-THIRD POEM in Levine's 1976 book, *The Names of the Lost*, a slim collection of elegies comprised of twenty-five contiguous poems in total, several of which could be considered long. "Ask the Roses" is composed in parsing lines, a leftover perhaps from his formalist days—Levine will move to more heavily enjambed lines in books immediately to follow—and it omits conventional punctuation, a rarity in his poems.

I mention these details not to bean-count, but to illustrate certain choices Levine made as a mid-life poet, just as his work was becoming more widely read. Technically his seventh book, *The Names of the Lost* was his third with Harry Ford at the great New York poetry publisher Atheneum (to become Knopf); he had recently been awarded a Guggenheim Fellowship, which supported the writing of the book; and he published nine of the book's poems, including "Ask the Roses," in *The New Yorker.* In other words, Levine was receiving a new level of national attention, and the poems' bodies as well as their contents reflect that attention.

Not all of that attention was favorable. In his 1977 review of *The Names of the Lost* in *The New York Times,* Robert Pinsky criticized Levine for adopting a "Stone-Breath-Light-Snow" brand of surrealism in the book, claiming that the poems displayed a deficiency of thought and a "monotony of feeling and repetitiousness of method [that] produce a dark, sleepy air." While true that Levine indulges in surrealist tropes throughout this book, as well as several books after, it may be more useful—given the advantages of time and perspective we're granted these decades later—to consider the specific needs and purposes of Levine's work in his middle years, highly productive years for him. In an America just out of Vietnam, Levine was finally reaping professional rewards within a poetry community rapidly expanding to include, among others, younger poets whose themes, according to Levine, were those of "unmitigated ugliness," and international poets whose work was being translated into English by writers of Levine's generation at unprecedented rates.

Levine learned Spanish, for instance, because he admired the Spanish anarchists and considered poetry in Spanish to include some of the best poems of any language. Spain is one place in "Ask the Roses," Barcelona and Tarragona specifically, where Levine had spent time living with his family, researching the Spain of the Civil War and growing a passionate allegiance to its roster of anarchists who, he believed, shared his "faith in the essential goodness of men and women." While Levine thought of himself as a cynic, he admired moral survivors; and in middle age, he had come to believe that social change would not be brought about by poetry. He considered it his duty, rather, as a poet of established reputation, to "memorialize" (his word). "Ask the Roses" fulfills that duty. But it is also a meditative long poem with inquiry at its heart, interrogating some of its author's beliefs about himself, his aesthetics and his politics.

The poem's title, while understood rhetorically, prepares us I think for the poem's reliance on the natural world and its abundance of imagery, both real and surreal, with its first line, "Snow fell forward forever," working in both realms. The next three lines introduce the first-person I, as well as the figure of the tree, which repeats as often as the figure of the rose—these resonant in ways Levine was shrewd enough to know well. Filling out stanza one is the first of the poem's series of questions, with no question marks: "What became of the sea's dream / to become spirit and range the sky / what became of the astronomy/of the gopher tunneling under the lettuce / and the onion that died like a saint / from the head down . . ." What I admire in these lines is their great democracy: the onion and saint, the gopher and astronomer, the sea and the spirit. But it is an elegized democracy, and in the stanza that follows, in a landscape shift as typical of Levine as any surrealist I know, the ominous marketplace of Barcelona opens the poem to its consideration of economics and accountability.

Pinsky's review unfavorably compares lines from "Ask the Roses" to masterful lines from Levine's titular poem of 1968, "They Feed They Lion." Pinsky is right to hear in "Ask the Roses" echoes of "They Feed"—I hear them arrive as early as stanza two—but they are not merely echoes of the earlier poem; they are further evidence of Levine's ability to code language, like Lorca or Vallejo, for example, for both aesthetic and political ends. They are also deliberate musical choices. Much has been written of the origins, meaning and music of "They Feed"; Levine himself confessed he used the rhythms of Christopher Smart's 18th century "Jubilate Agno." But of course we also hear, in this second stanza of "Ask the Roses," the apocalyptic / biblical rhythms of Yeats and Whitman, as well as Levine's beloved Dylan Thomas.

In front of everyone
I take out my money and count it
stacking the 50s, the 20s, the 10s
The House of Peace, The Mansion of Wisdom,
The Tenement of Beauty
and the Martial Arts, Survival and Torture
We drink to the health of the dollar

Let my people go, say the coins
herded into the black purse
and headed for Germany
No one is going anywhere
we've all come into our own
and we're staying

"Ask the Roses" is obsessed with money, or rather, obsessed with the world's obsession with money and its widening net of capitalism; no one seems immune to its attraction or influence. The heartbreakingly funny lines of the third stanza read as both an awakening, or apology, to the abuses of nature in the name of commerce and the poet's resignation to it, to the fact that neither his recognition of abuses nor his writing about them will change anything.

has anyone asked the roses
if they love bees who are
basically communists
and worship the female . . .
Perhaps it is too late, now . . .
   . . . I want to take
a vow of silence, every word
is a young mouse growing in my throat
stretching his paws
trying out his pink nails

Following a moving and autobiographical meditation on his mother and aunt—I find this poem, after all these years, almost shockingly feminist, despite its modicum of male bluster—Levine turns most directly to one of his pet obsessions, usefulness, which is related, for him, to the nature of a thing and whether or not it's behaving as its nature intends.

Let the leaves falling singly in my hair
get up and join the tree
let the unread books open
into the nests of barn swallows
or turn to twigs in the long grass . . .
        . . . my old cat
full of foolishness and hungers
Shall we dye her blue, call her
"California" and teach her how to turn
how to walk on stage, how to hold
the mouse in her paws
Every evening we show her television
blackening the screen when the lions
drink in the crowded stream

Aside from the criticism of marketability, a concept we know all too well today, Levine directs focus here on the wrong we perpetrate when we don't let things be: the trees we harvest for paper, the domesticated house cat that would be wounded to see how removed she is from her feline nature. "Ask the Roses" may not be Levine's first foray into the eco-poem, informed by Emerson and most famously practiced, among Levine's generation, by Oliver and Merwin, but it certainly isn't his last. The lines move with purpose and freedom through associative thoughts and images that serve, like the bees, the industry of nature, so different from the industry of man, of which, as poet, Levine is but chronicler and elegist; as a human, however, he is a full participant, with all that participation implies.

In a nod to Frost's edict about how a poem should ride like ice melting on a hot stove, discovering its journey as it goes and in so doing become itself, Levine begins the final stanza of "Ask the Roses," "The pen that told the truth melted / on the stove, the ink that held / in its veins the bones / of the eel, let go / They became dirt." Here again, what is taken from a creature of the earth for use by the poet is returned to earth in the great cycle of life, just as everything is taken from us in the course of our lives.

After a few proverb-like statements in this final stanza, Levine makes two unexpected turns. First, he introduces a realistic setting in which he, as a man, understands the threat he poses to a woman walking her dog alone. In a curious few lines in which the speaker becomes dog, assailant and redeemer—"If she cast her eyes to the ground / I would smell it and shake her head / until her hair caught fire"—he prepares us for the poem's focus to shift to the speaker, his past mythic and historical, his present needs unmet.

Smelling myself I think of old clothes
schoolrooms the rain entered and killed
of a leather purse lost at sea
of a mule bleeding along the whipped flanks
a wind passing through a burned hand
the black embers flaking
of air a dog wouldn't breathe
I am space alone, unfilled, waiting day
after day for two people to be together
or only one who could sigh and be still

Levine talked and wrote a lot about thought and feeling in poetry. He claimed the poets who had influenced him most were Thomas and Williams. From the first, he learned beauty and song, what I heard him call pyrotechnics. From the second, he learned the democracy of plain American-English words, and committed himself to representing the unadorned in his work. He loved the poems and letters of Keats too, explaining Keats's notion of negative capability to his students over and over again. It was not Coleridge's analytic mind he admired, but Keats's romantic one; not Stevens's intellectual and linguistic play, but Williams's work ethic—Williams, a very "useful poet," Levine has said. Best known as a poet of the working-class, Levine felt strongly the allure of money and beauty, and these conflicting impulses collide in his poems as he ages and his fame grows.

As many of Levine's later poems do, "Ask the Roses" careens between Detroit and other "useful" places, like Detroit's "rural counterpart," as he called it, Fresno, California, his primary home until his death in 2015. The poem ends on a highly personal note: the poet's Detroit school days, his factory days—those he said he hated but brought him all his poems—and the sun-drenched days of middle age when one questions it all. Does our poet-child wait for his deceased father to return to his mother in these final lines? Or does he long for his own return home, to his partner, to himself, or to the earth, unambitious and undisturbed, at peace?

In her vibrant 2010 essay on the long poem for the Academy of American Poets, Rachel Zucker writes: "Poets perfect short poems by cutting away everything that doesn't absolutely need to be there . . . But the long poem has a different mindset. The long poem embraces and rejects and re-embraces imperfection. Sometimes it does so because it's trying to describe REAL LIFE, and life is imperfect, messy, filled with loose ends . . . Sometimes the long poem is imperfect because striving for perfection is a questionable and problematic pursuit." Unlike many Levine poems we can name, "Ask the Roses" isn't trying to perfectly describe "REAL LIFE," but impressionistically responding to *his* life: American male consumer, someone's aging son, someone else's danger, elegist, public figure, family man. In loosely linked stichics moving from forest to city to the "kingdoms of memory," as Levine calls it, "Ask the Roses" questions what is and why and can resolve none of it.

What Pinsky went looking for in "Ask the Roses" and *The Names of the Lost* was "not themes but the strands of a life." Both are here. The twelve-year age difference between them in the '70s were crucial years, experientially. Levine trusted his intuition, prizing above all functional beauty and loathing global economic trends that valued product over nature and profit over humankind. "Ask the Roses" reflects those concerns, priorities the young Detroit line worker enlarged to include affections, allegiances and ambitions he could never have imagined at twenty, or even thirty-eight. To watch them all begin to slip away, after they'd been so hard-won, is not simply the premise of the poem but the life-blood of this middle age meditation.

CHRISTOPHER BUCKLEY

On "Belief"

MOST READERS OF POETRY know the poems of Philip Levine for their poignant elegiac narratives, their bold imagistic closures, their straightforward "vivas" for the dignity of the human spirit surviving in the adverse conditions of the world. When Levine was appointed Poet Laureate of the U.S for 2011-2012, the media continually referred to Levine as "the poet of working-class Detroit." (To be sure, he was enormously gratified to read for the AFL/CIO who bought many copies of his book for its members). When he died in February of 2015, the obituaries repeated the same storyline. Through the powerful testament of his own life, Levine has born witness to the inhumanity as well as to the beauty of much of life at the end of the 20th century and on into the 21st. Through hands-on examples in the factories and in the cities, in America and abroad, his poems exposed the political pretexts by which social injustice is protected, and the stories of his life became the stories of many lives, and they raised the fortitude of the worker and lives of common people, with dignity, into their own mythical element. However, while it is true that a substantial portion of Levine's work extols the fortitude of the worker and praises the lives of common people, lifting them into their own dignified element, it is essential to realize that Levine's poetry has a range in style and vision that far exceeds the limits of that working label alone.

The many poems of witness and elegy for the soldiers, poets, and people of the Spanish Civil war extend the scope of Philip Levine's important themes and subjects and should not be overlooked. His attention is intense and exact, and hauntingly accounts for the individuals who gave their lives then to oppose Franco and fascism.

However, the publication of *Selected Poems* (Atheneum, 1984) presented readers with a distinct turn in theme evidenced in poems published in the books just before *Selected Poems*. A significant number of these poems have a more meditative style, a mode less autobiographical. There are still the hallmark Levine poems of specific and concrete narration, the startling imagery and grit of factory life, the transforming inner light of the human spirit; but the books, *Ashes* and *Seven Years from Somewhere* (Atheneum, 1979) and *One for the*

Rose (Atheneum, 1981) offered an expanded vision, a turn toward fictive and speculative strategies which developed a more metaphysical cast in the poetry. Some excellent examples of this "turn" are "Lost and Found," "Ashes," "Any Night," and "The Rains" in Ashes; "Let Me Be," "Now It Can Be Told," "Dark Head," and "Let Me Begin Again" in *Seven Years from Somewhere;* and "On My Own," "The Fox" and "I Was Born In Lucerne" in *One for the Rose*. But the poem which most singularly intoned this new view, this texture, was the long poem "Belief " from *One for the Rose.*

While Levine's middle books—*They Feed They Lion, 1933,* and *The Names of the Lost*—showed us a poet less furious with creation, less defiant and more accepting, the work following often made a more noticeable break from the past and moved toward spiritual themes or resolutions, albeit fairly secular ones. In "Belief," Levine's strategy is to use larger, more mythic and elemental images. He does not ground a place, time, speaker, and social condition, but turns to images of water, light, breath, wind, and earth. His view is somewhat eastern in that he sees all aspects of existence as interconnected; man is part of, not apart from nature. Each of Levine's images shines with a natural life-force and therefore rises easily and accessibly to the level of emblem.

Levine then counterpoints the weight and run of images with short narrative sketches. Yet, there is no consistent narrative in the poem, no autobiography or biography of character beginning to end; rather, it is Levine's meditative voice and all encompassing vision that direct the progress of the poem. It is a concept-centered strategy, a symphonic theme-variation-recapitulation approach which is often a strategy in movement of long poems, and this departs from the occasional strategy of many other long poems which come before such as "Pili's Wall," "Silent in America," "The Sierra Kid," "Letters for the Dead," and "Ask the Roses"—(although the theme and variation strategy is largely employed in "New Season"). *In Sweet Will* (Atheneum, 1985), *A Walk With Tom Jefferson* (Knopf, 1988), *What Work Is* (Knopf, 1991)—we see speakers whose lives are largely fictive. In "Belief," although there is the first person pronoun used in a good deal of the poem, the voice is not the familiar personal voice of Levine, that voice we know with the rich authority of "I/we lived here, worked at this, witnessed this done, made this life, cherished that." Instead, the voice in this poem is a disembodied voice, a speaker not particular or necessary to the historical Philip Levine.

To be sure, much of Levine's distinctive style is still very much in evidence in the poem—a powerful three-beat fine, the anaphoric structures which order and advance ideas and stories, the forceful emotional rhythms. But this is not mere habit; it is a necessary and convincing technique to mesh the imagistic and narrative sections of the longer poem; by the last line, the poem is sharply focused and there is a weight and resonance in the rhythm and imagery. Throughout this poem Levine "educates"/sets up the reader for the ending which arrives at a credence in a metaphysical existence.

Readers are familiar with how well Levine sets a scene and creates character and milieu with specific and closely observed detail, but he takes a slightly different tack in "Belief." In the poem's first section, images are derived from the natural world, and their broad scope complements the latitude of his subject, that expanded notion of life continuum after death, and the longer scaffolding of the poem allows Levine to establish this landscape. He initially builds images of wind, sea, long black volcanic reefs, and water.

> No one believes in the calm
> of the North Wind after a time
> of rage and depression.
> No one believes the sea cares nothing
> for the shore or that
> the long black volcanic reefs
> that rise and fall from sight
> each day are the hands
> of some forgotten creature
> trying to touch the unknowable
> heart of water.

There is no particular coastline; such specific information would dim the focus on the elemental and its perpetual cycle. Right away, Levine is careful to allow images to have their natural connotations as well as a figurative and slightly elevated sense of life. In the first three lines "North Wind" is invested with the human characteristics of rage and depression, while the sea still has its traditional values of life and mystery in the image of the "unknowable heart of water." Also the choice of the "heart" metaphor, here as well as in later sections of the poem, elevates the natural image and charges that image with even more life force. After the narrative vignettes, the poem returns to the singular concentration on images of light, water, and trees:

> . . . the bodies of the drowned collect
> light from the farthest stars and rise
> at night to glow without song . . .
> for the first time among all my family
> and that the magic of water

which has filled me becomes me
and I flow into every crack and crevice
where light can enter. Even my oak
takes me to heart. . . .

Here is the cyclical life-force of the environment and Levine has become part of it; the water has "filled" him, and it "becomes me" as has the light which allows him to be among "all my family" and so, one more piece of that light. Moreover, it is the "magic" / mysterious life principle of water which allows him to be taken into the oak tree. Thus, Levine, the meditative consciousness of the speaker of the poem, becomes one with the elements, shares, more than a little pantheistically, their life source. Again, the heart image is used to amplify the nature of the oak tree, and there is an appropriate focus on the light as well, for it integrates with the water and saturates the scene at the end of the poem. Even when the waves break in the final lines of the poem, they are "radiant" and "full." By a careful concentration on the images derived from nature, Levine moves the poem forward past the limitation of personal history, complaint, and mortal circumstance, toward a vision that is grander than the usually acknowledged limits of life on earth.

To enlarge his vision and amplify his theme, Levine employs a long poem structure that intersperses narrative vignettes with the panoply of natural images, thereby integrating the usual and human span of life with the elemental and the cosmic. The poem is a long strophe and not divided into stanzas so that these vignettes work in a larger symphonic mode, establishing a particular vision, then varying that atmosphere and recapitulating at the poem's end. The most thinly narrative/historical section is the allusion to the life and death of Keats which occurs in the early portion of the poem. Levine chooses Keats' famous line—"Here lies one whose name was writ in water."—not only for its thematic resonance of the brevity of life in the face of our desire and our efforts, but also for its appropriate connection with the imagery he is using. "Water" is again used as a life source image / symbol and also paradoxically it is associated with death and mortality.

. . . the lost breath of a man
who died in 1821 is my breath
and that I will live until
I no longer want to, and then
I will write my name
in water, as he did, and pass
this breath to anyone who can

believe that life comes back
again and again without end.

However, the final effect achieved by this allusion and all that the great name of Keats carries with it is the spirit of a life passing on to another, the soul of a great man and his great art continuing. Metaphorically, by power of his vision and belief as well as actually, it is possible that Levine, and others, share the breath of Keats—the idea in his spirit and art, and of course, quite literally, the actual molecules in the air. Here, Levine is very clear about his theme / belief.

He continues then, to add to his theme by including another narrative portion. He offers one place name, "Depot Bay," and addresses the loss of a "you" in this section, a man who, "ate / the earth and the creatures of the sea / and the air, and so it is time he fed / the small tough patches of grass / that fight for water and air . . ." This man could be father or brother; Levine does not say as he usually would; only the general association of the familial relationship fits his purpose—to enunciate the connection of the elemental life and our human life, to show one translated in the other. Each bit of narration is circumscribed with the essential imagery and vision of his meditation.

There is also, as counter point and balance, the story about the stout Catalan gentleman standing on the beach in Castelldefels, outside Barcelona. This section works mainly by gesture. After "admiring" the women on the beach, the gentleman turns away "with specks of fine sand / caught on his socks to remind him / that to enter the fire is to be burned . . ." almost as if he tangibly could carry his desire with him, or not escape it and the material weight of his life. Finally, he dares the sea to take him away "on a journey without end," which I think we can read as a wish to at once openly confront the limitations of the physical life and to transcend it.

> He went away with specks of fine sand
> caught on his socks to remind him
> that to enter the fire is to be burned
> and that the finger he pointed would
> blacken in time and probe the still earth,
> root-like, stubborn, and find its life
> in darkness. No one believes he
> knew all this and dared the sea
> to rise that moment and take him
> away on a journey without end
> or that the bodies of the drowned collect

light from the farthest stars and rise
at night to glow without song.

The sections of vignettes then, become a kind extended image; they are selec-
tions of experience, not consistent to or dependent on a single narration. They
are there to detail the struggle and the paradox of a specific earthly lifetime
and a continuance of a cyclical existence envisioned by the speaker of the
poem, and their detail and illustration afforded by the longer structure serve
as both spiritual and material variations on that very theme, and thus the sym-
phonic structure of the long poem serves the vision.

Levine also chooses a voice that allows our attention to be directed toward
his theme and away from personality. He speaks at times as an entity outside
the body, outside time; in places, he is almost the voice of Keats, or the child
of his past, or of the elements of and around the earth. It is an elevated con-
ceit, but one which is the perfect equation for the vital force in the properties
of the earth, for the vision of life beyond the particular limits of one lifetime.
There is no sentimentality, only an adamant concentration on the light/force
that transcends personal histories. The "I" in the poem is depersonalized over
the mystic length of the vision/journey, for Levine moves outside himself con-
sistently, whether he is transferring Keats' life/breath to his own, or to another,
he is literally speaking from a position outside the body-consciousness as we
know it.

> No one believes that to die
> is beautiful, that after the hard pain
> of the last unsaid word I am swept
> in a calm out from shore
> and hang in the silence of millions
> for the first time among all my family
> and that the magic of water
> that has filled me becomes me . . .

It is a fairly omniscient point of view, as omniscient as the sea and stars, as
the light. By the end of the poem Levine still is speaking in the first person
but it is almost a collective "I," for he is speaking through the light of the sea,
through stars, through wind and sea sounds. Indeed, the anaphora throughout
the poem moves with the force of sea and winds. By the poem's final line, the
speaker has become part of all of the visible cosmos and the pronoun switch-
es from "I" to us—"follow us toward the first light." Even the "you" addressed
in the last portion of the poem is ambiguous; at times it could be his wife; at

other times we could correctly say he is addressing the reader, anyone who might doubt, who might believe. Levine introduces no personality or details to conflict with the "evidence" of a life flow beyond our avowed limits. We are not asked to believe a personal religious witnessing of one Philip Levine, but rather we have walked along with a consciousness that speaks in and through a basic and accessible physical world, which demonstrates a link to the light of that world which goes beyond it to a metaphysical level.

Finally, Levine is suggesting that the metaphysical world may somehow be contained in the physical or vice-versa; he addresses this paradox and resolves it in an accessible vision, one with immediate evidence and yet one with some spiritual heft, some carefully elaborated and distilled structure, and Levine's style here helps to carry this notion forward in the poem, helps to subtly resolve the ostensible paradoxes. Primarily, it is Levine's hallmark of anaphoric phrasing which resolves the imagistic and narrative sections as well as the life / death conflict. He chooses disbelief as a rhetorical starting point with the clause, "No one believes . . ." By admitting disbelief with this "disclaimer," Levine then begins to build his argument; he begins to introduce what he sees and does believe. Mainly, he does so by using the images that are apparently contradictory in their construction, but he consistently imbues them with life force, and their sheer weight and shining overwhelm the negative denotation of the anaphora until Levine achieves a closure that is both positive and convincing. Yet Levine's sinuous braiding of visionary witnessing and stance in nature with the specific vignettes of the man at the beach in Castelldefels, creates a structure and strategy that renders one a thematic coefficient of the other. To begin, he introduces the "North Wind;" this is an image usually of storm and violence, but Levine shows us a calm aspect of it. Additionally, the image of water throughout the poem is both a life-giving source and a source of death; the sea takes life and then gives it back in a larger spectrum of light in the lines: "the bodies of the drowned collect / light from the farthest stars and rise." Moreover, the voice by the end of the poem proclaims the contradiction that, "No one believes that to die / is beautiful" and in so doing proclaims its/his own death and then immediately the certain joy of being "swept / in a calm out from shore" to mix with the light "and hang in the silence of millions." Of course the poem's title is "Belief " and not "Against Belief." And really, the speaker of the poem is now one who is apart from life, the physical life as we know it, and therefore one who is offering "objective" testimony—one who is talking about what is usually not believed by others, those still in their lives. The sea returns his life and it is now part of the water, part of the light, part of life continuing outside traditional mortal strictures.

> . . . and I flow into every crack and crevice
> where light can enter. Even my oak
> takes me to heart. I shadow the yard
> where you come in the evening
> to talk while the light rises slowly
> skyward, and you shiver a moment
> before you go in, not believing
> my voice in your ear and that the tall trees
> blowing in the wind are sea sounds.

Levine closes on an image that again demonstrates his belief in life in and beyond the world; "First light" is an image found in several Levine poems, but it always has had the denotative meaning—dawn. I think we correctly read this closing image not only as dawn, but since the focus of the poem falls on this well-ordered final image, as "first light—primary principle—life source." In the largest sense, Levine has given up his life, his personality, to the world and the stars, and this makes for a startling and convincing strategy to motivate the reader to look beyond this life and to believe, nothing that could be accomplished in the standard lyric moment and length. And although he begins the last eight lines of the poem with the sixth repetition of "No one believes . . ." the emphasis is now on the positive and immediate evidence of his belief, for "tonight is the journey / across dark water to the lost continent / no one named." At this point he resolves the largest paradox of life / death and hones his vision on the light that comes out of the darkness; by this point the anaphora is undercut by the imagistic overlays of existence pulled from the elements earth. Levine now expects the reader to believe; and now he is not alone in his vision for we are to follow not just Levine, but Levine among all the living elements:

> . . . Do you hear
> the waves breaking, even in the darkness,
> radiant and full? Close your eyes, close
> them and follow us toward the first light.

PAUL MARIANI

The Song Old Rooms Sing:
"A Poem With No Ending"

HOW DOES A LIFELONG MEDITATION really end? Philip Levine begins his long meditation with a kind of koan. "So many poems begin where they / should end," he writes, "and never end." Levine takes his cue from poets like Wordsworth or Whitman, Yeats, Stevens, or Williams in their epic undertakings: all one's poems, all those poems written over the years—three, four, five, even six decades of work—do they in the end make up the song of oneself in a poem with no ending? Isn't that what Levine proposes here, that poems never really end but instead run on, "book after book, complaining / to the moon that heaven is wrong / or dull, no place at all to be"? And if an abstraction like heaven won't do it, then what's left for the poet but to interpose one's own song?

He's a Romantic, Levine: Keats in Detroit, Hart Crane in Brooklyn, Garcia Lorca in Fresno. Like one of his best teachers, John Berryman, the poet catching the absurdity of some momentary glimpse of heaven in the shape of a flight of ducks taking wing "only . . . to return/the gift of flight to the winds."

At five-hundred-fifty lines, "A Poem with No Ending" is the longest poem Levine wrote prior to 1985. It's a poem that comes years after his early "Sierra Kid," "Letters for the Dead," "Pili's Wall," "The Angels of Detroit" and some twenty others, though *A Walk with Tom Jefferson* which followed comes to some 600 lines. Still, he can feel the long encroachment of evening catching up with him, and so keeps coming back to his own beginning, something which hangs on him as it does with us all, until our last breath is gone.

"If you knew how I came to be," he begins, wondering how it is that he came into consciousness at all, only to find himself in a place like Detroit, recalling the loss of his father when he was five, the son of Jewish parents who emigrated from Russia not so very long before. "If you knew how I came to be / seven years old," he tells us, "and how thick / and blond my hair was, falling / about my shoulders like the leaves / of the slender eucalyptus/ that now blesses my driveway / and shades my pale blue Falcon." If you only knew. Which is what he will try to tell us in a poem which resonates with so many Americans of immigrant stock, or displaced persons everywhere. And like that, as in a Cubist painting by Picasso or Juan Gris, a distance separated by forty-five years suddenly cuts away, and Depression Detroit gives way to a ranch house in Fresno, California, in the early 1980s. East and West: the boy at seven, father to the man at fifty-five, a memory of him and his twin brother Eddie, his doppelganger, "pulling / wagon loads of stones across / the tufted fields and placing / them to build myself and my brother / a humped mound of earth where / flowers might rise as from a grave." Two seven-year olds in the summer of 1935, building what amounts to a memorial. Or is it just a pile of rocks? And a memorial to whom? His dead father? Or is it all of the dead who haunt the imagination?

Or are those rocks just one more heap of rubble seen from the air? What, after all, makes the difference, really? But if you saw this pile, he tells us, "you might understand the last spring / before war turned toward our house / and entered before dawn." The Spanish Civil War, that "pale stranger" hovering over his bed and his brother's, as now the dark angel of death enters his room, touching "the soft, unguarded faces" of his brother and himself, to leave "bruises so faint / years would pass before they darkened / and finally burned." For that is what war does, after all.

Europe's dark wasteland, where Hitler and Mussolini and Franco and Stalin planned their various strategies, and where, in the Basque town of Guernica, the German Luftwaffe's Condor Legion and the Italian Fascist Aviazione Legionaria obliterated much of the civilian population on April 26, 1937, on what would have been another Market Day. It's the war where some of the older guys on the street went off to fight in the Abraham Lincoln Brigade for the Spanish Republic against Franco and the Nationalists. Communists, Anarchists, Socialists, all those who plain hated what Franco and Hitler and Mussolini stood for, and which did not go down well with the Roosevelt administration, as some of them found out when they finally made it back to the States. Idealists who were poorly led and poorly trained, their leaders issuing life or death orders. And yet they fought: in Valencia and Madrid, in the Jarama Valley, in the battles at Zaragoza, Brunete and the Ebro River, some four-hundred-fifty of them, many of whom came home wounded or blinded, or never came home at all.

I remember going with Phil a few years back to see a collection of photos taken during that conflict. It was in a small gallery down in Soho somewhere, and there were only two or three others in there that summer's day: old men, who probably had some connection with the war. Mostly Phil was silent as we looked at the images of young men with outmoded rifles on the backs of trucks or in open fields or standing in doorways where the crosshatched sunlight filtered through.

But that was then, Levine says here, now, in this poem with no ending, in a sentence which effortlessly spans twenty-one lines, and never for a moment loses us. "If you knew how I came to be," the sentence begins,

> Seven years old and how thick
> and blond my hair was, falling
> about my shoulders like the leaves
> of the slender eucalyptus
> that now blesses my driveway
> and shades my pale blue Falcon,
> if you could see me pulling
> wagon loads of stones across
> the tufted fields and placing
> them to build myself and my brother
> a humped mound of earth where
> flowers might rise as from a grave,
> you might understand the last spring
> before war turned toward our house
> and entered before dawn, a pale
> stranger that hovered over each bed
> and touched the soft, unguarded faces
> leaving bruises so faint
> years would pass before they darkened
> and finally burned.

Now, in a moment of tranquility, as he sips a cup of coffee in his house in Fresno, a successful poet and devoted teacher at Fresno State College, he thinks back to what else he remembers of his years in Detroit: "how the rains swelled the streets," as they do in so many of his poems, and "how at night I mumbled a prayer because the weight / of snow was too great to bear / as I heard it softly packing / down the roof." Or recalling the incipient breezes coming off the Detroit River, or the iron ore boats on Lake Huron. Or, what he doesn't mention directly here, the death of his father that October of '33, when he was five, and the emptiness that left, as he tells us in so many of his poems, like a wound that will not heal.

Or there's the poem he never wrote, he tells us, the one called "Boyhood," placed between the "smeared pages of your morning paper," among all the important news so quickly lost to time. The blankness of it, the irrecoverable blank whiteness of it all, as the poem on the white sheet falls on the white tablecloth, only to be covered up and lost, as now he looks over his never-to-be-recovered past to write a "column of figures"—images, memories—which never seem to add up, like some poem "unread, not even / misunderstood, until it passed, / like its subject, into the literatures / of silence."

• • •

What happens, really, when you try to go back home again, if you're lucky enough to have the place still standing, and you walk up to the door where those "four trees" you grew up with are gone now? What happens when you screw up the courage to ring the doorbell? What will you tell the present inhabitants it is you're looking for? Your mother? Your father? Your *zaydee?* Your grandparents? They're all dead, now, and the woman thinks you're selling something or maybe this is another con game, so that before you can even open your mouth to say this is where you were born, this is where you came like an angel into this world, that you grew up in this city, worked here in endless miserable jobs, that this is where you slept, however fitfully, she is already shouting at you, that no, she's not interested, no, go away, and a child you can't see is asking the woman who the ghost at the door is.

All you can do now is try to imagine "the back of a closet," how it "burst into sky," and you stepped out at last "into a blue sky as undefined / as winter and as cold." No, this is not your childhood. That was something different. That was something that ended "in a single day," and not like the childhood you invented to ward against the cold, some magic childhood, where you could at last reach happiness if you just "took the first turn / to the left and eyes closed walked / a hundred and one steps and spoke / the right words," whatever the right words were, as if we could ever be sure.

One thing is certain: the poem, if it ever knows, isn't telling any of us. You sit and you sit before the "dusty window" of the past, as Levine told me he did when he and Franny lived on the twentieth floor of a building on 116th Street and Amsterdam during the time he taught at Columbia. And you sit there like someone waiting for the word that will tell you what it is you left behind when you lost your childhood.

That world is gone now, gone forever, every last whisper of it, and there's no getting it back, and the poem goes forward in time, even as the poet tries desperately to return to that lost past. And so, to protect himself, the poet has learned to regret nothing, not even the hands that have mottled and darkened over the decades as time ran south, the mottling reminding him of the speckled bird's eggs he once found as a kid "in the fields of junked cars." Like those old wrecks on the cover of the book that contains within itself this very poem with no ending: a black and white photo by Walker Evans dating back to that time, memorializing those wrecked Model-T Fords dotting Joe's Auto Grave-yard in a field somewhere in Pennsylvania.

And our lives go on, our hearts still beat, slowly, slowly, and the blood slides from behind our eyes into that half-familiar darkness we know, and then on to a darkness we don't know, and we begin rising beyond our lost childhood, like those untold generations before us have done, into the mystery of the poet becoming in time a man, "no different from my father / but slower and wis-er," if only because he has managed to outlive him already by a decade and more. And, really, "What could be / better than to waken" into the mystery of being a man?

And then the bird of life, the bird of time, enters the lit room through the dusty window, only to leave and re-enter the darkness. Isn't that the ancient allegory for life? Aren't each of us born "of the promise that each night" makes and each day breaks? And what if the cat's inscrutable consciousness stares back at our gaze and blinks, remaining as inscrutable as the quotidian sunlight which searches for each "closed face to waken"?

What is one's past made up of, really, if not those "tiny stories" your grand-father "told in which dogs walked upright / and the dead laughed"? Isn't it of those and of his "pocket of keys" and "his dresser drawers of black socks / and white shirts" and his "homilies / of blood and water," opening his eyes each morning like the rest of us until they opened no more? Isn't his past made up of those long walks he took into a world very much like Edward Hopper's, say on some Sunday, when no one passed him, and he seemed to float down the "long shadows of the warehouses," where a piece of paper, its message unread, if indeed it held a message at all, skips by on a breeze blown in from the river?

• • •

And now, in the fifth section of the poem, Levine recalls a Sunday afternoon in August 1936. He is eight and a half, and the Spanish Civil War is on in full force, and he recalls being on that "little island / where we came year after year / to celebrate the week." This is Belle Isle Park, Detroit's Coney Island, with its "shouts / of children at play," and Levine's twin brother Eddie is there beside him, trying to breathe through his asthma, though what remains most clearly is the poet's recollection of his own legs vanishing, and then his hands, until he is nothing more than "a presence in long grass," and then the grass itself, "blowing in a field all night," as the island "rides the river / between two countries." The U.S. and Canada, yes, but the country of memory and the world we call the present, where the young look at the strange old ones now, fifteen years after the death of King, shadow figures "huddled at separate tables" at the now-dilapidated park—blacks still divided from whites—"staring / off into the life they've come to," these, the living and the dead. 1984, and yet . . . "I was astonished," he told me once, "by how separate everyone was in the lunch and coffee shop on the island." It was, he said, yet one more "gift of our racial divide."

Fast forward to the following section (six) and yet another "present" in the ever changing river of time. It's a Monday morning, in mid-May, 1981, forty-five years on. This time it's New York City. Levine looks out the window of his apartment on the Lower West Side and catches a queue of trucks loading up "with parcels of everything," and in an instant he's thirty years younger and it's 1951 and he's back in Detroit again, twenty-two years old, "packing the van with frozen fish, household goods, oriental vegetables, wristwatches, weightless cartons of radium."

A real job this time at Railway Express, and the weariness and excitement of the time returns when they gave him "a shining badge / and a huge revolver to guard / 'the valuables.'" And how he hid the badge and the gun under the seat, uncomfortable with both. Then finding himself "in a two-room walk up," where "a dazed couple sat waiting for weeks / for a foot locker full of clothes / and kitchen utensils." And having entered that liminal space, we too wonder what their lives must have been like, living out their days like so many others, where "little / or nothing was done," when it seemed important "to smoke before / dressing and not to go out until / late afternoon." All those useless, essential rituals by which we pass our days, these newly arrived "homeless" who have come here to live in the very place where Levine too felt equally homeless.

Or the old man summoning him up to a third-floor apartment in another walkup, then pointing to the "massive steamer trunk full/of books he could take back to Germany now he could return." An educated man with books in Russian, French, and German—Tolstoy, Balzac, Goethe, all of which the man had read, and who was going home now that the War was over, impressed that some American worker in Detroit should actually recognize the names of those books, but scratching his head when Levine tells him that, invincible American or not, he really cannot carry a three-hundred pound trunk down those three flights of rickety stairs.

• • •

Like our memories which have little regard for the chronology of things, image begets image, as scene gives way to scene. Section Seven begins with

98

"The memory of rain falling" and it's Christmas 1965. The poet is thirty-seven now, married, with three sons asleep in the dark "in a narrow room without windows." He's standing alone out on the tiny veranda of some cheap hotel "above the railyards" of Seville. In the room adjoining his, a Spanish soldier has folded his uniform over the back of a chair and leaned his rifle against the glass door as his way of saying do not disturb, as Levine notes some "woman's clothes . . . scattered on the floor." Up and down the cluttered hallways peasants who have come into town to celebrate the fiesta have paid a few dollars to come in out of the cold to sleep. "Below the window," he remembers,

> the lights
> of the railway flash this way
> and that, and an old engine is firing up.
> Distant voices speak out, but I can't
> Understand their words. . . .

And what he feels now, on the twilight edge between waking and sleeping, as he observes the zigzag lights of the train yard below, comes down to this: fear and loneliness, the same fear and loneliness every child must feel "stretched out or curled up in bad beds / or on bare floors," and what he hears is that same old song he remembers as a boy, a "bird song or wind song" or just "the song old rooms sing when no one / is awake to hear." It's the song of human misery, isn't it? The song each of us contributes to, the "one full note" we are given in the symphony of life, so that for the first time now the poet realizes what everyone must come to realize at some point: that it is we who are the music, it is we who make up the long sad, wordless blues playing somewhere inside us.

• • •

How many of us actually possess a clear linear progression of our lives as they unfold? Don't we go backwards, then forward from there, then back again . . . and again? Now, in the poem's eighth section, the poet thinks back to a time when he hiked the woods with his youngest son, Teddy. One summer day in July, he tells us, he parked his VW Squareback somewhere in the high mountains of California, the two of them climbing "from the road's end and over a rise / of young pines," to descend "slowly for a mile or more / through a meadow of wildflowers." It's his son, this time, telling him a magical story, this one about talking bears, and how they "come into towns like ours to steal boys and girls / and bring them back up here and teach / them hunting," so that in time the children too grew "into animals and forgot / their homes and their brothers."

And suddenly the poet remembers how he realized he'd lost his way again, and that this was not something out of some fairy tale. What to do, then, but settle down in a small clearing and eat their sandwiches, and cool the cans of soda pop he has brought with him in the cold mountain stream they've found? And eventually the boy falls asleep, certain he's safe in his lost father's arms, and then the father too dozes off. And when he awakens it's darker and cooler and Teddy is doing what all boys that age seem to do: he's "throwing rocks as large / as he could manage into the stream / where they banged down a stairway / of stone and came to rest," for an hour or so building a house "below the water, dark now, and boiling."

And then the father comes up with an idea to extricate him and his son from the encroaching darkness by betting the kid a dollar he can't lead them out of these "dark / bear woods" and back to the car, which is somewhere out there waiting. And, by God, the kid does it, unaware of the situation the father has put him in. Unintentionally, it's true, but nevertheless the truth, as the boy enacts his own brand of magic which somehow gets them has back to the car again, and home, Teddy leading the way, little prince that he is, raised somehow by bears, it seems, as now he leads the way out of the woods, "switching a fallen branch before him / to dub this little tree as friend / or a tall weed as enemy, stopping once / to uproot a purple wildflower" for his father.

• • •

And then once more it's back a dozen summers before, to 1953, when the poet left Detroit for good, it seemed, packing up his own box of books and a rickety typewriter, and headed West for Iowa City and the Writer's Workshop there, weary of all those miserable jobs "that gave us / just enough and took all we had." Nor is he the only one leaving a desiccated and tired Detroit. Some are on their way back to Alabama and the exhausted soil they came from, who hoped once for a better life up north in Ford's industrial paradise, while others are going even further, returning, thirty or forty years on, "back to the villages / of Greece and Italy," the American dream having long since given up on them. And so a final meal together around some battered tin top kitchen table—"a drink, a pastry, and a coin to insure / a safe voyage" before sailing off across the Atlantic (or forward on to the River Styx), amid the soundless tears of goodbye as "each stands / alone and silent in the old pain" they have shared at one point or another.

It's one of the major motifs of this long poem, after all. In fact a major motif in Levine's body of work: a dream yearned after and too often lost, ending with a departure, as each of us inevitably "stands/alone and silent in the old pain."

• • •

The next section—the tenth of twelve—moves forward now sixteen years to August 1969 and yet one more departure. This time it's his oldest son, Mark, now nineteen, whose waving goodbye to his parents from the pre-dawn docks in Amsterdam. Like his father before him, he too is leaving. In fact leaving the country, on his way to Sweden to avoid being drafted into a war that no longer makes any sense. It's a year after the deaths of Martin Luther King and Bobby Kennedy and the war in Viet Nam has been raging on now for the past five years, with no end in sight. First it was Spain, then all of Europe and Asia, then Korea, and now this, all in the span of three short decades. "How many lives were torn apart / in those years?" the poet asks. "How many young men / went off as ours did but never / came back?" And so the poet bids goodbye, not knowing what lies ahead for his son, as he climbs "the gangplank / loaded down with duffle bags" and, true to the zany, hopeful culture of the time, "a guitar he scarcely played."

And then it's back to the streets of Amsterdam, and no magic bears this time to help the poet out of this lost forest. And having lost his son, he suddenly sees the face he's been searching since his own childhood that was snatched from him. And, just as he has looked all these years for his own lost father, he knows that, whichever corner he turns, his son too will not be there to meet him:

> Until late afternoon I tramped
> the streets no longer looking for
> the face I sought in childhood,
> for now that face was mine, and I
> was old enough to know
> that my son would not suddenly
> turn a corner and be mine
> as I was my father's son. . . .

Instead, there will be some distraught woman racing out of a bar, "screaming at her man," as the man himself brushes past him to hide himself down some alley, as the woman shakes a finger at the poet, damning him in a language you don't understand.

So, unable to find the words to comfort either his wife or himself, the poet dreams of returning to Detroit, to a home no longer his, and once more knock on the door of the

> house where he was born:
> It was quiet when I
> entered, for no one had risen yet,
> and I climbed the steps to my room
> where nothing stirred in all
> the rooms beneath me. I slept
> fully dressed, stretched out
> on a tiny bed, a boy's bed,
> and in that dream more vivid
> than the waking from it, the rooms
> were one and I was home at last.

• • •

"To get west you go east," Levine tells us in the following section, eleven. That is, to know who you are now, you will have to go back to the beginning. To drive back until finally, in sheer exhaustion, the poet pulls off the road to sleep "for an hour or a moment," who can say? And "If the windshield is crystalled / when you waken you know / the days will be getting colder and shorter." Or—conversely—to wake in a sweat and know the "year is turning / toward summer." It is Levine's version of the way up being one with the way down, in the endless grinding round of greased ball bearings, past towns and hills, through city streets or open fields with their "apple orchards and the barns /rotting and fallen," where none of it matters any more, and where "the magic eyes / that gleam by the roadside are those of animals come / down from the invisible hills."

And so those magical bears come down out of the woods again to reveal what the heart longs to retrieve, and walk toward those beckoning eyes, one's hand extended in greeting, only to find "a fence post / bullet-scarred and deckled with red-eyed reflectors." It is the final temptation, the Chapel Perilous, the Broken Tower, the final despair. Still, one can at least refuse to give up on the long search for one's home, whatever "home" comes down to finally. For there are magic animals out there after all, Levine tells us, bears who do actually "come down to stand / in silent formation by a road / you traveled," to console us: flame-eyed guardian angels sent to help us on our way.

•••

"We sat by the shore / together," the twelfth and final section of Levine's meditation begins, evoking Eliot's conclusion to *The Waste Land,* or Whitman's "As I sat alone, by blue Ontario's shore," where Whitman reflects on a war which took 600,000 lives and changed so many others for the worse, even as he dreams of a "peace return'd, and the dead that return no more." We are back in Spain now, and it's a Sunday afternoon, with a storm brewing off the Costa del Sol on the beach fronting Fuengirola, where Levine and his family lived in the mid-60s. The wine dark sea rises "in sharp / waves," turning a darker blue now, and all around him families are shaking the sand from their blankets and gathering up the remains of their picnic meals, their voices torn by the storm winds as everyone begins walking back to the train station. It's the final journey in Levine's poem with no ending, and it has the eerie feeling of some Shoah about it:

> The cars were crowded. The train
> stopped at each sea town to pick up
> the last stragglers, and we stood
> pressed together, groaning, as we
> jarred and jolted over the old track
> and finally entered the black tunnel
>
> that led to the center of the city.
> In the plaza young couples whispered
> together and soldiers passed in pairs,
> armed and silent, their faces
> glistening between the heavy wool
> of cap and tunic.

And then he's back in his room and the "empty crippled bed that held / a place" for him. It's not home, exactly, and yet it is home enough, a place where he has finally learned to make friends "with the seas / that work even while" you sleep. Sleep, and the brain which never really sleeps, like its dark mother, the ocean, the vast ocean of memory, where shore birds keep leaving the threshold of what he thought he knew as they venture out into the darkness, never to return again, for there is nothing to return to: no light here as he tosses restlessly, listening to the "unsteady tapping of an old man / going home and the young starting / out for work."

Harsh voices call out in the dark "to each other or / to no one in cries or in songs / that fill my sleep." And then, beyond the darkness: "the distant sky breaking into color and each wave taking / shape and rising landward," as the fitful dream of life goes on without end, except, perhaps, the final end toward which every life moves. Or, as Levine's teacher, John Berryman, sang it at the end of his own *Dream Song*, "Hard on the land wears the strong sea / and empty grows every bed."

A poem of over five-hundred lines, consisting of twelve journeys out and back, each line made up of five to ten syllables and three or four stresses, or even five, most of the lines running on without end into the next, and the next. Levine's language is every bit as much in the American grain as is William Carlos Williams', with hints of Detroit and New York and Fresno and—yes— Andalusia tossed in for good measure. "In the summer of '69," he told me once, "I became this compulsive walker trying to rid myself of my fears, especially for my son Mark. I had to go back to the States; I couldn't make a living in Europe, but the USA I'd left was truly frightening." You also hear Keats here. And Whitman and Eliot and Berryman, and even something of his other teacher, Robert Lowell, especially the Lowell who gave us *Quaker Graveyard in Nantucket.*

But what you hear most clearly, of course, is Levine himself. Not the poet who gave us "They Feed They Lion." That was the younger Levine, fiercer and angrier, the poet who, looking at what racial injustice in America had done to his beloved Detroit engulfed once more in flames, wrote something inspired—yes, inspired—by the acid graffiti painted on the slum walls of his city. "From pig balls," he wrote back then during the Detroit riots of '68,

> From the ferocity of pig driven to holiness,
> From the furred ear and the full jowl come
> The repose of the hung belly, from the purpose
> They Lion grow.

No, this is an older Levine, a father watching as his son sets out into the vastness beyond, no more able to protect him than he could keep his father from dying. This is the poet who reminds us that

> When the long day turns
> to dark and you're nowhere
> you've ever been before, you
> keep going, and the magic eyes
> that gleam by the roadside

are those of animals come
down from the invisible hills.
Yes, they have something to tell
or something to give you
from a world you've lost. . . .

But now the anger at the injustice of it all has turned to fear, the frightening realization that these were not animals in a safe haven, after all, but merely some "fence post / bulletscarred and deckled with / red-eyed reflectors." It's the nightmarish sense that if you strike back your right arm will fall off as in some nightmare, bringing home to you the realization of how little you sometimes feel you can do against either the darkness or the snowstorm thumping on the roof above your bed, against those inhuman forces that take your sons and daughters from you in the name of some larger, terrifying abstraction called terror or fascism or some virulent strain of confusion and demagoguery posing as democracy.

Against that, what can we do in the end which has no end, Levine asks us, but howl at the moon, reminding it, as if it cared, that the way things are "is wrong / or dull" and certainly "no place at all to be."

But no. There is something. Something more. A hope, a glimmer. . . .

"We sat by the shore / together as the sea rose in sharp / waves and turned a darker blue," the final section begins, echoing the close of Eliot's *The Waste Land*. But Levine, like William Carlos Williams in "By the road to the contagious hospital," moves out from that waste land and back into the light.

No, the last word is more hopeful, in spite of the darkness that pervades the scene as the first glimmers of morning enter the poet's world once more. It's Monday morning, early, and the beginning of another work week. "I / see in the ocean of memory," he tells us

the shore birds going out and nothing
coming back. No light enters
the little room, but I can hear
the unsteady tapping of an old man
going home and the young starting
out for work. It's Monday morning
now, and their harsh voices rise
calling out to each other or
to no one in cries or in songs
that fill my sleep.

And now, at the close of his poem with no ending, he gives us not an ending, but rather a new beginning. "I see beyond / the dark," he assures us, and beyond that dark rises the distant sky breaking into color and each wave taking shape and rising landward. Each wave, like each wave-like section of his long meditation, taking shape out of a dreamlike mist and moving, not out into the vast abyss of darkness, but landward as light, revealing so much human messiness and hope, breaks through.

CHRISTINE KITANO

Mythic Resonance in "Late Light"

PHILIP LEVINE IS KNOWN FOR his narrative, semi-autobiographical poems, so it is worth noting the manner in which he elevates the personal to the level of mythic significance, how he finds the universal within his own particular experience. This elevation is one of the main achievements of the long poem "Late Light," which was published in *Sweet Will* in 1985. In this poem, Levine shifts between two voices—a close, first-person voice used to recall personal memory and characterized by use of literal imagery and concrete detail, and a distant, almost omniscient-sounding first person voice, what I'm calling a "mythic voice," used to connect personal experience to communal experience, and often characterized by relative abstraction and an expansion of imagery. Levine's seamless shifting between these two voices creates an epic scope in the poem, a poem which works to examine what we can do to find connection and meaning in a life dictated by loss, suffering, and other events outside of our direct control.

"Late Light" is written in three sections, each section consisting of a single stanza. The first two sections are just over forty lines each, and the third section expands to fifty-nine lines. Levine's shifts in distance work to propel energy in this longer poem and enlarge the range of the poem's concerns. The poem opens in a mythic, almost Biblical voice:

> Rain filled the streets
> once a year, rising almost
> to door and window sills,
> battering walls and roofs
> until it cleaned away the mess
> we'd made.

The amplified description of the rain rising "almost / to door and window sills" creates this prophetic tone, as does the zoom-in to "cleaned away the mess / we'd made." The tensions are clear: the poem will veer between the mythic and the gritty, everyday drama of human struggle. The poet's longing

107

to find connection with others, whether family, friend, or stranger, will enact the everyday drama, while the poet's conviction that some deeper human connection must exist will enact the poet's mythic sensibilities. Following the mythic opening, the poem then moves to the personal voice and telescopes in on personal memory:

> . . . My father told
> me this, he told me it ran
> downtown and spilled into
> the river, which in turn
> emptied finally into the sea.
> He said this only once
> while I sat on the arm
> of his chair and stared out
> at the banks of gray snow . . .

For Levine, part of the struggle to define for himself the tension between the mythic and the personal arises from his own mythologizing of his father. The first section of this poem is firmly rooted in a scene from his childhood in Detroit, and demonstrates his re-envisioning of a moment with his father (who passed away when the poet was five). This lends emotional weight to the phrase "He said this only once," as it shows the poet elevating a somewhat casual moment to one of great significance. The repetition of the word "once," first in "Rain filled the streets once a year" and "He said this only once" creates the movement in scope between the large and the small, the mythic and the personal. The conflation of the personal memory with the mythic rainfall sets the stakes for the remainder of the poem: how does individual, personal experience find meaning in the scope of global events? Or, in other words, how do we make meaningful connections in the present moment when we know loss lies just ahead?

Levine then moves from this personal, intimate voice back into the mythic by dissolving the specific instance into the larger legendary mass of "childhood:"

> . . . All the rest
> of that day passed on
> into childhood, into nothing,
> or perhaps some portion hung
> on in a tiny corner of thought.
> Perhaps a clot of cinders
> that peppered the front yard

clung to a spar of old weed
or the concrete lip of the curb
and worked its way back under
the new growth spring brought
and is a part of that yard
still.

The word "Perhaps" tempers the movement into the mythic voice. With this word, Levine acknowledges that all memory is storytelling, and in doing so, begins to address another of the poem's concerns—that the individual always shapes their story in light of the present moment. The juxtaposition between the abstract phrase "passed on / into childhood" and the specific details that the poet might imagine about that day ("a clot of cinders . . .") demonstrates this tension between the epic and the personal, how it is the individual who must use language to make sense of and shape loss into the opportunity for connection. In this moment, Levine works toward connection and communication with the reader, inviting us into the myth-making mind, one that wants to memorialize the memory of the poet's father. Levine uses repetition in the remainder of this first section to enlarge the possibilities of the memory:

. . . Perhaps light falling
on distant houses becomes
those houses, hunching them
down at dusk like sheep
browsing on a far hillside,
or at daybreak gilds
the roofs until they grown
under the new weight . . .

The repetition of "perhaps" and "or" widens the scope of this section, as the poet speculates about all the possibilities of what might have happened on this day from his personal recollection. He maintains his gaze on the houses and concludes the section with "those houses and all / they contain live that day / in the sight of heaven," a clear shift into the mythic voice. This move mirrors the move at the beginning of the section, when the rain transforms from literal rain to a metaphoric cleansing. Here, through use of repetition to enlarge the memory, Levine emphasizes how imagination continues to shape and define the individual experience, and it is the use of imagination that enables the possibility of connection. The section ends "in the sight of heaven," which supports the shaping power of the imagination—the rain will always come once a year to clean away our mess; all happens under divine oversight. The Romanticist and optimistic close to this first section reveals the poet's longing to find peace with the events he cannot control. By using the imagination to connect his father's presence and impending absence to the mythic flooding of Detroit, he claims a larger significance for his personal recollection, and in doing so claims assurance that all events, large and small, happen "in the sight of heaven."

While Section I fulfills a satisfying emotional arc, the use of the long form allows Levine to further develop this tension between the personal and the mythic. In Section II, we move away from Levine's childhood in Detroit and into a memory from the poet's adult life at "the International Institute / of Social Revolution," presumably somewhere in Spain. He recalls drowsing off while reading the memoirs of "a Spanish priest who'd / served his own private faith / in a long forgotten war." In the midst of this personal recollection, the mythic voice takes over the memory:

> . . . That dust,
> fine and gray, peculiar
> to libraries, slipped
> between the glossy pages
> and my sight, a slow darkness
> calmed me, and I forgot
> the agony of those men
> I'd come to love, forgot
> the battles lost and won,
> forgot the final trek
> over hopeless mountain roads,
> defeat, surrender, the vows
> to live on.

Repetition of "forgot" announces this shift in distance to the mythic voice, and moves from the personal to the communal; as the poet falls asleep, he enters the book, in which his own experience conflates with that of the Spanish priest. The more abstract language here (in contrast to the detailed descriptions of Detroit in Section I) shows another way that imagination can bring us closer to other human experiences—in Section I, the poet imagines his father and with literal imagery ("a clot of cinders . . . clung to a spar of old weed") recreates this memory, finding connection with his readers. In Section II, however, the poet himself becomes the reader, and finds it is not through memory but through "forgetting" that he finds connection with the Spanish priest. Instead of active imagining, it is in the "slow darkness" between waking and sleep that he feels empathy and connection with the subjects he reads about.

However, instead of ending on this parallel moment between Section I and Section II, this movement into the enlarged scope made possible by imagination, the structure of the long poem enables Levine to add a variation on this theme. Here, Levine asserts that there are limits to finding empathy and connection. Loss and mortality will always intervene. Instead of ending the poem on the mythic drifting into sleep, which would imply our ability to imagine ourselves beyond the reaches of death, the poet is awakened by a girl "in sweater and American jeans." The specifics of the woman's clothing bring us back into the personal voice of the individual, who notes that she speaks "perfect English." We then move back into the mythic voice:

> . . . she swept up into a folder
> the yellowing newspaper stories
> and photos spilled out before
> me on the desk, the little
> chronicles of death themselves
> curling and blurring
> into death, and took away
> the book still unfinished
> of a man more confused
> even than I . . .

The simple documents on the desk take on larger significance in this mythic voice, as "chronicles of death," a harsh reminder of the poet's own growing sense of mortality. When the woman takes away the book, he recognizes the limits of the individual; time, space, death, and every day human action and inaction prevent him from making a connection with the Spanish priest. The section ends with the woman switching off the light and leaving the poet alone in the dark. If the poem were to end here, as it did when first published in *The New Yorker* in August 1984, the poem would present two contrasting scenes. The first section poses the question of how the individual can use the imagination to work beyond the confines of time, space, and mortality and ends on the Romanticist notion that all happens in tune with the natural and divine, while the second section posits that there is no larger project, no inherent mythic connection among people, that we are all alone in our individual human pursuits. Only in the moments between waking and sleep can we begin to grasp at a shared experience. The second section provides a harsh move into reality—for all we can do to imagine the experiences of others, we are ultimately left alone in the dark:

> [she] took away
> the book, still unfinished,
> of a man once more confused
> than I, and switched off
> the light, and left me alone.

The final version of the poem, published in *Sweet Will* in 1985, adds a third section, a move which allows the expansiveness of the long poem the scope to fully synthesize the tensions in the first two sections. Instead of ending on the harsh reality of sitting alone and confused in a dark library, Levine uses the third section to revisit the image of the library and the larger questions of memory and the imagination, only now allowing the personal voice more space to question the poem's original assertions. The section opens on a scene that parallels the ending scene of Section II:

> In June of 1975 I wakened
> one late afternoon in Amsterdam
> in a dim corner of a library.
> I had fallen asleep over a book
> and was roused by a young girl
> whose hand lay on my hand.

By directly stating the date and city, Levine grounds us in time and space, giving the personal voice prominence. This feels like personal memory, not a mythic dream-space as in Section II. And instead of being roused to be told to leave and then left alone in the dark, he wakes to find himself thrust into a moment of human connection:

> I turned my head up and stared
> into her brown eyes, deep
> and gleaming. She was crying.
> For a second I was confused
> and started to speak, to offer
> some comfort or aid, but I
> kept still, for she was crying
> for me . . .

The poet's confusion mirrors his emotional state in Section II, but here, instead of feeling separated from the world, he finds recognition. He realizes the woman is crying "for me, for the knowledge / that I had wakened to a life / in which loss was final." In this moment, the mythic voice takes over, a voice capable of knowing why this woman is crying. This move into the mythic voice turns the personal memory into a communal experience for Levine, the woman, and the reader—we all arrive at this moment in the poem with the realization that loss is "final" in all our lives. It is through this shared experience of loss that we might begin to imagine a shared connection. He closes his eyes for a moment to take this in, but when he opens them again, the woman is gone, and he is again alone and "the place was dark."

Instead of ending on this recognition (and ultimate disappointment), the poem continues—the shared experience of loss encourages the poet to return focus to the present moment, as this is the only antidote in the face of inevitable loss and death. This recognition arms the poet with a clearer vision:

> . . . I went
> out into the golden sunlight;
> the cobbled streets gleamed
> as after rain, the street cafes
> crowded and alive.

We stay in the mythic voice here and the description of Amsterdam recalls the description of Detroit in the first stanza ("after rain lifts halos / of steam from the rinsed / aluminum siding"), which creates a feeling of nostalgia. Both cities are gleaming after rain, and the poet here is rinsed of earlier hesitations about how to describe his experience. Being alive and awake in this moment prompts more memories—of his son who traveled through Europe as a teenager and "finally /—sick and weary—/ he'd returned / to us" and of his father "on the run / from an older war." These memories place Levine between generations, as merely one person in a long line of people who have moved through these same spaces in search of understanding and connection, fleeing wars both external and internal. The mythic longing for connection swerves into the personal, with the poet's wondering about the father he never had the chance to know. Levine writes:

> . . . I thought
> of my father on the run
> from an older war, and wondered
> had he passed through Amsterdam,
> had he stood, as I did now,
> gazing up at the pale sky,
> distant and opaque, for the sign

that never comes. Had he drifted
in the same winds of doubt
and change to another continent,
another life, a family, some
years of peace, an early death.

This is the most personal moment in the poem, with the poet's larger questions about existence turning inward into questions to a long-deceased father. And yet, these intimate questions take on the scope of the poet's existential questions, as both lines of questioning will remain without answer. In this moment in the poem, the personal melds with the communal, but instead of elevating the personal experience to mythic significance as he does in Section I, here Levine does the opposite—he finds mythic significance within his personal experience. It is in the direct questioning to the deceased father that he is best able to articulate his concerns—had his own father stood in this same space looking "for the sign / that never comes"? Had his own father "drifted / in the same winds of doubt / and change"? It is not space, or time, or loss, that connects or disconnects us, but instead, this questioning.

The poem ends with the poet, alone, walking through the streets of Amsterdam. The "late light" of the title appears to surface here: "I walked on by myself for miles / and still the light hung on / as though the day would / never end." Instead of the mythic light "in the sight of heaven" in the first section, or the "blue, winking light" that gives way to darkness in the second section, here we finally emerge into the real, natural world. The light hangs on as if the day will never end, but then it does: "The gray canals darkened slowly, the sky / above the high narrow houses / deepened into blue." Whereas the mythologizing of the father in the first section created a need to cast a supernatural, divine light over Detroit, and the harsh reality of the second section plunged the poem into darkness, in this third and final section the poet makes peace with the natural world. The natural world is filtered through his mythologizing and his imagination, and yet it will continue to exist, with and without him.

The description of Amsterdam echoes the description of Detroit in Section I, thereby returning to the original theme while synthesizing the poem's visions—"Perhaps light falling / on distant houses becomes / those houses, hunching them / down at dusk like sheep / browsing on a far hillside, / or at daybreak gilds / the roofs until they groan / under a new weight"—only now the poet speaks with more authority, confident with how his imagination shapes his perception:

> . . . The gray canals
>   darkened slowly, the sky
>   above the high, narrow houses
>   deepened into blue, and one
>   by one the stars began
>   their singular voyages.

Instead of the overwhelming Romanticism of the first section's ending lines ("those houses and all / they contain live that day / in the sight of heaven") or the devastating realism of the second section's ending lines ("the book still unfinished / of a man more confused / even than I, and switched off / the light, and left me alone"), the poem resolves on a moment of peace. The poet has recognized his own insignificance, but that it is this insignificance in the face of mortality and loss that creates the possibility of connection to others—the Spanish priest, the women in the libraries, his son, his father, even the stars on their "singular voyages." Time passes without regard for any of us but it is within this shared construct that we can begin to find connection.

The tripartite form of the poem allows this long poem by Levine the space to reach this moment of realization and articulation. When the poem was first published in *The New Yorker*, it contained only the first two sections, which creates an entirely different movement for the poem, something closer to the more usual lyric moment or vision. The two sections work as two contrasting options—on one hand, all is ordained, all loss and suffering occur under divine oversight, and on the other, there is no divine oversight, and therefore no larger significance to loneliness and suffering. The poem ends without the poet coming to terms with either option, though the ending image of the poet alone in the library might indicate Levine's inclinations. The expansion into the long poem format, however, offers the necessary latitude for synthesis, for the poet to recognize both options as too limiting, and therefore, untrue. The shifts between the personal and the mythic voice find their proper balance and fullest expression in this last section, a reconciliation that mirrors the poet's emotional and intellectual journey—his hope for divine oversight, his disappointment at the harsh reality of the human condition, and then, finally, his acceptance that his own insignificance, his own struggles with loss and doubt, are what connect him to the communal human experience.

RICHARD JACKSON

Philip Levine and the Extensive Poem: "Jewish Graveyards, Italy"

LEVINE'S BOOKS AND LONGER POEMS work by linking what Wordsworth called *spots of time* that continually redefine each other. Each "spot" as it were, expands and intersects its moment like circles from a few rocks thrown on a pond. This sort of expansion of the moment through others is the basic principle that generates the early "Letters for the Dead," for instance. The ten-sectioned poem reads at first like a sequence of lyrics where the narrator addresses the dead "one by one" in an attempt "to hold your faces" and "to say / something to each of you / of what it is / without you." Besides this merging of visions there is also an overall movement from dawn to dusk, winter to "warm days."

Later, "A Poem With No Ending" (from *Sweet Will*) uses similar principles though in a more narrative and less imagistic way than the earlier poem but, like the earlier poem, always moving towards a more encompassing vision. Even the posthumous book, *The Last Shift*, carefully ordered by Edward Hirsch, seems to collect the spots of times of various characters gradually moving towards the metaphoric last shift of his life until, in the end, "Those place where I had lived / all the days of my life were giving up / their hold on me and not a moment too soon."

If "Letters for the Dead" and "A Poem With No Ending" are long poems, there are also poems in between that Octavio Paz in *The Other Voice* calls the "extensive poem" where "the number of verses is not a criterion." He notes, for example, that for a Japanese poet, thirty to forty lines is quite long, while for Dante it is about a third of just one the thirty-four cantos that make up *The Inferno*, not to mention *Purgatorio* or *Paradiso*. In between he notes poems by Mallarm. and T.S. Eliot. Some writers—Poe in "The Poetic Principle," for instance—suggest that a long poem is a contradiction in terms, for a poem, he insists, is an intense and transient moment that excites and elevates us. It is certainly true that how a poet deals with the moments that constitute his or her poems is essential in seeing the kind of imagination at work in them.

For Paz, the extensive poem is made up of parts where "each part has a life of its own" while the whole poem exists as a complete unit. The key here is "variety within unity" and "repetition and surprise" in terms of rhythm, breaks, changes of mood and the like. In addition, in the extensive poem "the first person singular becomes the main character." This all sounds close to what Hardy in his "Apology" to his *Later Lyrics,* describes his poems as "chance little shocks" and the whole book as a kind of single poem that is a "juxtaposition of unrelated, even discordant, effusions." For Hardy, as for Levine, any sense of larger unity beyond a moment must accommodate the discordant elements and the poet has a duty to be honest in dealing with them rather than trying to create a false and homogenous unit.

As it turns out, Levine has written a number of poems that are, by Paz' definition, extensive poems, including "Letters for the Dead" and "A Poem With No Ending." As the second of these titles suggests, in these poems, and in this he echoes Keats' notion of the fragment as a whole poem ("Hyperion" and "The Fall of Hyperion"), there is a sense of an evocative world beyond the end of the poem: the fragment becomes an essential mode of vision. The poem becomes a moment, a Wordsworthian "spot of time" that extends outward spatially and temporally: indeed, the real 'subject' becomes what lies beyond. It is this beyond that characterizes Paz' notion of extension, a momentary sense of fulfillment that must be immediately supplemented. "For a moment / I feel my arms spread wide to enclose / everyone within these walls," he writes in "A Poem With No Ending." In an earlier essay, "The Long Embrace: Philip Levine and the Long Poem," I suggested that his poems often gather their fragments into a longer poem as in "A Walk With Tom Jefferson." I argued that the later books, too, tend to become constructed like long poems—Paz extensive poems. For example, *What Work Is* creates a Dantesque vision that takes us through a hell towards a provisional paradise where he "went down on [his] knees to you as to / a god or beloved." This trend towards books as completed "extensive" poems continues with *Breath* and *The Mercy* where themes and images start to echo against one another ever more extensively.

Most recently, we can see this in *News of The World* which is based on conjecture: it begins with "We don't see" and ends with a "hope to arrive," not an arrival. "Everyone loves a story. Let's begin with a house," one poem begins, and "Two young men—you might call them boys—" begins another. In "Alba," a poem of nearly ninety lines, he traces the story of the militia commander, Brilla, arriving at the spot of an atrocity long past and whose "lesson" is beyond words, left to speculation that is made of "words we spoke before we spoke in words." In fact, the unsayable is precisely the motive behind the fragment: one cannot quite get it right (write) and needs to try again: when the attempts start to come together we are faced, essentially, with the extensive poem. "Onward he flar'd," Keats would say, hoping to move closer to an unreachable end.

So it is in this context—a sense of reverence for what cannot be completed or fully expressed and is best evoked in interrelated fragments—that we might revisit an earlier poem, "Jewish Graveyards, Italy." The poem is in three parts—*dust, shade* and *rain*—each beginning by entering an enclosure and ending with an expansive gesture. The three somewhat independent segments move from morning to noon to evening, then end with a suggestion of dawn. Ranging also across several time markers—political, personal, and historical—the segments each end with a "luminous" vision that, like Keats' poems, are resolved poetically and structurally but not thematically. This sense of reverence towards the unknown is one of the marks of Levine's vision, a kind of humility that is rare in contemporary poetry.

If we are to understand this poem as an extensive poem we need, then, to look more closely at each section and how they interrelate. In *dust* Levine begins, "Within a low wall falling away / into dust" with the heat rising, and having been let in by an old man singing "a song I've forgotten" and a specific moment, "Now" and "before noon" on a summer day. These space and time markers are crucial for they set a scene of spatial and temporal confinement that is counterpointed by what is beyond:

> The large, swart flies circle slowly
> in air around something I can't see
> and won't be waved away.

Importantly, the flies, like the "crickets, salamanders and ants" are on equal footing with the speaker who is, with them, one of "us all." So later, when he hears other sounds that draw him beyond they too are anthropomorphized—

> and farther off
> the laughter of other birds,
> and beyond the birds, the hum
> of a distant world still there.

That "distant world still there" is precisely what the speaker is ever approaching as he approaches the graves themselves. Here, as in the other two sections, all the observed details act as a kind of deferral for the reality of a death the speaker seems reluctant to face, and yet also a way to gradually face it.

So, after noting some car horns and school children, he bends finally to the names on the stones to "say them as slowly as I can" as if the saying itself brought a certain reality. It is here that the speaker adds his own voice, reverently, to the sounds that have been echoing in the background since the opening. The paradox of the first section is that the names of the "vanished" now leave him to enter a world that transcends and dwarfs the outward movement he has been experiencing:

> vanished names
> that fill my mouth and go out
> into the deadly yellowed air
> of this great valley and dissolve
> as even the sea dissolves beating
> on a stone shore or as love does
> when the beloved turns to stone
> or dust or water.

The reference to the sea pulls us incredibly far in order to represent the absolute loss the stones represent: the whole movement is complicated and reveals the richness of feeling here. The sounds of names on the stones take us through the surrounding valley to the sea, then the stone shore, a kind of monument itself in this context, that brings us back to the graveyard but now on a larger scale. That movement allows for the introduction of what "dissolves," an image so opposed to 'stone,' and yet so present in the idea of loss. That in turn allows the speaker to broaden the idea of loss to the loss of love in such a way as to make the transcending movement at the same time more personal and intense. It is not, then, a confessional loss of love, but rather a sense of all that has been lost and represented by the stone monuments around him, a loss too great to understand. In the end he can only "bow again to what I don't know," what he perhaps thought he knew upon entering, now dissolving into the unknowable and unsayable.

The second section, *shade*, brings the quest to noontime and another cemetery, this one farther out of a city, a movement that seems to further the expanding vision of the first section. Again he doesn't see death but only "a huge symbolic spider" that ignores (again anthropomorphized) the snap of his hankie, a gesture that becomes in this second part a more frustrated sense of trying to clear away the names of death. Instead, he shifts not into the pasts of the buried, but into his own in a language that begins like a fairy tale:

> Once upon a time
> when even the weather proved too much, I would
> close my eyes and find
> another weather. The raw azures and corals
> of the soul raged across
> the great, black pastures of my childhood . . .

The alternating line lengths here suggest the elegiac, a more prayerful mode as indeed he says almost immediately: "That was prayer." And here, he can't find the graves of Keats and Severn though he does for an ordinary New Jersey woman. And again he hears traffic but doesn't hear in this elegiac mode "the music of a farther life beyond / this life." A sense of reverence now falls upon him almost unconsciously as he realizes "for I'm kneeling," and once again bows, but this time to the earth:

> I feel the damp of soil
> given back to the earth
> before the earth could take it back, and the heat
> familiar on my backbowed in poor shade of rusting alder.

The search for the meaning of death which is a search for anything beyond death keeps widening, but the provisional answers keep pulling him back closer and closer to the earth itself, to this life, the life of the attendant in section one, the spider and other creatures, the sounds of traffic, an ordinary woman from New Jersey. To the trees that give him shade and which will become transformed in the last section.

In *rain* it is evening, and this time an old woman opens a gate amidst the implements of everyday life close to the earth (a rusted barrow, shovels, etc), extending the references towards the end of the previous section. And she seems as mythical for she is a figure of a type who is "always" a type of the woman and a typical place: this extends and expands the personal fairly tale sense we saw in the second section. But now the sound comes not from an exterior source but from "a dull ringing / from within." There is a sense of unreality that he feels as

>   a man
>   in a romance I never finished
>   come to tell the rain a secret
>   the living don't want and the dead know:
>   how life goes on, how seasons pass,
>   the children grow, and the earth gives
>   back what it took.

In many ways this is the climax of the quest: what is beyond is what is right here in what is given back, in the stones that tell him "nothing I / hadn't guessed." The "truth that falls from the sky" is a paradox, taking the "shape I give it, and can't give it away." He is still, albeit in a more complex manner, confronting the unsayable. But his allegiance to the earth that parallels his hope in a beyond brings him to a stunning conclusion. "Before the last darkness" (an apocalyptic phrasing that again broadens the context) "new soft rays of late sunset / will fall through." This section that began in the evening, towards darkness, ends with a reference to morning with its paradoxical "luminous thorns," and with a dying Keatsian autumn where the light catches fire "for a moment on the young leaves," transforming the tree image from the end of the previous section to something more optimistic. Yet the vision is "for a moment," and so would require a series of such moments beyond the poem's end.

The extensive poem is by nature a quest, and true to Levine's Keatsian and Romantic influences, is, as I have suggested, always unfinished, looking towards tomorrow. When we look back over "Jewish Graveyards" we find a vocabulary of things "never finished," "a farther life beyond," "promising nothing," sounds from beyond sight, lives beyond this one. For the speaker it becomes a world of Keatsian wild surmise, paradoxes and fragments that express Frost's "momentary stay against confusion." For the poet, our powerlessness in facing death is all the power that is, an endless quest to understand how to submit to the forces of the earth, to our human nature. In this Levine is in line with a kind of Romantic stoicism. What we see in "Jewish Graveyards" is something that has been essential to Levine's vision. For example, in the last poem of Breath, thinking of two jazz players, he begins to "Listen to my breath / Come and go" and understand that this

> process has a name,
> A word I don't know, an elegant word not
> In English or Yiddish or Spanish, a word
> That means nothing to me.

The lines lead us to the ultimate unsayable, the experience of our own death, the unspeakable essence of ourselves. The poem reveals, in what isn't really spoken, something essentially human and yet also "unapproachable" in its "nearness." Breath is the body's music here, the language that links us in and through the language of the poem. Levine plays the endless variations on this theme in nearly all his books, a vision that unifies his books so that they become, more recently, extensive poems themselves, extending indefinitely, as he suggests at the end of *News of the World:*

> I had to put one foot in front of another,
> hold both arms out for balance, stare ahead,
> breathe like a beginner, and hope to arrive.

JAMES HARMS

On "Winter Words"

WHEN I WAS ASKED TO WRITE an essay on one of Philip Levine's long poems, the request came in the form of an email, which also included a list of Levine's long poems to choose from. Levine is an under-rated writer in long forms, and what impressed and, frankly, surprised me most about the poems on the list was their range and variety. As widely admired as Levine is, he is also seriously pigeonholed. His poems about growing up and working in Detroit, his tough vernacular and edgy narrations, and his identification with workers, socialists, and Spanish loyalists (folks for whom the basic notion of human dignity is both most precious and most under siege), make up a disproportionate bulk of his poetic identity.

Still, this perception of him as a working class hero of sorts was not something he discouraged: Levine was in many ways a quintessential poet of his generation, well educated (at Iowa, and by Berryman, among others) in the poetic traditions of the day, while at the same time pushing back against the conventional identity of the scholar-poet that predominated at the time; temperamentally, he was clearly no stuffy new critic, and yet he learned at the knee of poets deeply schooled in that formalist tradition. Frankly, it's an important source of tension in his work. Because even though Levine fashioned a voice for himself that was largely grounded in plain speech (and which valorized the working person), he also settled into a loose syllabic line at some point fairly early in his career, which he hewed to with some consistency (though there's little that's truly consistent about Levine, another unheralded strength of his work). His poems have a reliable look to them, often a single column of lines of roughly regular length; they look like Phil Levine poems, and this contributes to his monochromatic identity.

But, in truth, Levine is a poet of considerable rhetorical fluency, whose ambition for poetry (and the mechanics of poetry) is equaled only by his disappointment in structures of power and those who manipulate them, which creates a very basic and understandable math: The vastness of injustice and the astounding scope of human exploitation requires a large arsenal of poetic weapons, so, Power + Cruelty = a Poetry as flexible and varied as the many methods human beings have developed to strip their fellow men and women of dignity and hope. Thus, and again surprisingly, his poems are as varied in their voices and strategies as any major American poet of his generation, perhaps more so than many poets who were at one time considered experimental, like Ashbery or O'Hara, or who are as well known as he is for their social engagement, like Rich or Merwin or Bly.

It's useful to compare him to a slightly younger poet like Charles Wright, who long ago found his method and stuck to it. But where Wright's poems tend to look and sound alike, Levine's often lull us with their appearances into thinking they're just another "What Work Is" or "You Can Have It," when in fact they are trying to do something else entirely, perhaps even something less (and I'll return to this notion of a poetry that resists direct engagement, that strives for a little less).

Levine is, in fact, a restless poet, and the edgy prickliness of many of his better known poems—their narrative urgency and imagistic ingenuity—seems as much a symptom of aesthetic impatience as general frustration. In other words, he is as interested in finding new ways of speaking *through* his art as he is in speaking *against* the injustices he's witness to every waking moment. It would be difficult to think of another poet who has groused as beautifully as Levine about bourgeois values, but the complaints are rarely shrill, never dull, and often varied in their music: His is a song of objection sung in many different registers. And I think that statement would surprise quite a few casual readers of his work.

So as I read through the many long poems suggested to me by the editor of this project, I found myself more dazzled than certain. What did I have to say about this particular poet's engagement with length? How was he changed as a poet by duration, by an extended treatment of subject? Well, all this doubt and hand wringing on my part made me slow to respond to the invitation. Sure enough, the editor emailed a few days later to say that most of the poems had been snapped up by other folks, and that the few remaining were somewhat less well known. Was I still interested in contributing to the anthology? He asked in particular about two poems, one of which is titled "Winter Words." And then it hit me.

I ran upstairs to the shelf in our library where I keep the literary magazines I've been lucky enough to appear in. It's a dusty, neglected shelf, and I'm not sure how much longer I'm going to devote such valuable space to this sentimental expression of my literary heritage. I pulled down the very first journal that ever published me. So here's where I indulge autobiography to emphasize the way a happy accident can occur. Honestly, a great deal of what I love about poetry has to do with happy accidents, since the artifice of collecting the memorable in one place, on the page, as if the world in all its significance has organized itself into a container of language (a box of song if you're writing a sonnet, or a series of them as might be the case in "Winter Words"), strikes me as a careful cultivation of the accidental. But anyway, back to that shelf of literary journals.

I'll never forget the day the package containing my first published poem arrived at my apartment in Bloomington, Indiana. I was twenty-six years old, still in grad school, and as I carefully withdrew my two contributor's copies from the large envelope, I remember taking a deep breath and looking out the window. I suppose I imagined that something was starting in my life, that I was about to feel differently about myself, not necessarily better, but somehow more certain. I don't know what I saw out the window. But I remember forcing myself to pause before ripping the envelope completely open. I still have one of those contributor's copies, which after all these years is falling apart.

In those days, *POETRY* magazine, which prided itself on discovering young poets (thank God), printed the last names of all its contributors for each issue right there on the cover, and next to my name, in all caps, was the name LEVINE, in all caps, one of the biggest thrills of my life to that point. Frankly, it still ranks as one of the biggest thrills of my life. I opened the magazine to the first poem, which was titled "Winter Words."

I'm fairly sure I read the magazine straight through. I know I didn't allow myself to turn directly to my poem. Whatever the case, twenty-four years later (now thirty-two years later, thanks to the vicissitudes of the poetry publishing universe and the delay this project experienced finding the light), holding that same copy in my hands, I felt my decision being made for me: I emailed the editor to say I'd be happy to write about "Winter Words."

I'm not sure that what's most interesting about this poem is its length, and it's certainly no where near the length of another poem that appears in the same book it was ultimately collected in. The title poem of *A Walk with Tom Jefferson* is fifteen pages long and is much better known. It's also magnificent, more important, and more memorable than "Winter Words."

That said, "Winter Words" is a stranger poem, and nothing like the poems of Levine's I'd grown up reading, which, as I've suggested, tend to be more narratively direct in their treatment of content. There are plenty of exceptions to this rule, "They Feed They Lion," most notably, but "Winter Words" is somewhat of an outlier in a body of work that is unusually grounded and located, even as it slips among verbal registers; which is to say that it is an atmospheric poem, a quiet poem, which for me, was surprising. Incidentally, it's always seemed interesting to me that one of Levine's best-loved poems, "They Feed They Lion," doesn't sound like anything else in his oeuvre, which should tell us something: Levine may be known best for a poem that is nothing like what he usually wrote. Which is a way of saying that he was ultimately a vastly less predictable poet than he was given credit for. And "Winter Words" is not your usual Phil Levine poem.

Clearly "Winter Words," a sequence of six nonce sonnets (or reasonable facsimile of nonce sonnets), is using some of the modernist long poem's strategies for the treatment of theme (the gradual, non-linear accretion of details and images organized in discrete sections), but it seems simpler, less elaborate than that model. What we have here is actually a pretty straightforward meditation, though the phrase "straightforward meditation" is, by definition, something of an oxymoron: true meditations are rarely straightforward. The mind, when left to its own devices, meanders, and it's been the job of meditative poems for hundreds of years to map the mind's meanderings. Still, since the 1950s or so we've become ever more interested in honoring and enacting on the page the slippery characteristics of thinking, and giving such representations the quality of unmediated authenticity, as if by recognizing the legitimacy of meditation in the guise of a poem, a reader will commit to a shared cultural recognition, even an understanding of sorts.

In other words, meditations are no longer expected to arrive at encapsulated wisdom; rather, they exist to relate the significance of a shared (by the poet) activity of the mind. Each section of "Winter Words" begins with a description of the here and now, the place where the speaker sits observing the world around him, the New York skyline outside his window, New Jersey in the distance. Though elapsed time moves subtly over the course of the six sections (it seems we are observing the world over a few days, perhaps even an entire season, though an argument could be made that the poem takes place non-sequentially during a single, emblematic, day), the place is fixed; he is sitting in his high room looking out at the world and welcoming it into his consciousness, while at the same time inviting the past to make its appearance. Put simply, he is cultivating the activity of meditation. And so the poem begins by grounding itself and the reader in the activity itself:

> Day after day in a high room between
> two rivers, I sit alone and welcome
> morning across the junked roof tops
> of Harlem. Fifteen stories up, neither
> on a cloud of soot nor a roof of stone,
> I am in my element, urging the past
> out of its pockets of silence.

>   The friends
>   of my first poems long banished
>   into silence and no time leaving nothing
>   to tell me who they are.

I think any poet will nod in assent reading these lines, since "urging the past / out of its pockets of silence" is one of the agreed-upon jobs of poetry. But as important as the past is to this poem, it is more the past's *relationship* to the present that seems under scrutiny. In fact, the expression of the quotidian moment, and the reinvention of that moment via the soft pressure of the imagination, is exactly what happens when we read a successful meditative poem, particularly a long one that allows, as this one does, the mind to leisurely enact its presence in the present while at the same time encouraging an organic interrogation of the past.

Weirdly, "Winter Words" reminds me of James Schuyler's great poem, "The Morning of the Poem," which is sixty pages long and takes place over the course of a single morning, though it travels through time and space paratactically, moving almost without coordination or transition between the present and the past, one place and another. Levine is more deliberate in his transitions, but the sensation of wandering through memory is just as powerful, and it's not a particularly unfamiliar feeling. More and more we're recognizing that the fluidity of temporal and spatial movement is the most effective way of representing the mind thinking. For instance, the second section of the poem begins with what is happening right outside the window in Manhattan: "Sheets of rain falling in the descending / evening dark." But the section moves quickly into the past, Levine walking along the Llobregat River outside Barcelona many years before. He describes a particularly resonant memory, and then narrates that moment into the present, as if to more fully occupy the here and now by imbuing it with the past:

>   In the half-dark a child found three feathers
>   of a kingfisher and took them as a gift
>   of nature and gave me one.
>   I hold it
>   now on my palm for a moment.
>   It rises slowly and settles on no wind
>   but my breathing, the colors softened
>   to the usual shades of rain, night, sleep.

As I said, "Winter Words" is nowhere near as narratively paratactic as "The Morning of the Poem" (and no one would describe Levine as postmodern, as some might Schuyler), but its design, like Schuyler's, is intended to emphasize the blurring of space and time, even as the poem clearly emanates from a single lived moment. There's a fascinating passage right in the geographical center of the poem (section three) when Levine drills down further into the past, moving from another memory of a river (a more archetypal river than the previously mentioned Llobregat) to a single image from childhood, the far distant past:

> Once I slept
> beside a wide river whose current pulled
> both day and night. I thought it began
> at the source of all sweet waters and took them
> through seven small seas to a great ocean
> tasting of salt and our lives.
> When the sun breaks
> through the full clouds of boyhood, we are there
> waiting on the dock in our summer suits
> for bright lake boats with the names of islands.

This sort of meditative magic carpet requires a very specific fuel to truly take flight, primarily duration and repetition, so that the rhythm of the spatial and temporal shifts has a chance to work on us as readers, to enchant us into a particular state of mind. Which is why a discussion of this poem is part of the book you're now holding in your hands: it's long. Or longish.

Of the many things we might choose to examine in this poem (perhaps as a way of learning more about the construction of the effective and sustained meditative poem, or the appreciation of such a poem), the relationship between space and time, as noted above, is probably most important; locating the speaker spatially unlocks the imaginative movement into the past. This methodology also underscores the relationship between description and narration: Levine reasserts the meditative mode at the beginning of each section via pure description before moving into a narration of a memory. Finally, the relationship between stillness (which could be described as the goal of meditation and which might even be called emptiness, or "no time," a phrase Levine uses in the first section of the poem) and action (which might be termed plot or narrative) is in many ways performed via these dynamics. Stillness and action.

It's important to note that meditation problematizes narrative by imposing the default practices of the mind (humans are habitual describers; meditative writing formalizes the practice) on the artifice of storytelling and plot. But meditation is a dance with narration, a moving toward and away from plot. Which is what is happening in each of the sections of this poem (except for the fourth, which remains wholly in the present). If the meditative moment here is concerned with nothing more (a poem about less, remember?) than a self-conscious expression of the view from a particular apartment on the west side of Manhattan, then the dance, the narration, is the past as a series of places and small events: places that complicate the spatial sovereignty of the present location, events that inform and expand the current stillness, the lived moment. Here is the opening of the fifth section:

> Snow flakes racing across my window,
> then wind-checked, reversed, wheeling
> back east to west.
>   At Puigcerda,
> on the way back from the holy valley
> of Andorra, clouds of black starlings
> rising at dusk from the bare winter trees
> and the hard ashen fields of December,
> a twisting cloud above the road. They knew
> where they were going.

It's probably not necessary to point out that the drop line is consistently used as a way to indicate shifts in time and place. This seems to me a little fussy, a lack of nerve from a usually fearless poet: what works fabulously in the poem is the conflation of time, the collapse of space, and since Levine isn't using paratactic language the way Schuyler is in "The Morning of the Poem," I don't think it would have hurt the poem a bit to speed up the shifts by deemphasizing them on the page. In other words, the visual cue provided by the drop line just isn't necessary, and I say this only to underscore how successful Levine is at modeling the meditative mind in this poem. Within a few lines we're right there with him, traveling across the described landscape, into the past or back to the present, an activity as familiar to most folks as smiling. For example, at the end of section one, right after being introduced to "The friends / of my first poems long banished / into silence . . .", Levine shifts abruptly back into the here and now with a striking image: "A nail of sunlight / on the George Washington Bridge. The first cars / crossing to the island douse their lights / and keep coming." The description has an urgency that jolts us out of the reverie he has introduced in this opening, and it feels completely authentic, an imagistic snap of the fingers that relocates us in time. Honestly, it's thrilling to find ourselves in a poem that presents so matter-of-factly the yearning hold of the past (and its tenuous power over the living moment), as well as the ultimate dominion of the present, the place in time we must always return to, something we all understand, at least subconsciously. But of course, what is seen and remembered is wholly Levine's, however familiar its presentation might *seem*. The beauty of artifice, when it's successful, is transparency, which might be another argument against the drop lines (sorry): this is a seriously artful poem in its design and method. I'd prefer not to see any seams.

But what to make of the dedication *(for Tu Fu)*, and why might Levine have dedicated this particular poem to him? Just to place us all on level ground, Tu Fu is an 8th century Chinese poet of the Tang Dynasty, a Confucian, much beloved internationally, often described as the Poet-Sage of his culture. Like Levine, he lived through troubled times, times of great upheaval and war, and he identified enormously with those who suffered. He believed people could change, that the basic humanity of individuals was sacrosanct. In other words, there's a sympathy between the two poets across the centuries. And as a poet of his time and culture, Tu Fu was a poet of attentiveness, a descriptive poet, and perhaps just as important in the context of "Winter Words," he was a poet of friendship. Because in all but one of the sections of this poem, Levine emphasizes companionship, friendship, the eternal "we" of a non-religious man finding the divine in the eyes of others. And in fact, companionship might just be the solace the poem seeks and provides, even as the here and now describes a necessary solitude, necessary for the engendering of mediation. Oh, and the one section in which the speaker remains alone is the one that stays located completely in the present (no drop lines!), Levine alone in his little room above the rooftops, where, as he describes, "You can grow up here. / East I can see to Throg's Neck, a pale bridge / that leads to Connecticut, and above / the bridge a skyway of air the birds / could take if they wanted another world."

That's a transcendent image for Levine, who seems to recover his balance and his ideology in the lines that immediately follow: "Down below in an empty parking lot / I find my favorite, the sparrow / who picks about the gravel, and he invites / me in with a twist of his head, a knock / of his beak. You can grow down here." Even in this poem, which looks again and again toward the past, the future asserts itself as the promise of the working day, the working *life* that awaits "down here," which is an alternative to the contemplative life "*up* here," and just as attractive, just as important. The egalitarian in Levine is always on alert for opportunities for empathy and identification with real and symbolic figures of struggle. It seems no accident that, like Williams, the sparrow is his favorite bird, "who picks about the gravel" in the parking lot below.

What I'm trying to suggest here is that the architecture of a meditation can be as formal as the prosody of a sonnet (it certainly is in "Winter Words"), and yet each trusts the organic and associative powers of language, when harnessed to the imagination, to serve as an instrument of exploration; the poem sets out on its short or long journey not exactly certain where it will end up. Fourteen lines and a volta (along with meter and rhyme, etc.) might seem a confining set of logistics for exploring the intersection of the inner life and the lived moment, but aside from the three-minute pop song, what formal convention has proven more productive and flexible in addressing the lyric realities of our lives? Well, maybe just one: the catalyst of description followed by association: look at something, describe it, and you're on your way, very often into the past. And for the duration of that trip (the longer the better in this case) it's very likely that you will suspend the rules of time and place for a while, that the result will be a meditation of sorts. It's as reliable as oxygen, certain to bring color to the cheeks.

So, to reiterate: description of place engenders narration of memory, and observation of the immediate leads to a dissolving sense of the moment as the past bleeds into the present. In other words, the stillness of the lived moment, when attention is directed outward in order to quiet the yearning mind, is drawn into the stories of the past. What we're left with is an approximation of the actual: a truer representation of the present, which is, in fact, a nexus and not a fixed moment, a meeting place of the past, present and future. No one, not even the finest student of meditation, exists in the present for very long. The past always intrudes. The future always calls.

For years, in memory, I thought of "Winter Words" as a crown of sonnets even though it is clearly not anything of the sort. Or is it? It certainly wouldn't surprise anyone if Levine decided to invoke a particular form while feeling the freedom to break the rules of that form whenever it suited him. As I mentioned earlier, in some ways he was a prototypical poet of his generation, both yoked to certain traditions and somewhat dismissive of them, drawn to the idea and appearance of a crown of sonnets, perhaps, but unable or unwilling to commit to it—in fact, he seems constitutionally unable in this poem (perhaps in any poem?) to commit completely to formal restraints. Two of the sections are fourteen lines long, two are fifteen lines long, and two are eighteen lines long. That adds up to six sections, one shy of a crown. And none of the sections quacks completely like a sonnet. To mix my metaphors, I have a feeling he probably agreed somewhat with Williams' definition of writing a sonnet as a process akin to fitting a crab in a box by cutting off its claws (I'm paraphrasing). Levine's relationship to form and tradition ebbed and flowed throughout his career, as if the radical in him saw both alternatives as equally rebellious: eschewing the poetic past completely in favor of a poetry that spoke in the voices of those he'd grown up with and worked beside; and/or embracing poetic tradition while making it uniquely his own.

Still, it seems no accident that "Winter Words," in appearance, resembles a crown of sonnets, which is, of course, a cycle that links together short lyric meditations as a way of allowing for an accretion of power and meaning over a longer duration, and which echoes the ruminative methods of the mind thinking. And of course, a crown of sonnets concludes when it returns to the very first line of the first sonnet in the series, which becomes, in repetition, the ending of the poem. In fact, the last section of "Winter Words" begins by returning to the George Washington Bridge, mentioned first in the opening section; the speaker of the poem physically occupies the exact same spot he did when the poem began, though instead of morning it is now night:

> Above the bridge lights a rope of stars.
> Alone, late at night, my breath fogging
> the window, I can almost believe
> the sleeping world is the reflection
> of heaven.

But there is no heaven in a Phil Levine poem, and this final section shifts quickly (via the drop line) from the word "heaven" to the word "Detroit," and to one last memory of the past, the same "friends / of my first poems" he wrote about in the opening section, though they are no longer "long banished / into silence and no time leaving nothing / to tell me who they are." Instead he recounts a nearly ecstatic memory of a group of young men who camp out in "rough blankets" on the shores of Lake Erie and together toast the dawn:

> Detroit, 1951,
> Friday night, after swing shift we drove
> the narrow, unmarked country roads searching
> for Lake Erie's Canadian shore.
> Later, wrapped in rough blankets, barefoot
> on a private shoal of ground stones
> we watched the stars vanish as the light
> of the world rose slowly from the great
> gray inland sea. Wet, shivering, raised
> our beer cans to the long seasons
> to come. We would never die.

                              Scattered
to distant shores, long ago gone back
to the oily earth of Ohio,
the carved Kentucky hills, the smokeless air.

I don't believe there has been any sort of religious or spiritual evolution in
this poem, though I guess it depends on how you define the spiritual. Instead,
it's pretty clear to me that the activity of writing "Winter Words," that is, of
making art out of memory via the mechanics of meditative writing, has result-
ed in a reassertion of faith in the power of poetry to give voice and presence
to those who might otherwise have vanished into the "smokeless air." And so
an oddly atypical Phil Levine poem delivers perfectly on his lifelong themes.
Emboldened by its length and strengthened through formal innovation, "Win-
ter Words" stands as a renewal of his aesthetic and moral principles.

KELLY CHERRY

On "28"

PHILIP LEVINE'S NARRATIVE POEMS rove widely through time and space. In "28," a poem ostensibly about his twenty-eighth year, events and bits of information are by association linked to other times and places, much the way a short story or dramatic or comedic monologue proceeds from digression to digression. Although emotive power is generated by the particulars of each digression, it is the process of segue that confers on the poem a leisurely, if not languid, pace: the poem approaches meditation but retains the impact of its felt particulars.

The poem as river, perhaps. As journey. Or, best, as light from a star.

In 1956, at twenty-eight, Levine drove from Colorado to California in a green Ford, headed for Stanford University to work with, among others, Yvor Winters, whose first name was Arthur. We have come to think of Winters's own poetry as gnomic and academically dry and, as time went on, more and more retrograde, but he was an exacting and admirable craftsman and as such his influence was considerable in his time and perhaps still is. He was twenty-eight years older than Levine.

Levine, opening "28" with the declaration "At 28 I was still faithless" would not have meant he was unfaithful; rather, he was without faith. In God? Marriage? Friends? His work? Or might he mean he was not to be trusted? I take him to mean that, at twenty-eight, he was not passionately invested or attached or committed—was, rather, living in existential freedom. But existential freedom is not all that different from existential captivity, and since we know that Levine, writing "28," is not still twenty-eight—we learn from the poem that at the time of writing it Levine was fifty-six, the age Winters was when they met—we are aware that the speaker is chafing against his stated condition. With his first line he yanked us into the poem as abruptly as if he reached up from his desk to pull us into it.

The premise that he is faithless returns at several points in the poem and serves as a kind of bass note or recurrent chord until, near the end, the speaker says, "I was 29 now and faithless." Against this bass note we hear the mostly four- or five-beat lines of the poem as a steady yet lyrical development, carrying lightly the freight of detail.

> I could rise before dawn from a bed drenched
> with my own sweat, repack the green Ford
> in the dark, my own breath steaming
> in the high, clear air, and head for California.
> I could spend the next night in Squaw Valley
> writing a letter to my wife and kids asleep hours
> behind me in Colorado, I could listen to Rexroth
> reminiscing on a Berkeley FM station in the voice
> God uses to lecture Jesus Christ and still believe
> two aspirins, an allergy pill, and proper rest were proof
> against the cold that leaps in one blind moment
> from the heart to the farthest shore to shudder
> through the small sea creatures I never knew existed.
>
> (ll. 34-46)

Of course, the shift from "allergy pill" to "the cold that leaps" is huge, however reportorial the voice, and the duet of reportage and extravagant image parallels the themes of freedom and entrapment and contributes to the overall sense of the poem as a Whitmanic song—an obsessive song, perhaps, given the repeated returns to the bass note. Moreover, in "the cold that leaps" we brush against the icy terror of existentialism.

Again, "28" slides through time and space in the way a short story might. One may think, for example, of stories by Alice Munro or Elizabeth Spencer. Backtracking a bit, we find that from the mention of his trip to California he segues into the story of a motorcycle accident he later had involving a desperately close encounter with a Plymouth bearing a family of five. Then we return to the trip in 1956. And *then* we find out that the poet while writing the poem is in New England—and that a dropped lunchbox reminds him of the erstwhile Plymouth.

> . . . If only they had stopped
> all those years ago and become a family of five
> descending one after the other the stone ledges
> of Sweet Potato Mountain and found me face down
> among the thistles and shale and lifted me to my feet.
> I weighed no more than feathers do or the wish
> to become pure spirit.
>
> (ll. 61-67)

He has lost a tooth or teeth in the accident and broken his glasses, but now we touch the bass note again—"28 years ago, faithless"—and this time the poem takes us into East Palo Alto. The speaker meets "Arthur, my mentor to be," viz., Yvor Winters.

Arthur has "a voice ruined . . . by whiskey and coffee," wears "a green visor and stiff Levis," and proudly shows off his garden to his student. "He was almost happy," notes his student, but like his student, "Arthur too was faithless, or so he insisted." Arthur called himself faithless because he was without faith in a God who provides an afterlife.

> . . . His face
> darkened and his fists shook when he spoke
> of Nothing, what he would become in that waiting blaze
> of final cold, a whiteness like no other.
>
> (ll. 100-103)

Arthur "was dying," the poem tells us, "and he was ready."

In the preceding passage Levine has described his own faithlessness as "the bitter black fruit / that clings with all its life to the hard seed." He has not yet, he tells us, awoken to "mockers wrangling in my yard" or heard the waves at Bondy Bay (which can chase away nightmares) or "become a family of five" nor yet encountered the Plymouth. It is possible—the poem suggests—that these events, taken together, have made him faithful, or at least less faithless.

"By April" of that year, with the advent of spring, Levine decided that northern California was "a holy land," but he was still, he says, "faithless" and—"not the father of the man / I am but the same man who all this day / sat in a still house." In Wordsworth's poem "My Heart Leaps Up When I Behold" is the famous line "The Child is father of the Man." Levine tells us that in his case the Wordsworthian formula does not hold. He is not changed. Is he, then, still faithless?

Nevertheless something has changed. If not himself, then how he sees the world in which he lives. He is older; he lives far from California, in New England. Time and space have altered, and such shifting, or drifting, always entails a shift in perspective. He has lived beyond Arthur's death. He is in charge of his own family of five, holding "firm / to the steering wheel" of life just as the father in the blue Plymouth gripped the wheel and held fast to his course.

Far from California, the "still house" in New England is "no longer new or English" and the weather is autumnal and windy. He hears the children playing on his front porch, the crows "on the rain spout" cawing. He could, he assures us, write a poem called "The Basket of Memory" and place in it all his images of the past as if they were Easter eggs about to hatch.

Why Easter eggs? we might ask. And more: Why Easter eggs "waiting to hatch"? Surely because each image resurrects the past "as though I understood the present and the past." He does not, he confesses, understand the present and the past, no more than he understands why an eight-year-old girl waves to him "as she darts / between parked cars and cartwheels into the early dusk." Though he looks for connections among events, he recognizes that the events themselves may be random and inexplicable.

Easter eggs do not normally hatch, but an image might beget another image, a memory might lead to another memory.

When Levine was twenty-eight, Winters was fifty-six. Levine was born in 1928. At the time he is writing this poem, he is fifty-six, the age his mentor was then. Twenty-eight is not only the age to which he looks back but also the number of years that have lapsed between the move to California and the house in New England. ("Loopy numerology," Linda Gregerson calls it in her very smart review, published in *Poetry* in 1989, of *A Walk with Tom Jefferson,* the book in which this poem first appears, adding that "Levine's bittersweet critique of reason records the patent incapacity of form to structure meaning, all the while making meaning of vaporous coincidence.") If the poem is about his life at twenty-eight, and it is in part, it is more importantly about the distance between the past and the present. It is also, one must suspect, about acquiring faith. At fifty-six he can begin to trace contiguous connections, parallel events, the repetition and return that graph a life; at fifty-six he has acquired a sense of life as *plural.*

The poem's metrical steadiness supports the broad movements of the narrative, and because the voice is measured, we trust it and follow it on all the detours, torques, and switchbacks his memory takes. The several events within the poem, though not—purposefully not—described in chronological order, echo and resonate, with the result that, different as they are, they circle one another, becoming a unified "event" that is the transcription of—not memory, but of a theme, which on occasion may be a theme of memory. It is rather like serious music in that thematic exploration or interrogation in a sense is the subject of the work, as of the long poem. Narrative strategies in "28" include reiteration and segue, repeated return to the bass note, shifts in time and place that may seem ambiguous at first glance and oddly insistent at second, and efficient "naming" description ("blue Plymouth," "still house"). These devices are also musical devices and work to create the sense of a sustained song and they are simultaneously devices designed to grip the story-telling memory, as in the lengthy oral epics of ancient civilizations. Of course, it is because the narrative in Levine's poem is not epic that the poet is free to develop ambiguity wherever he likes: the reader can always look back to see when and where the poem hijacked him and brought him to the place he is in now.

In his essay "The Long Embrace: Philip Levine's Longer Poems," Richard Jackson has pointed out how Levine's poems tend to occur as a "moment" in a "temporary now," implicitly suggesting a "before" and an "after" in which things were or will be different. We do not see in this poem many historical events to persuade us that time is passing or has passed, but seasons are delineated and extended time is built into the poem or implied by its segues. With this heightened awareness of time changing, "28" develops a historical dimension and suggests that more poems will follow. Twenty-eight years is a long time for a human being and Levine's poem illustrates how years are stacked on years, gaining in complication.

Memory itself, we know, changes over time, invents and subtracts and distorts, and the very contours of it may shift and realign, like tectonic plates. Yet we do believe Levine's reading of his own memories even if we might wonder if some of the memories are fictional. That is to say that at some level the reader understands she is not expected to believe that the poet has remained "faithless." If "faithless" can mean uncommitted, and of course it can, "28" testifies to his desire to remember and to understand. He is committed to life.

And, clearly, to art, of which the poem itself is a considerable example. In one-hundred-fifty lines he describes the arc(s) of a life, pays tribute to a former teacher, and establishes a sense of life's continuity (though a life may be broken or briefly on hold), patterns and generations, especially generations of students, recurring and changing. This is what the long poem can do so particularly, and in Levine's hands so masterfully, well: seek out and shape from the confluence of materials a theme that holds the materials in place and in mind, which is to say, makes of them a coherent whole, a vision.

There remains a mystery in this poem: "Since then," he writes near the beginning, having informed us of the illness he experienced as he made his way west, "I have died / only twice." He was sick enough to sleep "almost fourteen hours in a motel / above Salt Lake City." The second time was the blue Plymouth/motorcycle accident. What was the other near-death experience? We don't know. Could it have been the point at which he became faithful, given that the transition—or transformation—from faithlessness to fidelity may be fully equal to the difference between child and father, or child and adult? Some will think so. But perhaps not Levine himself, who leaves us with the impression that he has written his "Basket of Memory" but is fully aware that none of it is comprehensible, that the particulars of a life, any life, are always both known and unknown to the owner of the life and cleave to no logic. What is important, we might conclude, is that we accept this and applaud the particulars. It is, after all, by living that we learn what life is.

ALEXANDER LONG

The Two: Levine's Walk with Tom Jefferson

FOR ALL THAT'S BEEN WRITTEN about Philip Levine's poetry, I'm lately drawn to that space of his imagination, his psyche, his source of ferocity and generosity: having been born a twin. I'm reminded of a few lines by one of Levine's favorite poets, George Oppen, his homage to Whitman, the poem "Myself I Sing": "Two. / He finds himself by two. / Or more. / 'Incapable of contact / Save in incidents' / And yet at night / Their weight is part of mine." Such a unique way—the miracle and burden of being a twin—to encounter experience has empowered Levine with an awareness that lays bare one of the most essential symbiotic relationships we have: how the physical cannot exist without the metaphysical, how they inform each other, how neither can exist in any meaningful way without the other. Levine's life as a twin, in short, shapes his vision and colors much of what he's written.

In Levine's imagination the pull between being an individual and being a twin is tidal, an original source of energy and vision. "A Walk with Tom Jefferson" reveals this energy and vision for an extended period with pathos suffused with quiet intensity, acute attention, and localized yet entirely expansive epiphanies. Consider the extensive list of dualities Levine unfolds then braids and ultimately unifies across the five-hundred-eighty-eight lines of the poem: the natural world with an urban landscape, the past with the present, father and son, Biblical and secular, the resonance of memory with the rush of experience, the African-Americans' experience with the whites', the human with the animal, the American south with the American north, and of course the poem's namesake (as well as the historical figure alluded to, the author of The Declaration of Independence who owned and fathered children with at least one of his slaves) with the poem's speaker.

How Levine sustains the energy and vision of the poem across five-hundred-eighty-eight lines are marvels to encounter. What's perhaps even more astonishing is that initial drafts of "A Walk with Tom Jefferson" nearly double the size of its final incarnation. Moreover, as Levine details in an interview with Guy Shahar, *(The Cortland Review,* Issue 7, 1999) the duration it took him to write it offers a glimpse into Levine's process of struggling and succeeding within the demands, strictures, and deceptive latitude of a long poem:

> I have a fairly long poem called "A Walk with Tom Jefferson."
> It was written in two fits and starts. I wrote the first hunk of
> it in two days. It was nine-hundred lines long. Then, in three
> or four days, I boiled it down to about three-hundred lines.
> It was going off in too many different directions the night
> before. When I was done with all that, the poem just stopped
> at a certain point, and I didn't know how to go on. So I said
> to myself, "What's the hurry?" I thought the answer would
> come within a week. Actually, it took over a year. I would
> pull the poem out about once every two weeks and reread
> what I had and think about, okay, where do I go from here?
> I realized exactly what I was missing. I just knew—instantly:
> I'm missing Tom Jefferson's voice. I don't have his voice in
> here. It's my voice that's dominating. Now I gotta' get Tom's
> voice in here. (He's a retired black factory worker in Detroit.)
> Once I realized that I needed his voice, I was on my way. I
> finished the poem that day. So my real virtue there was just
> patience and some kind of self-assurance: I'm gonna' get this
> goddamn poem. I didn't write all this for nothing. It's gonna'
> happen. Just don't keep pushing until you get the right idea .
> . . and it came. Maybe it was luck? Wasn't prayer.

These "too many directions," in conjunction with the staggered and loose and indented iambics, are precisely what sustains "A Walk with Tom Jefferson." The long walk of the poem proceeds uninterrupted by stanza and section markers; and once the reader enters the poem, he and she should be prepared for the absence of pauses, rests, and breaks. The duality of voices also helps sustain the energy down the lines and from page to page, and having Tom's voice chime in—albeit sparingly but sagaciously—vitally contributes to the poem's strategy, larger concerns, and overall purpose: patiently bearing witness in order to find oneself in others: "Two. / He finds himself by two. / Or more." A casual glance upon the page will reveal, even to a stranger of poetry, a pattern of something announcing two-ness. The lineation ambles down the page in steady two-step, the lines unfolding as though they were mimicking the exquisite machinery of bones and tendons and muscles and joints being pressed upon and into them, a rhythm borne by walking maybe home after a double-shift at Cadillac or Ford, or maybe some decades later after those, and other, manufacturing jobs vanished:

Between the freeway
     and the gray conning towers
of the ballpark, miles
     of mostly vacant lots, once
a neighborhood of small
     two-storey wooden houses—
dwellings for immigrants
     from Ireland, Germany,
Poland, West Virginia,
     Mexico, Dodge Main.
A little world with only
     three seasons, or so we said—
one to get tired, one to get
     old, one to die.
No one puts in irises,
     and yet before March passes
the hard green blades push
     their way through
where firm lawns once were.

It might serve us well to remind ourselves of the obvious: the first word of the poem is "Between." Easily overlooked, understandably, given all that follows. It's that space between that suspends us within the poem's myriad polarities, for it's a space the poem's speaker knows too well, but not as well as the poem's namesake:

No one recalls
a slender, dumbfounded
     boy afraid of fifth grade
home room teacher. Tom Jefferson
     —"Same name as the other one"—

"Don't preach," the poem's method suggests here. The image and the allusion and the prosody: they're enough, the stuff that give air and therefore voice and therefore credence to the fact—and the vast distances between—of the two Tom Jeffersons not-so simply sitting there.

    But, Levine is too shrewd and too compassionate to preach. He trusts his imagination. Truth will bear its fruit, not unlike how

The trunks of beech and locust
darken, the light new branches

take the air. You can
    smell the sticky sap rising
        in the maples, smell it
even over the wet stink
        of burned houses.
On this block seven houses
        are still here to be counted,
and if you count the shacks
        housing illegal chickens,
the pens for dogs, they tiny
        pig sty that is half cave . . .
and if you count them you can
        count the crows' nest
in the high beech tree
        at the corner, and you can
regard the beech tree itself
        bronzing in mid-morning light
as the mast of the great ship
        sailing us back
into the 16th century
        or into the present age's
final discovery.

This strange and surprising image of beech-tree-as-ship-mast serves multiple purposes that simultaneously elevate and deepen the scope of the poem. First, the extended analogy evidences Levine's intense imagination; it's a risky image that, at first glance, appears to be more of a non-sequitur or a flight of fancy than something integral to the poem's (and poet's) vision. Who can say which ship this is? Those that landed on Plymouth Rock? One of the thousands thereafter carrying Africans to be sold into slavery at American ports, thereby staining if not damning the entire soul of America? Was there much difference between them, after all?

    Tom Jefferson, after all, is African American, and like Joe Louis,

        . . . was up from Alabama,
like Joe he didn't talk
    much then, and even now
he passes a hand across
    his mouth when speaking
of the $5 day that lured

his father from the cotton fields
and a one-room shack the old folks
        talked about until
they went home first
        to visit and later to die.
Early afternoon behind
        his place, Tom's gathering up
the remnants of this year's
        garden—the burned
tomato plants and the hardy
        runners of summer squash
that dug into the chalky
        soil and won't let go.
He stuffs the dried remains
        into a supermarket shopping cart
to haul off to an empty block.
        The zinnias are left,
the asters in browns and dirty
        yellows, tough petalled
autumn blooms, even a few
        sticky green rose buds
climbing a telephone pole.
        Alabama is not so far back
it's lost in a swirl
        of memory. "I can see trees
behind the house. I do
        believe I still feel
winter mornings, all of us
        getting up from one bed
but for what I don't know."
        He tips his baseball cap
to the white ladies passing
        back the way we've come.
"We all came for $5
        a day and we got this!"

So much for The Great Migration. So much for The American Dream. Now, the extended analogy of beech-tree-as-ship-mast doesn't seem so arbitrary, so fanciful; yet, its risk is apparent, and successful. Now, the beech-tree-as-ship-mast all seems—no, is—part of a larger whole called American History, which is "not so far back/it's lost in a swirl/of memory." Tom Jefferson is a living, breathing, walking American History museum; and in the hands of Levine, he's at once an American treasure as well as simply and necessarily a man deserving of commemoration and respect and dignity, three things (at least) he's been denied for his seven-plus decades.

Here, at line 156, we're roughly a third into the poem. Consider what's become of Tom's (and the speaker's) Detroit neighborhood that endured two massive racial riots, one in 1942, another a generation later in 1967:

> His arms spread wide to
> > include block after block
> of dumping grounds,
> > old couches and settees
> burst open, the white innards
> > gone gray, cracked
> and mangled chifforobes
> > that long ago gave up
> their secrets, yellow wooden
> > ice boxes yawning
> at the sky, their breath
> > still fouled with years
> of eating garlic sausage
> > and refried beans,
> the shattered rib cages
> > of beds that couldn't hold
> our ordinary serviceable dreams,
> > blue mattresses stained
> in earnest, the cracked
> > toilet seats of genius,
> whole market counters
> > that once contained the red meats
> we couldn't get enough of,
> > burned out electric motors,
> air conditioners
> > we suffocated, and over all
> an arctic wind from Canada
> > which carries off
> the final faint unseeable
> > spasm of desire
> to be human and brings down

> the maple and elm leaves
> of early October. If you follow
> their trail of burnished arrows
> scuttling across the curbs and cracked
> sidewalks they'll lead
> you to a cellar hole
> of something or someone
> called Dogman. "Making do,"
> says Tom Jefferson.

The catalogue of urban decay—ten items listed here, but suggestive of so much more—is at once impressive and depressing.[1] Its impressiveness reveals itself in the intense specificity of the wide variety of the abandoned particulars of refuse. Its depressiveness (equally economic and emotional) can be felt not only in each particular item of refuse but also in their slow accretion (the catalogue takes on a nearly endless suggestiveness) and the lost lives implied by each item; moreover, this is where Tom lives, his modest house one of only seven left in the entire neighborhood. Tom's summation of it all are two words of hardened resilience borne by as much inner resolve as lack of options. Where, after all, could Tom go at his age with his modest resources?

Regardless of the superficial markers of race and age between Tom and the speaker, the speaker sees much of himself in Tom. Their shared experience of enduring Detroit's long and slow demise forges a bond between them that approaches empathy. The speaker, like Tom, has weighed his options of getting out:

> . . . Winter's in everything
> we say—it's coming on—we see
> it in the mad swirl
> of leaves and newspapers
> doing their dances.
> We feel it as iron
> in the wind. We could escape,
> each of us feels in
> his shuddering heart, take

[1] These lines may also remind one of the apocalyptic "They Feed They Lion;" the landscape is the same, but the speaker is entirely different. "A Walk with Tom Jefferson" is also twenty-one years removed from the 1967 Detroit riots, which were the triggering subject for "They Feed They Lion." The rage that fuels "They Feed They Lion" is replaced by something like resignation mingling with resilience in "A Walk with Tom Jefferson."

the bridge south to Canada,
            but we don't. Instead we
hunker down, slump a little
            lower in our trousers,
and go slow. One night soon
            I'll waken to a late quiet
and go out to see all this
            transformed, each junked car,
each dumping ground and battered
            hovel a hill
of mounded snow, every scrap
            of ugliness redeemed
under the light a street lamp
            or the moon.

What accounts for this source of hope in the speaker? After all that we learn the speaker is surrounded by—nothing short of a modern urban wasteland—another Michigan winter is coming on. Those who have endured such a landscape know in their bones that hope comes at a premium, if it comes at all. A few lines later, the speaker's mysterious hope dissipates just as quickly as it arrived:

            . . . For a moment
a few stars come out to share
            this witness. I won't believe it,
but Tom will. Tom Jefferson
            is a believer.

So it must be Tom Jefferson, the one with strongest arguments for hopeless-ness, who not only retains hope but offers it. Levine's speaker does all he can to accept it:

You can't plant winter vegetables
            if you aren't,
you can't plant anything, except
            maybe radishes.
You don't have to believe
            anything to grow
radishes. Early August he's got
            sweet corn

two feet above his head,
        he stretches
his arm to show where
        they grow to.
Tomatoes "remind you what tomatoes
        taste like."
He was planting before the Victory Gardens.
        His mother brought
the habit up from Alabama. She was
        growing greens
behind the house no matter how small
        her strip of land,
cosmos beside the back door,
early things
        like pansies along the fence.

The "cosmos beside the back door" is that little piece of Alabama in Detroit, a small strip of nature in the city, as are the vegetables Tom grows to keep himself tethered to the regenerative powers of creation in an otherwise desolate place. Later in the poem we learn that Tom is a widower and has taken up tending the garden in memory of his wife. As if that loss wasn't enough, we learn that Tom had a son:

It didn't take FDR
        and "the war effort"
to make a believer out of Tom.
        When he went off to war
his son Tom Jr. took over
        the garden and did
a job, the same son went off
        to Korea and didn't
come home, the son he seldom talks
        about, just as he
seldom talks about his three years
        in the Seabees
building airstrips so we could
        bomb Japan, doing
the war work he did at home
        for less pay.
A father puts down a spade, his son

picks it up,

"That's Biblical," he says,

"the son goes off,

the father takes up the spade

again, that's Biblical."

The Korean War was the war that came closest to drafting Levine, and it was the war that perhaps terrified him the most; and so to learn that his Virgilian guide through the Hades of twentieth-century Detroit has lost a son to that war must resonate with him. This, and another salient fact of Levine's life many of his most moving poems address: having lost his father at the age of five. I don't wish to portend some sort of psychoanalytic lens upon "A Walk with Tom Jefferson." I simply remind the reader of some facts of the poem that may meaningfully overlay some facts of Levine's life, which may bring us closer to comprehending the skill and vision and force of Levine's poetry. Paul Mariani writing about "A Walk with Tom Jefferson" in *The Kenyon Review* identifies this vision as

> the ancient pattern of fathers and sons repeat[ing] themselves, even as Tom Jefferson has seen the best of it—the hope of a better life, the hope at least that his son would have a better life—disappear in death and absence and the cold wind sighing off the Detroit River. One way or the other, Tom has learned, it's "Biblical" after all.

"A Walk with Tom Jefferson," we learn, is anything but a pleasant amble to proverbially get some air, though it may appear so to an observer, an outsider. Tom and the speaker saunter along and exchange few words, but when Tom does speak it matters:

"That's Biblical," he says.

"We couldn't even look

near each other

for fear of how

one might make the other cry.

That's Biblical,

knowing the other so well

you know yourself,

being careful the way she was

150

> never to say nothing
> or show the least sign."

All that grief simmering just beneath the surface, all that wisdom and experience summed up in two words. This is the second-longest string of dialogue Tom offers in the poem. His silences are sagacious, and Levine balances his speaker's prolonged observations with Tom's sparse wisdom masterfully. After Tom opens up, marginally, about the grief he and his wife have had to endure, he turns to something like nature in this desolate urbanscape:

> Tom picks a maple leaf
> stiff backed and brown
> from the gutter,
> holds it against the distant
> pale sky streaked
> with contrails. Maybe even
> war is Biblical, maybe
> even the poor white
> fighting the poor black
> in this city for the same
> gray concrete housing,
> the same gray jobs
> they both came
> north for, maybe that's
> Biblical, the way
> the Canaanites and the Philistines
> fought the Israelites,
> and the Israelites killed
> the Amalakites
> always for the same land.
> "God wanted Saul
> to kill them down to the last lamb.
> He didn't,
> and he went crazy. Back
> in the riots of '42
> they did not kill us down
> to the last lamb.
> They needed us making airfields
> the way they needed us
> making Fords before the war,

> maybe that's why
> they went crazy."

Here, by line 393 (roughly two-thirds into the poem), we get Tom's longest soliloquy, all of it twelve lines long. Notice the range in his points of focus and the clarity with which he offers them. Tom gets it, what it means to be an American who doesn't assume unwarranted wealthy, privilege, and power but nevertheless deserves something like it, and more. And Levine, the poet, knows all of this, which is why the poem must be as long as it is: it's got to earn these hard, simple truths too often not seen or overlooked or ignored by those who've got it just a little bit—or more than just a little bit—better for reasons entirely beyond their doing. "It's Biblical," Tom says,

> 'The way David plays for Saul so he
>   can weep, and later
> when his turn comes David
>   weeps for Absalom.
> It's Biblical, you cry,
>   it's Biblical you don't,
> either way. That's Biblical.'

To which Levine's speaker replies, if only to himself:

> What commandment
> was broken to bring God's
>   wrath down on these streets,
> what did we do wrong, going
>   about our daily lives,
> to work at all hours until
>   the work dried up,
> then sitting home until home
>   became a curse
> with the yellow light
>   of afternoon falling
> with all the weight of final
>   judgment, I can't say.
> It's Biblical, this season
>   of color coming
> to its end, the air swirling
>   in tiny cyclones

of brown and red, the air
           swelling my lungs,
banging about my ears so that
           I almost think I hear
Tom say "Absalom" again, a name
           owed to autumn
and the autumn of his hopes.

These crushing epiphanies are also what help sustain such a poem of this length and breadth and depth. One might want the poem to end because it's all too much, too painful, too real, too Biblical. But no, Tom reminds us:

                . . . 'We need
this season,' Tom has said,
           but Tom believes
the roots need cold,
           the earth needs to turn
to ice and snow so a new fire
           can start up in the heart
of all that grows.
           He doesn't say that.
He doesn't say the heart
           of ice is fire waiting,
he doesn't say the new seed
           nestles in the old,
waiting, frozen, for the land
           to thaw, and even these streets
of cracking blacktop long gone gray,
           the seven junked cars
the eye can note collapsed
           on slashed tires, their insides
drawn out for anything, he doesn't
           say all this is a lost land,
it's Biblical.

Indeed, Tom doesn't say any of this. We learn, through Levine's speaker, that Tom has embodied it all, exudes it all, has lived it all, and then some. What shorter poem could embody, exude, and live it all, and then some? What's now made apparent (if it hasn't already been established) is that the poem's subject demands its form.

153

The question at this point for both the poet and the reader is how to wrap all this up, as if the truest version of American history can be wrapped up. Tom's hard-won sagacity suffused with his wearied understatement provides perhaps the only answer: "Tomorrow." Levine's student and friend and unofficial editor Larry Levis, three years later (1991) in his book *The Widening Spell of the Leaves* asks: "What does it mean, American?" Tomorrow, one must surmise, because all the yesterdays and todays have proven too barren, too painful, too unbelievable.

And yet, where else can the pained memory go but into the past, all of that which has triggered an awareness of such an utterly corrupt and morally bankrupt landscape of American capitalism. Levine's speaker has the final word; Tom, after all, has retired from their walk:

> The place was called Chevy
> Gear & Axle—
> it's gone now, gone to earth
> like so much here—
> so perhaps we actually made
> gears and axles
> for the millions of Chevies
> long dead or still to die.
> It said that, "Chevrolet
> Gear & Axle"
> right on the checks they paid
> us with, so I can
> half-believe that's what we
> were making back then.

"A Walk with Tom Jefferson" is a testament to endurance in its long form, its subjects, and its vision. It's Biblical, indeed, the implications of "Biblical" serving as a necessary coefficient of the length of the poem. In this essential way, "A Walk with Tom Jefferson" encompasses a life.

M.L. WILLIAMS

"Hard Task to Analyze a Soul": On "Burned"

ADAM HILL ROAMED the English department hallways at Fresno State in a kind of ecstasy. Philip Levine had given him a copy of "Burned" before it came out in *Poetry*, and Adam was telling anyone who would listen that it was Phil's masterpiece, a tour de force that would seal his immortality as a poet. When the rest of us in the workshop had a chance to read the published version ourselves, we fairly seethed over its ambitions for poetry and the poet's imagination, its elegiac sweep, its luminous ferocity, and its unsentimental tenderness and delicacy toward creating a poetry for the people. I'm sure most of us in the workshop truly failed to understand the poem, because we hadn't read enough, but we could feel its epic power and its grandeur of voice, its length and its fragmented, allusive play. It made some of us feel that we should quit writing, because none of us would ever write a poem approaching its magnificence. "Burned," we knew, would be recognized as one of Philip Levine's masterworks.

What Work Is received the national accolades we all expected, including Levine's second National Book Award. While I believed "Burned" would be the breakout poem of the book (to be sure, Tom Disch in his review for *Poetry* called it "the longest and quite the best poem in *What Work Is")*, the collection bristled with so many outstanding poems that this long and ambitious centerpiece has generally received, with the exception of David Baker's illuminating three paragraphs reading "Burned" against Whitman's "Song of Myself " in *Heresy and the Ideal: On Contemporary Poetry* (2000), only passing comment, even when it is praised. Critical attention is primarily lavished on the book's shorter poems, especially the compelling and poignant title poem "What Work Is," which remains, along with "They Feed They Lion," perhaps Levine's best-known poem. Yet "Burned," a poem he had begun fifteen years earlier, was the final poem he selected for the book.[1] Given his meticulous attention to book craft, finishing his selection with such a long and ambitious poem suggests that, at the time, Levine was confident in the poem's merits. Levine's

---

[1] Osen, Diane, Interview. https://www.poemoftheweek.com /philiplevine

return toward such an autobiographical project at this point in his career is perhaps surprising, but he was also already writing the mostly autobiographical essays that would culminate in his next book, *The Bread of Time* (1994), a book of personal essays that he calls an "episodic, unorthodox approach to autobiography" that marks a turn away from his typical Keatsian attitude that "the poet 'is the most unpoetical thing in existence'" (vii). In that sense, "Burned" provides a poetic bridge between *What Work Is* and *The Bread of Time*, and reconnects Levine to the autobiographical epic traditions of Romanticism, to Wordsworth explicitly and Walt Whitman, as well as to a broader epic tradition that includes Blake, Milton, Dante, and certainly Homer's Stygian underworld. Perhaps surprisingly, his personal response to "Burned" following the publication of *What Work Is* has been noncommittal. In the unedited transcript of Jeff Rumiano's *Five Points* interview included as an appendix in his dissertation, Levine simply concludes, ". . . I'm not that proud of it." [2] Nevertheless, for many poets, "Burned" remains the apocalyptic, fevered centerpiece of *What Work Is*, and it deserves consideration as one of his finest and most revolutionary long poems.

• • •

In exchange for a bottle of 1981 Caymus Special Selection, Philip Levine was kind enough to visit a class of my Fresno High students during the time he would have been finishing up *What Work Is*. His talk was compelling and the students were rapt, which was especially surprising given that he visited during the last class of the day when the clock on the wall looms largest. While the students soaked up every word, I was most surprised that the first poet he mentioned was William Wordsworth. In workshop, he spoke of many poets, especially William Carlos Williams and Walt Whitman, Antonio Machado and Miguel Hernandez, Robert Frost, and even Sir Walter Raleigh, along with contemporary rivals and friends that he would needle humorously, but he had never, as far as I recall, mentioned Wordsworth. Yet during his visit, he informed my students that every poet writing in his generation (except for James Dickey, he joked) owed a debt to Wordsworth for reintroducing "the language of conversation in the middle and lower classes" or "the very language of men" to poetry in his editions of *Lyrical Ballads*. He moved on quickly to Williams and his famous quote about how his poetry came "from the mouths of Polish mothers" (later to become the title of one of Levine's own poems),

---

[2] Rumiano, Jeffrey Edmond, "They Know 'What Work Is': Working Class Individuals in the Poetry of Philip Levine." Dissertation, Georgia State University, 2007. https://scholarworks.gsu. edu/english_diss/24

and then he talked about his own relation to poetry and its continuing necessity to the world, even in a culture that seemed to have less and less room for it. He was truly inspiring and generous.

Wordsworth's *Prelude,* begun in 1798, is Philip Levine's primary touchstone[3] for "Burned." Ed Hirsch, characterizing Levine's early work as an attempt to "create a poetry of the urban landscape," notes in "The Visionary Poetics of Philip Levine and Charles Wright" that Wordsworth's sonnet "Composed upon Westminster Bridge, September 3, 1802" (which provided his title for *Sweet Will),* "reverberates through all his work" as his poems move out of "silence and failure" toward "the defiant transformation of blankness into language" (Parini, 780). While the sonnet betokens a "glittering" urban landscape of enormous potential in its sleeping houses and "all that mighty heart . . . lying still," Levine's engagement with The Prelude allows him to interrogate the poet's necessary relationship to that sleeping potential and to lay out the responsibilities of the poetic imagination to the mighty urban heart.

Certainly, Levine's attempt to compose his own "Growth of the Poet's Mind," as *The Prelude* was called in manuscript, also implies a criticism. Yet I propose that the criticism is not of the poem's egalitarian impulses inspired by the French Revolution, but rather of the poet himself, who increasingly turned away from revolutionary ideals toward Edmund Burke's conservatism, nationalism, and elitism. In "Burned," Levine implicitly studies Wordsworth's ultimate betrayal of that revolutionary spirit as he confronts and explores the growth of his own poetic imagination, as well as his relationship to the political anarchism foundational to his poetic ethos. So it is perhaps an advantage that Levine approaches his own epic of imagination and revolution from a state of exhaustion, of being burned out in the underworld of a denatured urban landscape, rather than repose, because he cannot adopt Wordsworth's

---

[3] Philip Levine encouraged his students to identify great touchstone poems and to consult them as they composed their own poems. Given that the genesis of "Burning" was in the mid-1970s, it might be tempting for some critics to read "Burned" through the lens of Harold Bloom's *Anxiety of Influence,* which, to oversimplify, argues that contemporary poets must struggle with and rise above the influence of their great poetic progenitors. While Phil, in conversation about doctoral programs, said he liked Harold Bloom as a colleague at NYU and respected his incredible intellect, I got the sense that he didn't think much of Bloom's elaborate theories about authorial anxiety. Levine's ideas about touchstone poems are more pragmatic and fundamental and more obvious to poets, so I use "touchstone" to consider "Burned" and its response to *The Prelude.* Nevertheless, I have consulted criticism that would have been standard at the time of the composition of "Burned" for a sense of general commentary available on *The Prelude,* including Harold Bloom's revised edition of *The Visionary Company* (Ithaca: Cornell UP, 1971), and others, as noted. Furthermore, Bloom's revised edition was designed by Harry Ford, Levine's editor at Atheneum and Knopf.

retreat to nature's sublimity and a desire to reflect in a retirement that led him away from the revolutionary ideals of his early work.

The earliest version of Wordsworth's manuscript, the two-part *Prelude,* urged on by Samuel Taylor Coleridge as Wordsworth is still reconciling his revolutionary ideals with the French Revolution's excesses and ultimate failure, begins with the repeating question, "Was it for this . . . ?"—initiating what is, according to M. H. Abrams, "one of the most grandiose" projects ever in the extended examination of his poetic imagination, its relationship with nature and the sublime, and "his claim to be ranked with the greatest poets," especially Milton (19). Levine, in contrast, initiates the first section of his twenty-section, mostly visual blank verse masterwork with the anchoring phrase "I have to . . . "[4] its urgency igniting a need to act because "it's too late" to reflect quietly:

> I have to go back into the forge room
> at Chevy where Lonnie still calls
> out his commands to Sweet Pea and Packy
> and stare into the fire
> until my eyes are also fire
> and tear away some piece of my face
> because we're all burning in the blood
> and it's too late.
>   I have to walk
> the long road from here to Bessemer,
> Alabama, and arrive on a June night in '48
> after work when the men have crowded
> around a stalled car and tell them

---

[4] I quote exclusively from the poem as published in the September 1990 issue of *Poetry* rather than the poem as it appeared in *What Work Is* due to edits made before publication in the book, as will be discussed.

Anxiety of Influence, which, to oversimplify, argues that contemporary poets must struggle with and rise above the influence of their great poetic progenitors. While Phil, in conversation about doctoral programs, said he liked Harold Bloom as a colleague at NYU and respected his incredible intellect, I got the sense that he didn't think much of Bloom's elaborate theories about authorial anxiety. Levine's ideas about touchstone poems are more pragmatic and fundamental and more obvious to poets, so I use "touchstone" to consider "Burned" and its response to *The Prelude.* Nevertheless, I have consulted criticism that would have been standard at the time of the composition of "Burned" for a sense of general commentary available on *The Prelude,* including Harold Bloom's revised edition of *The Visionary Company* (Ithaca: Cornell UP, 1971), and others, as noted. Furthermore, Bloom's revised edition was designed by Harry Ford, Levine's editor at Atheneum and Knopf.

there's no place to go and
let them take turns beating me
with hands turned to pig iron.
                                        I have to
climb the shaking ladder to the roof
of the nitro plant and tear off
my respirator and breathe the yellow air
the Chaldeans called "the air you must not breathe,"
and sing in the voices
of my fathers calling the children
into prayer while below the stubby canisters
pass labeled "Chicago," "Amsterdam,"
"Belsen," "Toronto."
                                I have to swim out
into the flat waters of the great sea
at dawn when the small fishing boats
are coming in and climb aboard the one
with the face of a goddess and the tail
of a goat and let my left cheek
brush against the rough, unshaven cheek
of the old man whose tears—mixed with wine—
watered the beach twenty one years ago.
                                                    And
keep going past the last marker
until I am lost forever, until the sea
and the sky are one, the waves have ceased,
no tide pulls us toward anything and there are
no cries from the drowned.[5]

His biblically anaphoric repetitions move through scenes of work and labor
strife and draw fire from the book of Daniel, only to end up "in the flat waters
of the great sea" on a ship "with a face of a goddess and the tail / of a goat . .
. ," the ship of capitalism presenting its beautiful, false face, its deceitful prom-
ise up front, while the dehumanizing work of scapegoated labor takes position
aft (where a good Marxist would point out the rudder is), and "the old man"
with "tears—mixed with wine" a figure of someone used up in offering to false
gods. The sea itself both echoes and contrasts with Wordsworth's:

[5] The strophe in "What Work Is" ends "no tide pulls us toward / the cries of the drowned."
The *Poetry* version suggests utter oblivion, while the revision maintains the nightmarish,
audible "cries of the drowned."

> oh then the calm
> And dead still water lay upon my mind
> Even with a weight of pleasure, and the sky,
> Never before so beautiful, sank down
> Into my heart and held me like a dream. (2. 211-15)

Levine substitutes the "weight of pleasure" with being "lost forever," and "dream" with the apocalyptic dead tide and "no cries from the drowned." Levine's final "I have to" verse paragraph reimagines the climax of *The Prelude* at the very beginning of "Burned":

> I have to climb
> the slag hills again, but this time not
> as a child, and look out over the river of iron,
> and hold it all in my eyes,
> the river, the iron mountains, the factories
> where our brothers burned. I have to repeat
> the prayer that we will all go back
> to earth one day soon to become earth,
> that our tears will run to the sea
> a last time and find it open, and our fires
> light someone's way home.

"[T]he slag hills again" are Levine's Mount Snowdon from which "this time not / as a child" he must look out over the "iron mountains" and his molten Detroit Derwent, "a river of iron," to "hold it all in my eyes." For Wordsworth, the ascent of Mount Snowdon signifies attainment of his visionary achievement as he overlooks Derwent's riverine symbol of his life emptying into the great sea in the distance, the vision signaling his full becoming as poet. But for Levine, this is not an end, but a beginning of the poet's work, and initiates a reversal of Wordsworth's ascent. The "slag hills" are a place of witness, to see "the factories / where our brothers burned," his hopes for the shed tears of sacrifice that will "find" the sea and "light" their "fires" that will "light someone's way home." Levine's Snowdon is not a platform for visionary self-realization, certainly not the kind that ultimately resulted in Wordsworth's increasing self-absorption and withdrawal from his revolutionary ideals. Levine's is a vision of and for others—his burning brothers and sisters in the factories, the inhabitants of the burning streets of Detroit, his family, those exploited and abused by capitalist greed—and his hope at the end of it all in this visionary opening is not for himself, but for "someone" among the collective exploited who needs light to find a way home. The remainder of "Burned" allows Levine to offer up his own "spots of time" in memories and in reflection upon the growth of his poetic imagination and poetry's relationship to the world, not anchored by nature recollected in repose, but by the common theme of fire, of being burned, and of a burning desire for collective connection and social justice. To accomplish this, he must descend and be among the people.

In stark contrast to the chronologically reflective *Prelude*, however many its perambulations and narrative disruptions, "Burned" lacks obvious temporal contiguity, as though images and narrative fragments issue forth out of the speaker's fever rather than reflection in repose. The second section reveals a young Levine, aged sixteen, "Summer in Detroit" during World War II in a collage of memory that initially suggests a kind of nostalgia, a girl coming of age, a young man named Leo reading from *The Tempest* "his skin / chilled by the glory of language," until the speaker admonishes the reader:

> I have not brought them together
> so their hearts may stutter or stop
> with a love they can't bear. It is 1944,
> Moradian has landed on a Pacific atoll
> to become his life forever, Esther's husband
> sees the Sherman twenty yards ahead
> go up in a flash and knows his is next.

The shift forces awareness of what the trauma of war is stealing from the community despite continuing daily existence or "Bernard and Arthur's vow / to give themselves to music and to poetry." But he can't take the place of those in their commitments to war or to art because he is "too young, / too exhausted, too busy." In this scene, he is in the realm of family, making a sandwich "the exact way my grandmother taught me" and

> humming one of my grandfather's tunes,
> one he groans out himself when he sings
> himself to sleep, tapping his foot, swinging
> from side to side as though he were burning.

The young Levine in exhaustion from school and work is caught between the antipodes of war and high culture, exploitation and higher human achievement, but the mature voice signals that this is also a point of departure to "The other kingdom." He grounds the image of "burning" here as both passion and destruction, the boy grounded in family on the verge of becoming a man in the midst of human extremes. Here we also encounter the beginning of Levine's version and revision of Wordsworth's "Two consciousnesses" (II. 30) as he introduces the boy that will father Levine's mature imaginative vision.

The speaker in mature voice revisits the site of his former neighborhood, which is no longer there, in the third section, and he slips into a memory of a friend, possibly an early love.[6]

> A burned car left in a field
> of sassafras, the long green shoots
> through the windows and doors where no
> doors remain. The kids don't come by
> after school to carve their names
> on the dashboard or pull the steering wheel
> to avoid the inevitable. Rocks, tires, cases
> of empties, an old couch sagging
> into weeds, the cushions blooming.
> I lived here once, in a house
> now gone.

The landscape remains remarkably denatured, the hope of "long green shoots" and the music of the word "sassafras" overwhelmed by the wreckage of the burned-out car, weeds, empty bottles, the ghosts of houses and absent children who otherwise might have made the space a playground, a place the young would mark their names. The scene provokes a memory of a relationship—the simple tenderness of a gift and the silences of profound friendship, and perhaps love:

> A friend visited me
> at dusk, and she brought a paper parcel
> of cookies tied with a ribbon. Even then
> we were scared of the silence that followed
> whatever we gave each other. I would
> walk her to the bus stop on Second Avenue,
> and we would wait in silence in the dense air

---

[6] Cf. Philip Levine's essay "Nobody's Detroit" in *My Lost Poets* (Knopf 2016): "Half a mile south of the stadium the plumbing-parts factory where I'd worked for a year was gone, and nothing was in its place except a field of nettles and weeds and three abandoned cars, their wheels gone" (38). Also, "The home of Dolly Basil, whom I truly loved for two months, has given way to a six-lane highway" (43).

of a March night as slow rain
fell into the last snow. I'd come back
alone, sober, singing to the starless sky,
singing recklessly out of a boy's
throat, past the darkened rows
of sleeping two-storey houses
that have all gone up in smoke.

The astonishing last sentence conflates both times, as the speaker is "back alone," both in this desolate space of the "burned car" and in the living memories of this community after leaving his "friend" at the bus stop. The mature poet is "singing recklessly out of a boy's throat" as he passes those houses in the penultimate line, but in the true present of the speaker in the last line, they are "gone up in smoke." The section moves from nature denatured to human connection to oblivion in beautiful, poignant language, yet what lives at the center is the simple act of the gift, the silent connection, and the aforementioned "sleeping" potential once held in all those houses brought back to life here in this profound elegy.

The fourth section in much shorter lines moves to Los Angeles much later. His mother, a bookseller, had moved there from Detroit, presumably to be closer to family. It's "Yom Kippur / in the New World. Los Angeles hums / a little tune—" and "blinking" faces make their way through the morning dark up the coast highway to Monday market. The hopeful mood first gives way to her reverie after gathering, after atonement, perhaps, then to loss:

My mother dreams
by the open window.
On the drainboard
the gray roast humps
untouched, the oven
bangs its iron jaws,
but it's over.
Before her on the table
set for so many
her glass of fire
goes out.
The childish photographs,
the letters and cards
scatter at last.
The dead dream alone
toward dawn.

The elegiac mood continues, but the loss is not literal death, as Levine's mother was still living in Los Angeles when the poem was composed. Rather, this section suggests the scattering that naturally occurs to families as children relocate and parents age. The "New World" here is Los Angeles, and the old world is less Central Europe than Detroit, one of Levine's "Holy Cities" and the source of "fire" in the poem—passion, connection, rootedness, and destruction—despite the pleasures of the west coast and the attempt to maintain tradition after leaving so much behind back east, in Detroit.

Eight questions[7] and a statement in their midst comprise the fifth section of "Burned," and the questions reveal the poet in crisis and express the desire for an intermediary, a muse figure. "Why am I going away from the glass of wine, / from the loaf of bread?" The speaker questions first his refusal of biblical sustenance, and then perhaps nature in his inability to "mourn[ ] the tiny death of the sparrow" who was "drawn into / tall burned grass." The next question, the most important one for the poet, is also a kind of answer: "What will I say when the nights grow, / when the day dies into the violet haloes / of exhaust?" Indeed, what to say is the first question for the poet against the pressing nights, that burnt air that is both waste and a reflection of the speaker's exhaustion. Next, the one statement suggests, not simple loneliness, but the absence of a muse: "No one takes my hand and leads me to bed, / to the mouth-to-mouth agonies of darkness." And the section concludes with an appeal:

> How will I know I was and I was alive
> when this passes?
> Who will take my hand and lead me to you?
> Who will take my hand that is on fire,
> that smells of earth,
> that is burning now to autumnal rust?
> Who will lead me?

The burning hand of the poet, the quest for a voice, the desire for a muse to "lead me to you"—you, the poetic imagination and ultimately, you, the poem—regathers the vatic impulses of "Burned" and reconnects it with *The*

---

[7] The two-part Prelude also contains eight questions. This section was slightly revised in the version published in What Work Is. The section is not punctuated except for capital letters at the beginning of sentences and one comma in a new line added after "longer and longer": "the dawn is barely visible, a grudging / of yellow light"; he also deletes the phrase "that is on fire," perhaps to cut a redundancy ("on fire" and "burning"), so that the line in What Work Is reads "Who will take my hand / smelling of earth . . ." (47).

Prelude's objective, yet as Levine moves beyond both religion and Wordsworth's grounding Nature toward a poetry of community, he seeks to establish the growth of this poet's mind, not merely to recast Wordsworth's project. This prophetic section certainly plays on the trope of the muse as lover, but in the only statement, "mouth-to-mouth agonies" also betokens a desire to be a part of a community of speakers to engage that darkness and to become a voice against it.

The sixth section disrupts the interior memory of the previous sections as the speaker encounters a woman who might fit into an updated canto of Dante's *Inferno*. She explains to the speaker that she "was burned," and shows him the scars on her belly, "still smooth."

> "He
>   said he adored my white skin, creamy.
> Can a Jew imagine what a real
> white woman looks like all over? All
> your life you dream of someone like me,
> every night of your life." Her green eyes
> on fire with her own memories
> of herself 40 years ago. She shakes her head
> awake and still goes on. "Not with cigarettes,
> you moron. Would a man like that, richer
> than God, burn his only beloved with
> cigarettes? Cigars, imported Havanas, nothing
> but the best!"
>   And she's gone, thank God,
> slamming the door on me, gone back
> to the one life she clings to. The room
> is quiet, ashamed, the books gawk down
> from their shelves, not one
> with a word to tell me what it is like
> to enter a fire of your own making, naked,
> day after day, until the burning becomes
> a sweetness.

Levine presents this first and striking direct encounter with another person as an abject failure to connect, and it results, not only in his silence, but in a silence profound enough to render even the books in his room mute. After such a plea as "Who will lead me?" she is anti-muse, abused, racist. Her dignity has been burned out of her and replaced with the "sweetness" of capitalist corruption, her old lovers' abuse bought off with "only the best" and most expensive instruments of torture, Cuban cigars. As in any capitalist system, she is "beloved" only as object, and she has succumbed not only to his abuse, but to its dehumanizing reification of her as thing. The section also presents a challenge to the poet, in that the answer to "What will I say?" requires a new making, one absent from his shelves that initiates a critique of capitalism into his developing aesthetic.

In sections seven through fourteen, Levine introduces the critical "you" that will dominate the heart of the poem. In *The Prelude*, "you" is Samuel Taylor Coleridge and, later, Dorothy Wordsworth, but "you" is also the landscape around Lake Como, "Imagination!" in the crossing of Simplon Pass (1805, VI 528), and "Thou Soul that art the eternity of thought." (1805, I 432) Levine's "you" is also multivalent and initially mysterious:

> The day you left I walked
> alone for hours down the crowded streets
> hearing and seeing no one until I
> caught the cries of a broken woman
> behind me. She had lost her husband,
> left him in a bar, was alone, frightened,
> calling for help. I kept walking
> with her behind me, calling.
> The houses along the canal were closing
> up, turning their eyes inward
> listening to the rumbling of their furnaces
> or their human groans. This day will end,
> I told myself, this pain will pass.
> I will waken to my life.

All we know of "you" is the crisis absence provokes, sending the speaker headlong into crowds invisible and silenced, in his consciousness, because of the trauma. He finally hears "the cries of a broken woman," but chooses to keep walking, to turn, like the houses, his own "eyes inward" at first in hopes of future solace against his loss. This passage recalls the crowded streets of Wordsworth's London, when, shortly after his vision of the Blind Beggar, Wordsworth hears "The feeble salutation from the voice / Of some unhappy woman now and then / Heard as we pass, when no one looks about, / Nothing is listened to." (1805, VII 641-44) Levine hears, too, a woman's pain echoing his own, but in his decision to stop and hear her out, he encounters not the woman, but something of a vision as the "broken woman" transforms into a "little girl":

> The evening
> spread from the great oaks
> that lined the emptying boulevards
> or descended in bits of ashes and dust
> from a deepening sky. I turned at last
> to behold the woman whose grief
> was louder than mine. There was
> only a child, her right hand closed
> tight on a handkerchief knotted at one end
> with some coins and a note, a little girl
> who seeing my eyes filled with tears
> began to cry as she smiled.

The visionary moment is enhanced by the narrative's ambiguous time and place, the unexplained metamorphosis, and the unread note, and is marked only by the precipitating absence of "you." He may be seeing through time, through the woman herself back to and made whole in childhood, the note a cipher he must solve to "waken into . . . life." The loss of "you" opens up, in his turn toward another, the possibility of metaphysical human connection and empathy.

Levine's epic continues with a catalog of family artifacts in section eight: "Two ten-inch phonograph records, *Bluebirds,* / going white, that won't give up their music," his uncle's book on "the secret of electric growth," his father's "Victoria Cross" war medal picked up "at an automobile parts convention" and "white gold pocket watch

> a Howard, that runs and stops and runs
> to keep his time. His naturalization papers
> claiming he was born in 1898 in Poland,
> without a mention of his years at war.
> My brother's smeared grade school drawings
> of Spitfires, Stukas, ME-109s,
> his "Withdrawal from Dunkirk," the beach
> crisscrossed with small black lines
> that could be abandoned arms or the arms
> of boys hugging. My stillborn sister's
> wish to mother a child, to breathe
> the stained air that blows in at dusk
> from the parking lots, to walk with us
> on Sunday afternoons. Your fingerprints

on the final application for release.
A bitten fountain pen, a dry stamp pad.
Two clear drops of fluid that catch
and hold the artificial light, that glow
with their own light when that's gone
as eyes in stories are said to do.
Now in the dark they could be you,
they could be me, they could be anyone.

The list begins with and is anchored by memorabilia, records, a book, his dead father's medal and watch, papers, drawings, the pen and stamp pad, but the speaker's imagination wells up at the drawings when he envisions "the arms of boys hugging" on the beach at Dunkirk, and, most poignantly, his imagination pursues the life and simple human desires of a sister born dead. Then his "you" again in fingerprints on an ambiguous "application for release" that suggests a particular "you." This sentence remains in the realm of the speaker's poetic imagination, and so may also represent a shift from "she" to "you," rendering his sister present even as the artifact that brings her to life in memory may be the application to release her body to the family. The gnawed pen and dry pad seem to bring us back to the realm of simple, junk-drawer objects, but the pen also suggests a writer at work. The catalog concludes with two glowing tears in light and storybook darkness that could be "you," "me," or "anyone." But the admission of "anyone" into this mournful and nostalgic list opens beyond the "you" and "me" of the reader and writer to "anyone" who might feel this sense of human connection so deeply that elegy offers a continuation of life.

Following this catalog, Levine presents an ecstatic "you" in section nine, in that "ecstasy" literally means to stand outside oneself. Whoever else the "you" might also be, here his poetic imagination speaks to him as he seeks answers. He "stop[s] at the borders of dreams," but not in the dream, and he "ask[s] who you are" of the voice in his "ear all these years," a voice he has confided in and "said all I can say." The speaker and the poetic imagination both turn to his "two hands" raised "upward toward the light," as if in prayer or supplication:

> That is the shape
> of eternity: five long fingers
> and a palm broadened and carved
> by use. When I looked
> in my heart and found only

questions, when I walked
beside the ditch at dusk
and asked the sun,
the answer was curled
quietly in my pocket. "Look at
them both," you say, "turn them
over and place them on the table
before you. Don't be afraid.
They are you, familiar at times,
overlooked, despised. Now,
go back the way you came, down
the same old streets where you
grew to a name and a single face.
That was home, you said, and today
it is nothing, not even a closet
of unread books. Here is home.
Close your eyes. You are on
a dark plain. The hot winds
breathe in and out. You are laughing!
You asked for a home, you crossed
the earth, you sat speechless,
you questioned the closed door,
'Are you there?' No one answered
because all the time it was you."

The "dark plain" and "hot winds" mark this as Levine's version of Wordsworth's famous Arab Dream (1805 Book V, 71 ff), but instead of the richly symbolic stone and shell the Arab will bury that represents Wordsworth's desire "to save Imagination from the abyss of desert and ocean, man's solitary isolation from and utter absorption into Nature" (Bloom 151), Levine's "guide" tells him to look to his own two hands. The true source of poetry for Levine is not tied to any kind of external capital-lettered entity such as God or Nature, which are human projections anyway, and in the passage above, even "eternity" maintains lower-case status. The poetic imagination arises from and through those hands, from the mind that conceives and uses them in an act of work, of making, of poetry, and it is poetry as a kind of manufacture, a work, that connects Levine to the broader community of labor. Ecstasy for Levine here is a recognition that the answers he seeks come from the self through those hands, the self outside himself that connects him to others through work and the deep, communal meaning of work.

The speaker appears to be much older in the tenth section, a domestic scene, and the "you" he speaks to therefore takes on a more intimate, if still forcefully guiding, character:

If I called you "my soul," you'd
laugh in my face. If I went
down on my knees to you as to
a god or a beloved, you'd turn
to the window, shake your head,
and talk to the last of the garden.
At the end of September, I may
ask the trees to hold still
in the west wind. I may scold
the flicker hiding in the shade
of an orange tree. His feathers
scatter and settle into the trough
of each wave. He is not
a religious object nor is
the wind sacred, smelling
as it does of cold salt
and sea life. I have been
here so long the bleached hairs
quivering on my hands remember
the years before the flood.
The whites of my eyes, no longer
white, stared into fire when fire
was ours, and I am only
so much salt, water, and stone
smelling of iron. I can talk
to you, and though my answers
will scatter like feathers in the wind,
you may write them down on paper
that burns even in sunlight.
Get what you can, says the flicker;
remorseless, he shoulders his way
into light and then into air.
What does he care that the year
winds down? That the west wind
smells of ice? That what went out
as lies and so much bad breath
came back as the final truth?

The "you" here continues as poetic imagination in negotiated reconciliation with the speaker, now aging, and it chides him for confusing his poetic imagination with his "soul" or "a god or a beloved" or, in Wordsworth's final capitalized parlance, "that awful Power." (1850 VI, 595) This section may continue in the antediluvian visionary rhetoric of the vatic poet on the surface, but mainly to undo it, as this section lays out the speaker's powerlessness. He may ask the trees to be still in the wind and scold the "remorseless" flicker, but they are not "sacred" and neither is nature. They don't care. This could almost be parody, but the "you" becomes his hands again that can write down his scattered answers on "paper / that burns even in sunlight," and the "lies and so much bad breath" that the flicker doesn't care about can come "back as the final truth." The "you" here is grounding, anti-visionary, despite the speaker's quest for poetic vision, and while that grounding demystifies the poetic imagination, what remains is the poem, the truth. Moreover, anyone reading the beginning of this section who knows Philip Levine personally will find it hard not to envision his "beloved" wife, Frances Levine in the "you," but she would tell him to stand up if he was on his knees. She wouldn't abide such rhetorical extravagance and very well might shake her head and say so to him while looking out on her garden. The veiled suggestion of her presence also grounds and reinforces the section's demystification of the poetic imagination, while contributing a subtle humorous layer. As muse figure, she is no-nonsense, advising the poet to stop looking outside himself in search of "that awful Power."

Section eleven nods toward modernist poetic forbears and the reconciled "you" is absorbed into a royal "we" in Levine's reversal of Eliot's "Unreal City":

> The outskirts of our least favorite city,
> the one bombed and burned from the inside
> by its own citizens—along the fence
> small climbing roses bloom in April,
> the hardier ones hang on long
> past the better days, and late autumn
> brings tiny crystals glistening
> on the cheeks of the blackened petals.
> Spading the gray soil, I think
> of begonias and how their buds redden
> even without rain and of the wild iris—
> flags we called them—that won't live
> in the rich beds, though they survive

171

fire and hail, outbattling tough weeds
to spring up where houses once were.
Poking among these ruins for rocks
for the garden, I unearth bricks
from a familiar fireplace or a slab
of stone that crowned a hearth, remnants
of my lost neighbors. Spilling
the kernels of carrot seeds
into my palm and the black pips
of radishes, I know something
will come from this root and wood
thickened ground. With a stick
I scrape a trough for planting. I remember
the unloved lamb become a sheep I saw
on his way to slaughter. Like me, he shook
his head as though he knew
the way home, that head dirty with curls.

This gives Detroit as T. S. Eliot's "Waste Land" in a cruel April of its own "bombed and burned from the inside" making, roses and begonias instead of lilies and tubers, and embellished by the apparition of Ezra Pound's "In a Station of the Metro" in its "crystals on the glistening cheeks of the blackened petals." The "fragments shored against my ruins" (poetryfoundation.org) come from the "remnants" of Levine's "lost neighbors." The speaker plants a garden here in the burned out neighborhood. The "you and I" become "we," allowing Levine's preferred Keatsian poetic imagination to obtain in a landscape rich with objective correlatives. The speaker is not Levine, but rather Levine almost certainly become the urban gardener he names Tom Jefferson for his book *A Walk With Tom Jefferson*. He recounts meeting this urban gardener and guide on a trip back to Detroit in "Nobody's Detroit" *(My Lost Poets* 38-40), his fenced garden planted without permission in an empty lot where a two-story house had been. The speaker in the poem, breaking "root and wood thickened ground" with "a stick" to plant seeds while identifying with a sheep led to slaughter, deepens the scene toward myth, for the speaker becomes a kind of Abel figure, an everyman Fisher King for this Detroit wasteland.

Sections twelve and thirteen feature the ecstatic or double consciousness of "you" and "I" in less fraught, more intimate conversation:

I was small once, hardly bigger
than the laughter of a lemon, and like

a lemon, I had come into a life
no one would question, an oily rind,
closed volumes of flesh, and seeds
as smooth as pearls. Even then
you could talk, you were immense
with desire to touch each leaf,
each small animal that rose
from its lair. Later,
even you who could love rind,
seeds, oil, flesh, let your name slip
from your tongue to become
nonsense, let salt rain down
into the fields and surrendered
all you'd seen, you who had
eaten the earth gave back ashes.

Here the poetic imagination "hardly bigger than the laughter of a lemon" addresses the poet, with the playful imagery of Lorca, in a lifetime's arc from a youth "with immense desire," to the surrender of his name, and finally to the biblical finality of "ashes." This vaguely echoes Wordsworth's birth-to-death poetic journey, perhaps, yet, rather than following the figure of a stream to the all-enveloping ocean, Levine follows desire, fruit, and flesh—all images of appetite and taste, of eating the earth, of sapience—on through nameless-ness, to the residue of burning. This is not about the death of the speaker, but rather about the process of poetic creation in which the poet gives over the self or the ego completely to the poem. This, of course, is Keats again,[8] or in his former student Larry Levis' parlance, the poet "becoming threshold." The poet giving up the self is akin to death, but for the imagination, this is a point of visionary poetic reckoning, a point of departure. "[I]t's time we left," he says, suggesting a journey, but perhaps also indicating an act of leaving behind time, a movement toward the lyric. The voice instructs the poet to gather items that seem initially to be memorabilia:

[8] "A Poet is the most unpoetical of any thing in existence; because he has no Identity—he is continually in for—and filling some other Body—The Sun, the Moon, the Sea and Men and Women who are creatures of impulse are poetical and have about them an unchange-able attribute—the poet has none . . . . I feel assured I should write from the mere yearning and fondness I have for the Beautiful even if my night's labours should be burnt every morning, and no eye ever shine upon them. " "Letter to Richard Woodhouse," October 27, 1818 (Wikisource).

> Take the small, empty purse
> your mother carried across an ocean,
> take the little book of songs
> the children taught you, take
> your teeth and your fingernails
> and the white scars on your belly . . .

However, the white scars recall the cigar-burned woman earlier in the poem, so rather than memorabilia, these are simply images from memory, building blocks, perhaps, for poems. After instructing the poet to meet "where the road/vanishes into the hillside," the imagination offers puzzling instructions:

> How will you know me?
> I won't be tall or dressed
> for dinner or carrying a dark bag,
> I won't be whistling like a bird
> or your father coming home from work,
> I won't be anyone you ever
> spoke to or fell asleep beside
> or wakened to. I won't be sorry
> for you, I won't take your hand
> or come forward and touch
> your hair or kiss your cheek.

The figure merely offers a list of the consoling figures "I won't be" or actions that "I won't do" in negation after negation rather than any identifying information, and the voice invites the poet to look "between the two sullen elms / without leaves, the ones that died / years ago," and asks if he can "see a shadow." The voice lists several conflicting possibilities for what the poet might see, what the shadow "could be": "the birth we gave back to the rain" suggesting, perhaps, Levine's stillborn sister, and "silence after love" and "pain without hope" and "the need to dance." The shadow "looks alive even, in darkness" and it is "growing," but, after the enjambment, "smaller and smaller." It's not melting snow, but

> It could be
> a whisper, a secret never kept,
> everything your heart knew
> and you forgot. Don't ask.

The poet is in the space beyond the road at "the hillside," at the base of poetic possibility ("the slag hills again"), the blank page, and the section closes with the most direct explanation of negative capability that only Philip Levine could have come up with: "Don't ask."

The voice that "won't take your hand" will, however, in apparent contradiction,

> accept it if it is given:
> Give me your hand, and I'll count
> each finger twice and put them to sleep
> with a name more cold and remote
> than a star's. They don't move,
> not even to breathe, not even
> to search for water or embrace
> another hand. This is the way
> things become as we return closer
> and closer to air that simply is,
> stained by a day not yet here.

This final giving up of self through hands allows the poet's doubled ecstatic consciousness to unify away from name and need into the ontological possibility of poetry, "the way things become," by approaching the "air that simply is," the element in pure form a priori of speech, of voice, in a state perhaps akin to that "sleep" in which Wordsworth's childhood images rested awaiting "maturer seasons." (1799, I 428) However, the staining here, the shrinking shadow above, suggest the imperfectability of this process in this movement that can only move "closer and closer," and denotes the indelible presence of the human. The poet in this visionary state is not some kind of god. Disruptively, the rest of the section turns to a vision:

> A woman gets out of bed and goes
> to the window to see if the birds
> have wakened and sees the houses
> have gone, the trees have turned
> inward to become so many pages
> unmarked by mistakes. She says
> nothing to herself. She makes
> the bed, and washes the one plate, the cup,
> the little spoon and fork. She dries
> them carefully and lets them fall
> one by one into the garbage.

This recalls Levine's mother at the window with a set table in the Yom Kippur section, but Detroit is where the houses have vanished, so this moves from immediate observation of birds through a window to the utter collapse of time and place. That "trees have . . . become so many pages" pushes vision to words, and the section ends surreally as the woman washes her dishes "carefully" and drops them into the garbage, as though she will never set her table again.

The final section of the ecstatic dialogue between the poetic imagination and the poet, with a note of schadenfreude, echoes again the apocalyptic Arab dream in Book V of *The Prelude* from which Wordsworth awakens "in terror." (1805 V 137) Bloom calls the Arab quixotic, since "he pursues a quest that is hopeless, for the deluge will cover all. Wordsworth hopes that his own quest will bring the healing waters down, as he pursues his slow, flowing course toward his present freedom." (151) Wordsworth believes that he can redeem mankind by realizing his poetic vision. The voice here suggests otherwise, that apocalypse is unavoidable and perhaps necessary, and, in his criticism, hints at another kind of work for the poet:

> Here it comes.
> It's been quiet. If you'd bothered
> you'd have heard the finches in the trees
> and the wind out back and the wires
> singing in the voices of wire, you
> could have heard a country asleep
> except for the people down under
> stoking the furnaces and the ones
> way up, changing the light bulbs.
> No more, because here it comes.
> The big wave the moon's been holding
> back and the Rocky Mountains
> of ice water. Now the clouds of locusts
> waiting since Genesis swoop on Kansas
> and eat wheat and carry off the cows.
> Hear the constant hum? That's California
> on its knees chanting to keep safe
> its vintage wines and swimming pools
> and the false gods of their movies
> and the true dead ones in our hearts.
> Los Angeles, Seattle, New York City,
> Detroit, Washington, all down the drain.

Now you can hear again, finches
in the golden voices of finches, the wind
saying its best as only the wind
can, blowing over centuries of nothing,
blowing every which way it wants, blowing.

What "comes" here—the plague of locusts, the tidal wave, "the Rocky Mountains of ice water," the wind—will be inevitable and unstoppable whatever prayers are chanted to save the luxuries of prime beef, wine, and movie stars. The great cities from coast to coast and the vast expanse of what lies between won't be spared regardless of the poet's talent or status. The critique—"if you'd bothered"—suggests that the poet's job is to pay attention, to listen to the birds (whether flicker or finch), the wind, the wires, and most importantly to hear those who work to keep the lights on and the houses warm while the city sleeps. The poet's work is to witness and to speak of these people, not to awaken the "dead gods" or appoint oneself divine poetic savior. For Levine, a lifelong atheist, there is no promise save oblivion—the wind "blowing over centuries of nothing," no stone nor shell to bury against the deluge, no knowledge to save but in the living people.

The ecstatic dialog between poet and his poetic imagination in the center of "Burned" casts Philip Levine's idea of the poet's calling and how he came to it against Wordsworth's iconic epic and other important influences, and he uses the multivalent "you," first as poet seeking, then as poetic imagination responding, to excavate a different visionary path for the poet. But the very first "you" of this sequence, the one that begins "The day you left" and whose leaving precipitates Levine's quest most likely represents an amalgamation of the two people who initiated him into an awareness of social justice and his belief in anarchy: Florence Hickok, who cleaned and cooked for the Levines, and the presser he calls Cipriano, "the perfect embodiment of the human spirit." ("The Holy Cities" 43) He recounts the importance of their influence on the development of his ethos, and both depart from Detroit shortly before he finds poetry that same autumn at the age of thirteen. "My teachers were leaving, and I suppose it was time for me to become a man." (44) They are the spark for Levine's vision quest, as well as grounding so that he doesn't presume to rise above his people.

In the poem's closing sections, poet and imagination fully reconciled, the speaker turns his attention to others and to relationships with others. Still, epic tropes continue, as Levine begins the fifteenth section with a sequence of impoverishments and instances of avarice tied to journeys. The first suggests an encounter with a possible Charon figure in a Paris park when an "old wom-an/seized two coins nesting on my open palm." He fought to get them back, and

> . . . she gasped and tore at my hand
> with her nails. At least one dark tear
> dripped from her nose and the two coins fell
> into the grass. When I put a shoe over them
> she cried to the low clouds scudding overhead
> that all men were strangers and sons of whores.
> Leaving the coins, I stood and walked away.
> I did not have to turn to know that smile—
> I'd seen it on my own face, I'd known
> the same hump in my shoulders, the cold
> gleaming in my eyes, and wanted not to see.

After her accusation, he leaves the coins in "the grass" for her and turns away so he won't have to see her greed, "that smile" he imagines that shows this as other than desperation, and that he knows too well in himself. Giving up both coins also means that he won't be able to purchase his trip back from this cap-italist underworld.[9] Where the coins land, however, signals an answer that he initially misses:

> "What if grass were bread?" my son asked me
> the week before when the plane broke through
> the dense rain and we beheld the green world.
> I had no answer. When we landed
> I bought money with money, forgetting
> that each dollar spent was so much time
> staring into faces that answered nothing.

Of course, forgetting that he is "caged" in a deeply abstract capitalist sys-tem that separates things from people and their work, the literal connection between grass (wheat) and bread eludes him. But the deeper connection here is through Walt Whitman, as Levine echoes Whitman's response to a child's question—*"What is the grass?"*—in section six of "Song of Myself"

---

[9] For example, in Psyche's quest to the underworld in Apuleius' story of Psyche and Cupid, "Psyche's two coins . . . are a payment for a round-trip ticket." *Phoenix Stevens,* Susan T. "Charon's Obol and Other Coins in Ancient Funerary Practice" Vol. 45, No. 3 (Autumn, 1991), 215-229.

(poetryfoundation.org): "How could I answer the child? I do not know what it is any more than he." Nevertheless, Whitman "supposes" what grass is, beginning his lengthy conclusion: "And now it seems to me the beautiful uncut hair of graves." So the coins the speaker throws in the grass purchase nothing but a greedy smile, but his son's question stays with him when he confronts an old Parisian concierge who wants Levine to contain the anarchy of his children playing on the elevator: "When he came to my door to complain / I answered that in the West grass was bread." As the concierge, one of those "faces that answered nothing," "deliver[ed] his truths of waste and use," Levine could only wonder "How many days / had he ended by reheating lunch and praying?" In what for the concierge is merely a responsibility of the job and so part of a commercial transaction, Levine tries to imagine something of his life, and he can only envision its emptiness. The tense shifts to present as he considers again the grass in "the long fields that blaze / in March across the lower hills / of the great Sierras," but he "cannot answer" his own questions about the concierge's life and the account of his "days" of "praying." Presumably the concierge continues speaking as Levine drifts off into a memory of another theft:

> of the village of Lorca where I bought bread,
> the women smiling at me and giving me
> the first place in line. Bread so stale
> it shattered into shards as sharp as glass
> when we tried to break it. My kids,
> my wife, and I howled with glee.
> The father had returned, his face full
> with trust, bearing the gifts of earth.
> It was afternoon, cold, and we had hours to go,
> we had sour red wine and empty stomachs.

What appears to be an act of "smiling" generosity in Levine's beloved "village of Lorca" is merely a trick so he will purchase their stale bread. Economic greed in Franco's fascist Spain ruins the "gifts of earth," and the family upon his return can only laugh together at his folly. What Levine has forgotten is that he was spending money bought with money, that he was trapped in and by the falsely smiling promise of capitalism. Levine's consideration of the concierge's nightly prayer sparks this memory, which ends in inedible bread and "sour red wine," recalling communion and its promise of an afterlife. But here there is no body of Christ and the blood is sour, and their journey, such as it is, must continue together buoyed by collective laughter. There is no *viaticum*, no *obol,* to a better world or to an afterlife beyond the grass we will one day become, and the abstract promise of some better world amplified through the further abstraction of capitalism only separates us on the one journey we have together. While every epic demands its journey to the underworld, Levine shows us that the hell we must pass through is here and of our own making.

Levine next takes us back in section sixteen to the Detroit that begins the poem—the burning world of factories and work and slag heaps—just after a shift as a young Levine and another worker, Leo Maryk / Marikowski, discuss religion and love:

> To enter the fire
> is to be burned, said Leo Maryk, slumped
> on the loading dock behind Kelsey-Hayes.
> He'd read it somewhere, maybe the Epistles
> of Paul or one of the early Fathers,
> Augustine or Ambrose. On a night like this
> they all ran together in his head.
> "Some kind of priest I'll make," he laughed.

Interestingly, Maryk quotes neither Paul nor Augustine nor Ambrose directly,[10] but "To enter the fire is to be burned" reprises the same sentence in Levine's "Belief,"[11] published originally in 1981 (*New England Review,* Spring, vol. 3,

---

[10] While Levine quotes himself, the speaker supposes that Maryk's sources include "the epistles of Paul," most likely I Corinthians, 3:15 (If any man's work is burned up, he will suffer loss; but he himself will be saved, yet so as through fire" NASV), Saint Augustine's *Confessions* ("My thoughts, the intimate life of my soul, are torn this way and that in the havoc of change. And so it will be until I am purified and melted by the fire of Your love and fused into one with You" (Penguin, 2003), and Saint Ambrose, whose references to "fire" are many, but perhaps the phrasing closest to Levine's is this, quoted interestingly in a footnote to Canto 27 of Dante's *Purgatorio* (translated by Robert Durling): "The great Baptist . . . will brandish the flaming sword saying . . . : 'Enter you who dare, who do not fear the fire'" (Oxford University Press 2003).

[11] The sentence occurs in a lust-inflected, surreal encounter with two women "dressed in almost nothing" sunbathing "at the beach at Castelldefels in 1965" during which a "stout man" in a suit and bare socks holding his coat and vest and shoes in his arms

> pointed to those
> portions of them he most admired,
> and he named them in the formal,
> guttural Spanish of the Catalan gentleman.
> He went away with specks of fine sand
> caught on his socks to remind him
> that to enter the fire is to be burned
> and that the finger he pointed would
> blacken in time and probe the still earth,
> root-like, stubborn, and find its life
> in darkness.

no. 3, and *One for the Rose*, Atheneum). "Belief " is one of several "visionary poems whose metaphysical cast and resolution rise far beyond the chronicles of work and the elegy for the individual" according to Christopher Buckley (*Plume #47* Newsletter, 2015), and the poem rises out of references to John Keats' life and death to suggest a metaphysics of enlarging pantheism as the speaker in death becomes one "among all the living elements." In "Burned," however, Levine inscribes this metaphysics within the realm of the workplace, in the grueling lives of those who work in the factories, as the self-deprecating Maryk, an aspiring priest, struggles to remember his source. "Even in the cold . . . the sweat / running down [his] long, jagged nose" connects Maryk to the "old woman" her "one dark tear / [that] dripped from her nose," but in stark contrast. The speaker turns away to avoid seeing "the cold gleaming" greed he expects to find in the old woman's eyes, whereas Maryk is a source of warmth despite the cold of the loading dock, "the steam / rising from his enormous chest as from/an oven as he clenched and unclenched / his gloved hands." The voice of his poetic imagination above commands Levine to look at his hands, yet now he looks at another's hands, witnesses Maryk's clenching and unclenching struggle, signaling an understanding not simply of the poet's becoming, but his connection through hands with the human community, with making in its purest sense as communal activity. After laughing at himself, Maryk reveals the fear that perhaps explains his desire to join the priesthood:

> "A man the size
> of me terrified of every little woman,
> afraid to live the life my father lived.
> I even changed my name." Marikowski asking me
> what was love if he couldn't feel it
> with his body? what was it? Asking me, a kid
> more ignorant than he.

A fear of women so profound that Maryk felt compelled to change his name from Marikowski and become a priest because he couldn't "live the life my father lived" or feel a love for women "with his body" may suggest that he was struggling with his sexuality, but that is not most relevant. What matters is that his warmth is real, that the "kid" Levine listens and doesn't judge. Instead, he connects, with his anguish, with his failure, with his genuine warmth, making this one of Levine's "vivas for those who fail." The scene enlarges under "a low sky" to the "slag heaps burning slowly toward a day / that never came." Despite the apocalyptic imagery, the supernatural apocalypse will never come, the day of judgement for which Maryk is trying and failing to remember the source. The tempering occurs here "for the others—men and women—/ passing into and out of the same fires / they never saw into the world," not another world, but *this* one, with its fires of passion and cold fires of oppression most are oblivious to, but a fire that burns from within against the other that burns us, if we can only see it, and here Levine sees it in Leo Maryk, whose generous and deeply human spirit counters the greed represented by the old woman and the concierge and the Spanish bakers.

As "Burned" approaches its close, two quiet, brief vignettes, sections seventeen and eighteen, dwell primarily in image. In the first, the speaker acknowledges a change in his belief that "I lived those closed / rows of tenements, the shotgunned houses / bunched uselessly against the coming / of another day." He finds himself at a remove from the lives he has witnessed, and he is outside those tenements, though still on the same level, and not above them. This suggests a more mature understanding of the poetic imagination—that witnessing isn't the same as having "lived" those lives or looking down from a lofty viewpoint, and that however much he identifies with them, the fundamental act of representation creates implicit, but necessary, separation. He is outside, looking in, but it places him where he can envision a greater context. Human activity occurs in a landscape in which nature is not completely extinguished. Stars come alive in reflection, and the speaker's belief magnifies, connecting those in the houses with the stars, the river they delight in, and the seven seas beyond.

> Now the stars settle
> down, easing themselves into the river.
> Shivering with delight, they almost
> go out, but a high wind fans the little
> separate points of flame. An ore boat
> passes upriver. Riding soundlessly
> the other way, another parts the waters
> toward seven oceans and an older world.

Nature only appears to be extinguished, as the wind awakens the "separate points of flame" in the waters. The two ships headed in opposite directions, like the fishing boat in the first section, signify capitalist enterprises, but they also recall ancient journeys and deeper connections with the greater, "older world," and echo Wordsworth's spiritual connection of river to the great ocean. The work that the people in those tenements do matters and is honorable, despite their ill treatment by corporations, and the ships and the sailors in them bear the product of their work, their livelihoods. Those tenements at night are not "bunched uselessly," because the lives in them are a source of hope, like the stars that reemerge in the river when the winds relent. They are a source of human potential and abide here in beauty as seen from this distance.

Next we are granted a peak at pre-dawn lives in a scene that recalls again the sleeping potential of the pre-dawn town in Wordsworth's "Composed upon Westminster Bridge, September 3, 1802." The "windward motion of the stars" and the "rain falling for hours / between the squat, closed houses" regathers the wind, stars, water, and houses—all the human potential—in perhaps the most hopeful and nostalgic section of "Burned":

> The silence, the town asleep, the light
> not yet arrived where a single shade is torn
> or a door leans ajar. A wagon pulled
> down the bricked alley, and there is milk,
> bread in cold packages, white, untouched.

We are not at the outskirts, as in Wordsworth's sonnet, but closer, and even before the people awaken, people are working to deliver milk and bread to homes. We expect a prelude to a day of work, but the speaker commands us to imagine instead a day of rest:

> Imagine the darkness drawn away,
> the new day dawning equitably
> in the valleys of the living. Imagine
> all the long morning fathers rising
> with their wives, children making way
> for children at sink and table on a day
> without work or school until dusk
> shatters the golden windows.
> Imagine it.

The poem carries through the interior rhyme of "drawn" and "dawning"[12] to the surprise of "equitably," an ungainly, unpoetic word, but perfect in this psalm that bears us through "the valleys of the living," this idyllic day off during which fathers, mothers, and children can simply be families resting together and enjoying the fruits of their labor on a secular sabbath. He

---

[12] The What Work Is version substitutes "falling" for "dawning."

commands us to "Imagine it" because this is what was taken away during the industrial revolution and what unions in most of the twentieth century were fighting to restore, the human dignity of the worker. The second iteration of "Imagine it" commands us to envision the halcyon scene again, but it also announces a veiled irony for another kind of reader who may think it hyperbole to present a day off for the working class as a kind of utopia. The privileged reader will likely take such a day for granted and may read this command to see something so fundamental as merely sentimental. Imagine, he reminds such readers, having to imagine a day off.

The poem closes with two returns home in sections nineteen and twenty. The first is Barcelona, where he takes his family to live in 1965 during the reign of military dictator Generalissimo Francisco Franco. They enter "late afternoon, Friday" on a road crowded with traffic, "trucks and old cars spewing/everywhere," passing "closed warehouses," "factories," and "laboratories grinding out antibiotics and/corn plasters." In his essay "The Holy Cities" Levine explains: "We had travelled halfway around the world to discover this Detroit of Europe." (49) Having secured a room, they "entered the darkness / together, holding each other /. . . in the hope / we would be home." The darkness of the room reflects the darkness of Franco's Spain, but "hope" and "home" ring out against this darkness:

> Morning. On the street
> a tiny man leans back planting
> his heals as six greyhounds tug him
> toward the single tree. Our old friends
> the sparrows busy in the gutters turning
> yesterday's papers for a hint of the truth.
> A blue sky enters from nowhere. A truck
> delivers oranges and red sacks of milk.
> Air so clear I can see all the way down
> the Ramblas to where the sea goes out
> on its one voyage, all the way up
> to the Holy Mountain from which the devil
> said, "Behold, it shall be yours, all
> the kingdoms below," and we made our choice.

[13] He describes the men he saw the morning after arriving in Barcelona: "It was as if I'd known these men before I saw them, these men in their wool caps, smoking and hollering in their course voices. Their faces unshaven, rough, spare, worn down but not worn out, these were the men of my boyhood and my growing up. In spite of or perhaps because of the decades of Franco's oppression, their anger was palpable and fresh" ("The Holy Cities: Detroit, Barcelona, Byzantium" 49).

Levine sees hope in the man with his dogs[13] and finds solace in the sparrows, "old friends" picking out "a hint of the truth" in the newspapers of a nation corrupted by fascist capitalism. The scene is beautiful and "clear." The delivery trucks with their milk and oranges reprise the previous idyllic scene, and he can see "down the Ramblas" to the "sea [that] goes out on its one voyage," and he can also see "all the way up to the Holy Mountain . . ." The necessary elements are present for Levine's own Mount Snowdon epiphany—clarity, the sea, the voyage, the "Holy" mountain in the land of his anarchist forbears—but instead he turns to a different epic in the biblical story of Christ's temptation on the mount. This is an epiphany, but it is an epiphany of a betrayal, the choice "we" made as a nation still mired in isolationism not to intervene on behalf of the Republicans against the Nationalists and ultimately against fascism and its engine of corrupt capitalist oligarchy. Yet Barcelona is also truly a home for him, for his poetic ethos, because Barcelona and its resistance is the source of Levine's anarchy and the burial place of his anarchist heroes: Francisco Ferrar, Buenaventura Durruti, and Francisco Ascaso.[14]

The poem closes in Fresno, and so the Friant-Kern Canal stands in as a kind of anti-Derwent. If, as Geoffrey Hartman contends in *Wordsworth's Poetry*, Wordsworth's conclusion at Mount Snowden is "an astonishing avoidance of apocalypse" (61), Levine avoids such an avoidance, and in the first strophe presents it as the fact of things in this degraded and commercial body of water within walking distance of his residence.

> Rain falling into the dry canals
> east of here. Old couches, magazines,
> dinettes—their legs skyward—car seats
> unstick slowly from the gray mud and drift
> spinning toward the little dams and weirs.
> A skirt, stained with wine or blood, fills
> with water and swirls to the surface,
> a carton of empty beer cans like trophies.
> A black setter comes toward me, springing
> easily along the bank, his long head
> hung low, his coat soaked and heavy,
> and passes without a sign.

Unless snowmelt from the Sierras is unusually heavy, the canal is empty when not in use as a source of water to irrigate the arid commercial farms, so

[14] He recounts their histories and describes visiting their graves and composing his poem "Francisco, I'll Bring You Red Carnations" in "The Holy Cities: Detroit, Barcelona, Byzantium."

the flooding here suggests the annual springtime release of water, which will eventually be channeled into fields by farmworkers, a historically exploited class of workers. Local inhabitants frequently abuse the canals as convenient dumping grounds, and the detritus—the fragments of our broken capitalist consumer culture and the specter of the skirt "stained with wine or blood"— swirls in a flood that is no one's dream, the passing wet dog no omen. Levine's vision is very clearly of this world. That the speaker locates the canals "east of here" (the actual canal is a short walk south of the Levine household) and includes abandoned car seats connects this landscape with the empty field that replaced his old neighborhood in Detroit in the section above. The next strophe presents "Another day," peaceful, presumably in autumn as the clouds have departed and the "sun [is] still up past six," though it's "darkening." "The water" is high in the canal, concealing detritus that recapitulates earlier images in the poem, and it

> moves swiftly beside islands of calm
> and darkness. I glimpse a root, bare
> and silvery, groping upward through air,
> the open hand of black branches breaks
> the surface for a moment and then
> turns under and closes up. Somewhere
> a light comes on in a living room,
> someone I don't know pauses at
> the window before the last light goes
> and speaks to me.

The "groping root" recalls the more hopeful, fertile "root and wood/thickened ground," but here it is "groping" for air against the flood. The hand is given as the source for poetic imagination earlier in the poem, but it sinks and "closes up" in this current. What the figure in the room presumably says to him is unstated; syntactically, however, it is the "light" that speaks, the darkening sky itself. What appears to be calm at the surface fails to dissemble the sense of foreboding, and the flooded figures foreshadow the memory of a drowning in the final strophe, in the "One great room" we share together, this world, and

> the moon
> sliding through the trailing wisps
> of clouds or dust clouds. The child
> gone under in clear water years ago,

the sad yelps of brothers and sisters
that went on and on until morning
quiet at last. The earth's own sighs,
the day's last breath going out,
my own silent cry of denial. They're
all asleep, all the windows from here
to the end of the world are open,
and I can hear the even breathing
of all that was wordless and final
singing together tonight
in the rising voices of the unforgiven.

The poem ends in a very human apocalypse of water: the memory of a child drowning, possibly even in the steep-banked and swift canal the speaker stands beside, imagining the terrible voices of grief in the throats of siblings that only quiet by exhaustion into sleep. This is Wordsworth's sleeping city recast as elegy, as the day dies into night and the exhaustion the speaker imagines in the siblings of the drowned child becomes his own "silent cry of denial" in images that touch back to "no cries from the drowned" and the "too exhausted" young poet introduced at the beginning of "Burned." The image expands to include everyone sleeping, and their windows "from here / to the end of the world are open . . .", completing the apocalyptic trope of the poem unambiguously in "the end of the world," yet the open windows symbolize hope in the collective breath of those who have been exhausted, those who have lost, those who now sleep.

To complicate any reading of "Burned," two different versions of the ending were published: the first in *Poetry*, as quoted above, and later in *What Work Is*, in which the last two lines are deleted, ending the poem on "all that was wordless and final." The revised ending is elegant, suspending the poem in collective breath, suggesting the kind of pantheistic metaphysics that Christopher Buckley notes in his discussion of "Belief " and other poems, or the Whitman-inspired transcendental dissipation of the self into artistic completion that David Baker explores as something Levine acknowledges and resists in his reading of "Burned." It is a Levine ending, to be sure, but one that privileges the metaphysical collective that points forward to such poems about namelessness and oblivion as "Burial Rites." The *Poetry* version, on the other hand, ends on a note that recalls Levine's more overtly revolutionary poems, including "They Feed They Lion.," and tracks the ethos of the poem back to the "angrier" work of the early and mid-seventies, when he first began composing "Burned." This version moves beyond the open window into breathing as collective "singing," their voices "rising," suggesting voice, song, and poetry are foundational to collective action or revolution before transcendental completion can become possible. That they are "unforgiven" undermines any notion that we are to take this as a kind of afterlife or transcendence. In the Poetry version, the hard work of revolution lies ahead, and the poem finishes with a deeper connection to the working people that the poem presents from its fiery beginning. It is not, perhaps, the more beautiful ending, but one that better honors Lonnie, Sweetpea, Packy, Leo, Florence, Cypriano, his Spanish anarchist heroes, and his family in a poem that calls for basic human dignity in this world. It is the better ending for a poem that begins "I have to."

M. H. Abrams argues that *"The Prelude* is a poem which incorporates the discovery of its own *ars poetica"* (78), so its epic project affords Philip Levine with both framework and foil to explore the growth and development of his own poetic mind in an extended *ars poetica.* Yet "Burned" is not simply a long, epic poem of self-discovery; it is a poem that insinuates the transcendental Romantic spirit into a political poetics that emanates from and expresses the need to rise against urban capitalist industrialism. "Burned" acknowledges the necessity of political change, and even revolution, but it envisions a metaphysical collective that completes the human spirit in this world. Human dignity cannot achieve the metaphysical collective in a capitalist system that impoverishes human beings, turning them into capital, into mere data points in the vast dehumanizing abstraction of market-based economics. "Burned" as *ars poetica* is not about the poet rising into the power of the imagination, but the poet coming to terms with the necessity and human importance of witnessing as a poetical and political act—one that envisions a hopeful, collective future *because* of the act.

The relationship between "Burned" and *The Prelude* is complicated, but it isn't necessarily fraught. Levine isn't correcting Wordsworth's attempt "to write a new kind of poetry" that creates "the union between the mind and the external world" or Nature (Abrams 78, 79), one that speaks in the voice of common humanity. The project of *The Prelude,* after all, intended to establish the visionary attainment of the poet as a new kind of prophet to set the stage for his greater but never completed work, *The Recluse,* in which he expected to foster an egalitarian future unblemished by the failures of the French Revolution. His revolution-inspired project arising from the voice of the people inspired Levine, and he has admitted Wordsworth's importance openly. Yet Wordsworth failed to complete his project, and, as he grew older and adopted stringently conservative Burkean views, he failed his vision, revising *The Prelude* from its more revolutionary origins into a poem that, in its final form, serves mainly to bolster his claims of poetic achievement.

So it is Wordsworth's failure to fulfill his vision as a poet that I believe serves as Levine's foil. Levine completed "Burned" at a time when he was grappling with his own evolution as a poet and as a political human being. He had achieved success in poetry, winning grants and awards, but in his view he had compromised his anarchist ideals by buying a home, owning property, an act that he "never regretted," he explains in "The Holy Cities," but which "deprived [him] forever of the right to say, 'Property is theft.'" (46) During the trip to Spain in 1988 to lay flowers on the graves of his anarchist heroes, he confessed that he was "no longer an anarchist" (64), and as a crowd of people celebrated the sacrifices made by those who fought Franco, he had to recognize both their attainment and their failures:

> What I had said to Ascaso was true, his Barcelona was gone, but so was mine, the Barcelona in repressed rebellion and fear under the thumb of Franco. This was a new world, though not the one Durruti claimed to carry in his heart, not the anarchist ideal. (65)

When he met young anarchists and informed them of the work of the Industrial Workers of the World, the Wobblies, in North America, they showed incredulous interest in the unimaginable possibility of an anarchist labor movement in the U.S., but they were less sanguine about their own political forbears, condemning the terrorism of the *pistolero* anarchists and Durruti's compromise to join the Republican government in the fight against Franco, yet Levine was undeterred in his adulation of them and their sacrifice despite their compromises and excesses. They remained his heroes despite his own "failure" to live up to "The Idea." (76)

Two years later, in Paul Mariani's class at the University of Massachusetts in a discussion of W. B. Yeats' "Sailing to Byzantium," a student questioned Yeats' admiration of Byzantium and his avoidance of problematic aspects of the culture. Levine, in answering, at first agreed, but recognized that his agreement and its implied criticism of Yeats' admiration of Byzantium was an unjustified moral simplification, and that his own relationship with Barcelona was essentially the same:

> . . . that I'd chosen a holy city and my allegiance to it was far more powerful than anything I'd managed to express in my poetry. I'd made my pilgrimages to Barcelona over and over and unquestioningly accepted all its lessons. I'd made certain of its heroes the high priests of my life. I needed my

> Barcelona, I needed to uncover somewhere in the history of
> the failed attempts of men and women to create a decent
> society an experiment that worked, and, having half-found it
> in the violent struggles of Spanish anarchism, I'd clung to it
> no matter what. . . . (75)

Levine then goes on to read from a history about an act of anarchist terror-ism, the massacre at the Bay of Sitges. Such events in the French Revolution horrified William Wordsworth, and the excesses of the anarchists no doubt horrified Levine, yet he chooses not to repudiate revolution, for, he argues, "the centuries of violence done to these workers had to produce an equal vio-lence." (76)

Levine brings the essay to an end in a kind of invocation as he views the scene of the class, and himself in third person as "the guest," as they "bow their heads to attend" to the end of Yeats' "Lapis Lazuli." The bell rings and the students leave, as "the guest" "stares out the window." (76-77) What he says refers to the "gay" artists depicted in the carving observing human trag-edy from their mountaintop view in Yeats' poem, but his comment applies as well to Wordsworth's lofty epiphany, his claim of poetic achievement, on Mount Snowdon, and to Levine himself:

> Let the guest realize that no matter what he has climbed
> toward, he has never left the world below, that tangled mess
> he would only escape at his own peril. And what has he
> climbed toward? "Perhaps a lofty slope where it still snows,"
> perhaps a sky unsullied by our human blunders, perhaps the
> holy cities of the world and of the imagination, Detroit, Bar-
> celona, Byzantium, stained with our blood. (77)

"Burned" is an astonishing and conflicted epic that attempts to reconcile the poet's ambitious quest for poetic imagination and literary accomplishment with his desire to annihilate the evils of capitalism and its impoverishment of human dignity. The poem does not truly end, because its collective transcen-dental audience cannot exist until the dignity of the working class is restored, and the *Poetry* version implies more explicitly that this will only occur through revolution, through an awakening from that collective sleep into collective action. Certainly, both versions of "Burned" point with hope toward a col-lective sublime, but the *Poetry* version more clearly emphasizes that it is only attainable, only worth attaining, if the people all rise together as equals on a level plane. In "Burned," Levine certainly sets out to seek his place among the

Visionary Company, but finds he must come down from the mountain, look to his own two hands, and even accept responsibility for the blood that may flow in this world before any new world can arise. "Burned" is thus a magnificent crossroads poem that connects Levine's "angry" early work to his later metaphysical poems as it navigates a remarkable ambivalence to become one of the most important and revelatory poems in Philip Levine's oeuvre.

Works Cited and Consulted

—, "Belief," *One for the Rose,* Atheneum. 1981.

—, *What Work Is,* Knopf. 1990.

—, "The Holy Cities: Detroit, Barcelona, Byzantium," *The Bread of Time,* Knopf, 1994, pp. 33-77.

—, "Nobody's Detroit," *My Lost Poets,* Knopf, 2016, pp. 37-51.

Abrams, M. H., *Natural Supernaturalism: Tradition and Revolution in Romantic Literature,* W. W. Norton & Company, 1971.

Baker, David, "Against Mastery: Adrienne Rich and Philip Levine," *Heresy and the Ideal: On Contemporary Poetry,* University of Arkansas Press. 2000.

Bloom, Harold, *The Visionary Company,* Ithaca: Cornell UP. 1971.

Buckley, Christopher, *Plume #47* Newsletter, 2015.

Eliot. T. S., "The Waste Land," poetryfoundation.org.

Hartman, Geoffrey, *Wordsworth's Poetry,* Yale University Press, 1971.

Hirsch, Ed, "The Visionary Poetics of Philip Levine and Charles Wright," *The Columbia History of American Poetry,* Parini, Jay (ed. & introd.); Millier, Brett C. (ed.). Columbia UP; 1993. pp. 777-806.

Keats, John, "Letter to Richard Woodhouse," October 27, 1818 (Wikisource).

Levine, Philip, "Burned," *Poetry,* September 1990.

Osen, Diane, Interview, https://www.poemoftheweek.com /philiplevine.

Rumiano, Jeffrey Edmond, "They Know 'What Work Is': Working Class Individuals in the Poetry of Philip Levine," Dissertation, Georgia State University, 2007, https://scholarworks.gsu.edu/english_diss/24.

Stevens, Susan T, "Charon's Obol and Other Coins in Ancient Funerary Practice," *Phoenix,* Vol. 45, No. 3 (Autumn, 1991), 215-229.

Whitman, Walt, "Song of Myself," poetryfoundation.org.

Wordsworth, William and Jared R. Curtis, *The Prelude* (1798-99, 1805, and 1850). *The Poems of William Wordsworth: Collected Reading Texts from the Cornell Wordsworth Series,* Humanities-Ebooks, 2009.

DORIANNE LAUX

On "Magpiety"

THE POEM BEGINS WITH A WORD borrowed from Miłosz, which captures a mixture of observation and emotion, and opens to a world where time is fluid, a flash, a rush, a wing. "You pull over to the shoulder" is a simple enough entry point. Then within the prose-like quality of the lines, oblique rhymes begin to form, *over / road / going/oaks,* then hurry and valley. *Day* and *rain. Wondering* and *comes.* Just as we become accustomed to these near rhymes, Levine changes them up, like a jazz musician, and begins the next sentence, the next movement, with staccato bursts of repetition and alliteration: "noon / noon," "short shadows," "little life." Playful, gentle, serene, until the poem shifts in vision and rhyme and begins to build in power and intensity: "pass / dark / black / stab." All of these techniques are replicated and reinvented in varied sets of patterns as the poem progresses. Throughout, we hear a craftsman at work.

But what's the poem about? A vision within a vision within a vision, and then a clearing that opens into another vision. A series of moments. Time, multi-layered, splayed out, casts its yellow nets over eternity. This is intensified by shifts in person, perspective, and narrative voice, disorientation occurs, a sense of the mystical, and that oceanic feeling that Neruda was often able to achieve as well, having the effect of shattering the ego, merging the poet now with the poet in the past, the reader blending with the "you" and the "me," the bounds of time and personality in shards, both terrifying and exhilarating at once.

This poem searches for the density of experience, which is why it must be as long as it is, just as a blanket must as long as the body it covers. This is a poem of the moment made so elastic it vibrates. Expansive in scope, we see the small gesture within the larger field. A noticing, and thinking about the noticing, and a thinking about the thinking about the noticing.

A man stops his car on his way to the ocean and wonders where he's going, or more importantly, where he is, who he is, why he is. The moment of opening is the movement of the lizard, that "trick of sight," that flash of being we all are—here and gone in an instant, hardly seen—then the flare of wing, black with white patches, peripheral, transmutational, transformational. We can't merge with nature or step entirely out of it—we must embrace the difficult middle. All attempts to establish a comfortable permanent residence in either the merger or the ego are false.

Next comes the caught sound of human breath, loud as the sea, wide as the landscape the human is lost in, dwarfed by, the whirling mind within the body working to apprehend the spinning world he stands on top of, dizzying, so he must reach out and grab the earth, steady himself, and slowly lower his body onto the ground, reclaim his bearings: Central California, San Francisco. This confusion of consciousness, this momentary unsteadiness, is something we might feel when an epiphany is about to occur, like the feeling poets often experience when entering act of creation before re-emerging to translate it, though that translation is never perfect. For now, we are lost inside the rooms of the heart and mind, personhood expunged, only the light of being left.

And then the poet emerges, that trick of sight now become a trick of voice: "not I, not you." And yet, as soon as we are settled into this new truth, the poet takes it from us: It is the poet, the man of thirty-two, that younger self, fashioning the lines the poet can't believe are his own. Then the magpie, snoop of a bird, meddler, the one who would steal the ring, the marriage symbol, circle of joining and wholeness, as one preens before the mirror, the rough towel rubbing the skin alive, happy in one's body, in one's life. That bird is the wiseacre, the "otherwise," and gives the ring to "a king or a bride or an old woman asleep on her porch," iconic figures of power, love, wisdom. We've entered the kingdom of story, of myth, of imagination. But it's primarily the figure of the old woman that brings us back to earth, to this life, to the carp, that flash of orange.

This is a poem that can't be understood fully with the mind. It's a poem that asks the reader to live through the experience, moment by moment, to wander around with the poet, though Fred Marchant says a Levine poem "cascades down the page," and that's also true. There's a simultaneity at work here: through the poem we fall both into and out of time, slowing down even as we are washed into its rush and froth.

In the back of my copy of *The Simple Truth*, there's a note that says the poem is a response to a Milosz poem with the same title. I've reprinted it below with the word "magpiety" removed.

_____?

The same and not quite the same, I walked through oak forests
Amazed that my Muse, Mnemosyne,

Has in no way diminished my amazement.
A magpie was screeching and I said: _____?
What is _____? I shall never achieve
A magpie heart, a hairy nostril over the beak, a flight
That always renews just when coming down,
And so I shall never comprehend _____.
If however _____does not exist
My nature does not exist either.
Who would have guessed that, centuries later,
I would invent the question of universals?

Even with the central word deleted, we see how the poem retains its mysterious cohesiveness. We also see how we could easily replace the word "magpiety" with the word "poetry," or any universal. Mnemosyne though, becomes a good guide to Milosz's poem—and Levine's, I think—the mother of the nine Muses, the personification of memory. Memory is the key to unlocking both poems—memory with respect to language and the ways in which we construct our memories using language. Notice right before the last stanza of the Levine poem we get the Mnemosyne figure overtly: "an old woman asleep on her porch" who could "change your life" and then again, later in the poem . . . "an old woman waited on her wide front porch."

I think the main point of both poems is that as we grow old, despite our ability to critically break down the world—to parse it into memories we ourselves make—we still end up being confounded by it, wordless before what goes into making a life. Though as Milosz says, it "in no way diminishes his [our] amazement."

Interesting, too, is the juxtaposition of images and ideas in both poems. The language of each of these poems is becoming as "real" as language possibly can be on the page, trying to get at the lived life through words—to quantify it and get it down.

Of course, we can never actually do that, which is why Milosz says "I shall never comprehend magpiety," though, by writing these poems, Levine and Milosz have comprehended something grand about that incomprehension: we can never be simultaneously merged with nature or separate from it; like the coinage here we live on the boundary between self-forgetful merger and self-conscious emergence. Writers who have not known that self-forgetting are unlikely to tell us anything of value; writers who do not return from that state will tell us nothing at all.

An echo of both versions of "Magpiety" can be seen in Li-Young Lee's line from the poem, "One Heart," "Look at the birds / even flying is born / out of nothing"—and so say Levine and Milosz: If "flying is born out of nothing," memory is too. And poetry. And talking birds. And this mysterious life. How we got here and why is anyone's guess. What are we supposed to do? How easy to become lost in those questions, mute before them. The bravery of this poem is the heart and mind that stops to take it all in, and rather than being silenced by it, dares to call out. A body, a being, that rises from the vast landscape like a wisp of smoke and makes the fire of its presence known.

SUZANNE LUMMIS

On Dust, and Philip Levine's Poem "Dust"

I

IT ADDS UP. Each year billions of tons rise from the earth and float through the air, desert dust, salt flecks from the seas, organic chemicals exhaled from growing things, together with massive contributions of ash from volcanoes, from burning trees, burning *anything*, and then, of course, all that human skin. And to this mix we can add certain exotica, the eyes of flies and legs of spiders.

For these specifics I thank the 2002 body of knowledge, *The Secret Life of Dust*, by Hanna Holmes, which I found many years ago, gathering, yes, dust in a second-hand bookstore. I never did read far into those pages but kept it lying here and there, visible to guests, because—I have a dust problem. Or rather, this place I live in has a dust problem. And the book cover seemed to say, 'Yes. I know. But my dust has a secret life.'

When I took on the project to write a review, an assaying of, a musing upon Philip Levine's long poem "Dust," I became possessed by the notion that I couldn't begin until I found *The Secret Life of Dust*. My bookshelves long ago filled up, and books spill out of them and travel into different rooms, onto surfaces, or disappear into baskets or other receptacles. *The Secret Life of* . . . had gone missing.

Philip Levine's poem touches upon most everything that dust touches but doesn't end there. He also notes the failing struggle by some against both soil and soiled things. Therefore, it seemed fitting that I finally found the missing book in my clothes hamper, not among clothes already washed but those needing to be. That might be a poor omen for a different sort of undertaking. However, if we have somewhere among us a great poet of the Disinfected, a laureate of the Spic and Span, surly it's not Philip Levine. I hope—I don't think—he'd mind me saying that.

II

It's composed of five sequences this poem, "Dust," each standing alone on its own page, the first 3 twenty lines each and the last 2 twenty-one, so that the facing poems mirror each other. Almost all lines run nine to eleven words. Two in the series settle on a single story, one location; in the others, references, memories, knowledge, and imaginings tumble over each other. And what's it about, this quintet? Wonderment, disorder and decay, labor and livelihood, transformation and transcendence, and dust—and love. Especially that last one, love. It's about that. The series will begin and end there, in love, and in silence. The poet relates a story his wife told him, recollected from decades earlier, a memory from childhood when she came home from school to find no one. So, unafraid, she simply waited:

> The house was still, holding its breath,
> the late afternoon sunlight streamed in
> the unshaded windows and turned the dust
> into golden planets floating
> before her. Sixty-four years later
> she declares, "It was beautiful," and goes
> on to describe the sense of awe and peace
> before this vision of the universe
> that descended from nowhere or perhaps
> rose from within. . . . (I)

If it is not a love poem exactly then it's something akin to that, a poem that describes one of his wife's remarkable qualities, a quality that throws light upon why he loves her. And it showed up early, this ability to fold herself in silence, to observe the smallest particles the eye can see, to be alone, to be enchanted—early indeed, age six.

The poem that follows begins suddenly, and with a sharp reversal:

> A woman who thought she loved me once wrote
> a story in which "dust motes danced on and on."
> It may have had a narrative, I forget. . . .
> the story won a prize, was published, brought
> her momentary attention and money
> enough to take me to lunch. I hated
> the way she ate, her clothed arms close to her sides,
> one hand clutching a napkin with which
> she feverishly dabbed at her lips as though
> ingesting her chicken salad were an act
> against God or some vast cosmic principal . . . (II)

He does not think much of her prize-winning story, nor of prizes. He does not love her. She is unlovable and I, by Nabokov's criteria, am a bad reader, too caught up in the character's circumstance to pay attention to what the writer wants me to notice, and in this case, not even the character of greatest interest, a small supporting player. Yet I am both fascinated and appalled, and rather on the side of this woman, poor thing who wrote an O.K. story, won her first and perhaps last authorly distinction, and now, in her horror that she might get besmirched by mayonnaise, is making a bad impression on the man she thinks she loves. Which is, as we all know, the second worst thing to actually being in love. (Admittedly, I take this poem, and others in the "Dust" sequence, to be inspired by true events—always a good way to look like a perfect fool if one is found to be wrong.) She spent some of her prize money, but it was not wasted. After all, a poem came out of it.

Just as the first makes vivid for us the qualities of mind and soul he loves in his wife, so does he reveal here characteristics that repel him—a fixation on propriety and cleanliness that seems life denying. In closing, he notices his own hands, "nails begrimed with grease, the yellow callouses / thick on my palm and cracked fingers and felt / spectacularly pleased to be me, / a dirty Detroit Jew with bad manners."

We recognize the sentiment, one he shares with Neruda who called for an "Impure Poetry"—"Let that be the poetry we search for, worn by the hand's obligations as by acids, steeped in sweat and smoke, smelling of lilies and urine . . . a poetry impure as the clothing we wear on our bodies, soup stained, soiled by our shameful behavior." (from *Towards an Impure Poetry*)

And then there's that mighty disgust-filled playwright-poet, whose experiences of WWI followed by the rise of the Third Reich earned him the right to be as disgusted as he pleased, Bertolt Brecht. He so rarely wrote out of tenderness, but he, too, has at least one poem of affection, "Of all the works of man I like best / Those which have been used. / The copper pots with their dents and flattened edges / The Knives and forks whose wooden handles / have been worn away by many hands: such forms / Seemed to me the noblest." (from "Of all the works of man")

Throughout these five sequences, those who strive for purity, unmarked cleanliness, *newness*, will fail in the end, but they might succeed in improving the surface of things. Surfaces—poems III and IV concern themselves with those, and so do the figures in these tales.

> I live now across from a funeral parlor
> where even on Sunday mornings the hearses
> are taken out and first hosed down for hours,

then dried carefully and polished, slick black
'88 Lincolns tailored for their jobs
so that the dead of North Carolina
can be smoothly and dustlessly chartered
to their earthen holes. (III)

It's also work, doing one's best to put a presentable face on this business. For the sake of onlookers let the deceased travel dustlessly, up to the end, the being lowered into the ground part.

The sequence above begins with a quote, "Without the body there can be no love." Nor we might add, any death. But there it is again, love. And death. And the body. They will roll around and show up in different forms, varying situations, among this series.

Long ago, when he was waiting for a friend, Levine, or—at any rate—the "I" in this episode, idly wrote "Dust Me" on the spreading leaf of a large household plant that had accumulated pollen, fibers of cloth and rotting leaves, hair fragments from cats and wildlife, particulates of ocean salt and the toxic productions of coal fires, and possibly an eye of fly or leg of spider. Many years after his friend would tell him that the little gesture had deeply wounded her mother. This account begins sequence IV. Had this been one of Levine's long trailing poems and not a twenty-one-line portion of a longer poem, he might have speculated about this woman, a Mrs. Kurian, so easily hurt by such a slight gesture. But these relatively short takes leave a degree of responsibility to the reader, or a freedom—to make out of this event what she will. What he will. And that, too, is one of the demands or invitations of poetry. A poet labors but where does it say the poet's supposed to do *all* the work?

III

Left to my own my devices, I think of the term housewife, rejected in the Women's movement of the 1970s when woman across the country declared, "We're not married to our houses." As a small child I remember marveling at colorful magazine ads of women pushing Hoovers across the floor. This was promised me, when I grew up I would vacuum in ballgowns and pearls.

The Life-Changing Magic of Tidying Up has sold millions of copies in multiple languages. The other day I caught an interview of Marie Kondo on my car radio, heading west. Through an interpreter she revealed that before her own smash-hit publication debuted, another contribution to the field by a different author had sold well in Japan, *Women Who Cannot Tidy.*

I'd like to avail myself of an English translation of *Women Who Cannot Tidy* and leave it lying around together with *Women Who Run with Wolves*. "Dust," by Philip Levine, made me think of this.

IV

In this narrative, after the "thoughtless act that (he) in his merriment / thought clever," the Kurean family begins to collapse, like matter into particles. Death takes each one and returns them to anonymity, save for their appearances in this poem. But before that, the house is looted, the husband mugged in his driveway, a violation of the home, on the body, that dwarfs the tiny impertinence that so hurt Mrs. Kurian.

> A proud man, Roy,
> he died in a rest home in San Jose
> among strangers years after the house was sold
> to a city councilman who raised pigs
> illegally in spotless pens in the backyard. (IV)

They're clean, these illegal pigs, they keep a nice pen. And maybe the man breeching the local ordinance is also, at least clean enough to serve as City councilman. One element wandering in this mix must be the paradox particle.

V

Some dust does more than reveal one's imperfections, one's overlookings, it rises en masse. Some dust will kill. On the worst day of the Dust Bowl, April 14, 1935, Black Sunday, a cloud hundreds of miles long, thousands of feet high, rolled across the plains blacking out the sun. Levine remembers a photo spread in *Life* magazine.

> . . . a farmer
> and his woman run toward shelter while the earth
> they tore some living from rises against them
> with all its plenitude . . .
> These two borrow a Ford with bad tires and worse spares;
> They have themselves and three kids to feed, and so
> like the wind they head west where perhaps the land
> has settled down . . . (V)

Sure enough, the land settled down out west—though few fleeing Oklahoma and neighboring states would be welcomed by westerners or find solace here.

However, in the final lines of this sequence and the poem, Levine stills the air.

> Tonight my wife
> Holds a glass of black Catalan wine up
> to the candlelight and drinks to my New Year
> and I to hers, acts as good as any
> to stall our time from whirling into dust. (V)

In life, even the raising of a glass would release into the air new flecks with their mischief and secrets, and stir up a micro storm—but this isn't life. It's a poem. In a poem a woman can hold up a glass of deep red, almost black, Catalan wine and it seems like an offering of light. For a moment the dust stops whirling. It holds off. And at the same time, the poem acknowledges our mortality. In the right hands, soiled though they may be, a poem can do that.

DAVID ST. JOHN

On "Naming"

—Until he dies, a boy remains a boy.

IF MEMORY IS THE TRUE ENGINE of mourning and human celebration, then we've long ago learned that Philip Levine's poetry has always held within it the most powerfully built, highly-charged and finely-tuned engine ever to have escaped the confines of Detroit.

Memory is both recovery and recuperation—the recovery (active and healing) of those times, people and experiences that would otherwise remain bound by or lost to the past. Memory allows the retrieval, the recuperation (again, a healing act) of the individual lives of those who are—or have been—the touchstones of our daily passage, family or friends, as well as those who've somehow become emblematic presences in our own lives, those who arise—in our stories and writing—as both salutary and cautionary figures.

Philip Levine's poetry has from the first shown an intricate web of these personal and linked memories just as his poems have often celebrated the men and women he pictures in his narratives. Throughout his career, Levine's own family has often stepped into view, at times clearly to full center stage as in his book *1933*, which I've always thought of as the poetic equivalent of a family album.

Just as Levine's poem "Letters to the Dead" served as the centerpiece for *1933*, the sonnet sequence "Naming," in Levine's stunning book *Breath* (published in 2004), acts in precisely the same way, providing a self-reflexive and autobiographical core around which *Breath's* other poems gather and revolve. The twenty-five sonnets of "Naming" are each fifteen line sonnets and each is composed of stanzas of eight and seven lines. Levine has self-consciously staged "Naming" to be read as a sonnet sequence (or cycle, if you prefer) in that long poetic tradition. As in the poems and family album portraits of 1933, each sonnet is a snapshot of a moment in time—sometimes panoramic or broad in scope and at other times minutely focused.

The sonnets combine, echo and reverberate as individual scenes of "Naming" reflect the story line and arc of Levine's own life, beginning with the birth, in the "state of Michigan in 1928," in Detroit—that hell next to the River Styx—of twins, Levine and his brother (Phil and Eddie, neither referred to by name here), called by Levine in this opening sonnet, "the wise and tiny children of the wolf," like the twins Romulus and Remus, but whom Levine names as:

> In the endless month of that year's winter came
> the wise and tiny children of the wolf,
> Last Hope and First Curse disguised as boys,
> even at birth brimming with the knowledge
> of who they were: the eyes and ears of hell.
> They would record the green leaf 's bursting out,
> the gray rain's song, the sparrow's rise and fall.

So begins the story of Levine's childhood, of his own seasons in hell-as-Detroit:

> The seasons changed around them and they changed,
> slowly growing into the names they answered to
> until they thought they were those names—
> soldiers and conquerors, though in the streets
> just kids fighting to be kids, kids who knew
> they had their special work cut out:
> the crushed cat dying to be heard, the oil
> along the curbs, the sun transformed in filth.

Each of the two brothers, the twins, will find his own artistic and individual way by which to navigate those other seasons ahead:

> So one took on
> the sparrow's conscience and sang to no one
> the nothing he knew, the other found
> his colors in muffled light or none at all.

Levine is a supremely deft shuffler of time and intimate familial details. Yet, in his history of writing long poems—and within his compendium of narrative strategies in those long poems—Levine's decision to use a sequence of linked sonnets as his staging and framing device is deeply compelling. Just imagine "Naming" as a deck of twenty-five playing card sonnets, a deck with its occasional King/father or, more often, its Queen/mother, yet always a deck most conscious of its twin Jacks, the sons, in their various incarnations or disguises (embodied in one sonnet as Castor and Pollux, more mythical twins) and at the many shifting stages of their lives. (In "Naming," deuces are often wild.) These cards, these sonnets, are turned over (so their "faces" will show) in sequences and scenes that merge the present speaker with his memories or reflections upon his lost childhood and past, upon the figure of his father, from a vantage point of the years:

> Count on the weather. Seventy-one
> years ago my father climbed the stairs
> to the back porch with two bottles
> of frozen milk. He stamped the snow
> off his wing tips. A few stars
> sparked in his hair and slowly
> faded away. The cream rose through
> the bottle tops. The first bite thrilled.
> When my father sat down to coffee,
> a cigarette, and the Free Press
> while he hummed "Home on the Range,"
> it was I who smashed my fist down
> on the table. Where was oatmeal,
> where was my orange? I howled for what
> was mine and got laughter instead.

Yet the next sonnet in the sequence alerts us to the imminent loss of that father ("Over and over we live / that perfect winter of '33"), who dies in 1933:

> Sooner or later the death angel enters
> these lives or others. Let the day be bright
> in early autumn, let it be morning
> with sunlight streaming through broad windows
> on a usual school day. Pushed to one side
> of what we thought was ours, we stand for hours
> wondering, Who are these people in our lives
> talking in voices that were never theirs?
> Soon this will end, we think, and we'll go back
> to who we were. But it won't be that way.
> Something is missing. Look in the closets,
> or under the bed where Mama would look,

search every face. Something is still missing,
though we search the cupboards, the sofa,
all our pockets, even our memories.

The mother and the sons, including a son elder to the twins (Eli, also unnamed in this poem), are shown in snapshots shuffled through those times leading up to WWII, which is, for Levine, a time of struggle and reckoning: "To be alive, nameless, / still young, searching for anything. . . ." Then, still finding his place within the constellation of the family, Levine shows himself:

Late summer of '45. My older brother
back from war. Awake, waiting for light
to flood the room when a voice cries out,
my voice in dreams. Later he and I tramp
through the empty fields at the edge of town
and into the shaded woods. I show him
a tight nest of broken eggs, a fresh hole
the field mice made, a wren's gray remains,

all the small secrets that contain me.
He doesn't ask if the cry was mine.
He says nothing about the daylight raids
on the French villages. Though it's still August
the seasons blow around us, night and cold rain
waiting in the air we breathe, two brothers
held together by what they can't share.

It's at this point that "Naming" unfolds its vision of a far larger world that includes a cast of characters drawn from those times. Levine begins moving through these landscapes unleashed from the chronology of time, yet held in memory to their particular Michigan contexts. They are the lost, the dead, the men and women of this past who are to be named and reclaimed, recovered from the erasures by time, and therefore reclaimed from the anonymity of their deaths. Levine has always memorialized those unseen by the world and given names to those with whom he's shared his life whether in the factories of his youth or the many cities of his adult travels. He calls out their names in poems to register their being and presence in our world; he calls out the names of the lost to inscribe those names both of his heroes of social justice and political change as well as those musicians he loves ("Call It Music," which concludes *Breath*, is in my view one of the greatest of all of Levine's poems) who, for Philip Levine, have helped to mark and alter the tempo of the passage of time. Again, from "Naming":

> Always there was music, Clifford and Max
> one month, Miles the next, Lester Young
> near the end, half sober, the high off-
> center wail of the horn like a
> voice heard before we heard voices.
> On the Saturday singalong from the Met
> In the back of D'Angelo & Ferente's
> French Cleaners & Fine Alterations,
>
> the tiny Sicilian coat maker
> on tiptoe to reach the high notes
> along with Björling. Della Daubien
> on the crosstown streetcar as dusk
> rises from the trees. If you go back
> you'll hear her rough alto echoing
> down the bombed-out streets of heaven.

As in the poem "Letters for the Dead," in the poem "Naming" Levine will address those dead named in the poem and those unnamed yet still present, those dead who need to know they have not been forgotten as well as those whose names can never be called often enough:

> Each spring you come back to us
> in the blossoms of the pear tree,
> in the lost language of the spruce
> trapped in sunlight, in the cry
> of the one gull circling,
> you come back in the cold rain
> falling all night on the tin
> roofs and the dry canal beds.
>
> Again the earth drinks all that's
> left of you and asks for more.
> Beginning April, I go out
> to the dawn fields where last
> year's yellow grass still hangs on,
> and I say your names, numberless,
> into the wind, and it's not enough.

Echoing the concerns of other of Levine's braided long poems, "Naming" reminds us that we move forward in a life, towards a future in which landscapes and cities appear like promises and dreams, even as we move away from those foundations of our own pasts. Yet we're able to recall the names of places and people, and we can, as Levine does in all of his poetry, call out those names as a way that frees time—if for only that instant—from the velocity of its passage. For the brothers of his experience as well as his own actual brothers, both named and not named, Levine ends the penultimate sonnet of "Naming" with this gorgeous invocation of the future:

> Something amazing's always ahead,
> a city like no other, and their lives
> waiting. When they drown the headlights,
> the whole dime store of the night sky
> blares into view, so let's leave them there,
> both still young, still full of pleasure
> in each other and in themselves.

The final sonnet of "Naming" is yet another reminder that even the dead grow lonely over the years, and confused, sometimes calling (to) us in dreams from those lost times, and sometimes reminding us of who we were, which we must understand ("over time" as we say) is also, Levine says in closing, who we will always be:

> "Does the wind have a name?" Eugene asks me
> from a phone booth outside the old grease shop.
> (This must be a dream.) "Does the what?" I say
> pretending I haven't heard. His voice fades out
> as the jet fighters take off at dawn and set
> my house roaring as though invaded
> by an ocean. The operator breaks in to ask
> if I'll accept the charges. Eugene's alone,
>
> it's winter in Michigan with snow falling
> in the twilight and hiding the stalled cars
> on Grand River. Head whitened with snow,
> Eugene lets the receiver slip from his hand.
> I can see his eyelashes weighted with ice,
> his brown eyes slowly closing on the image
> of who I was, who I will always be.

In Philip Levine's long poems, he consistently looks to embrace a larger and more complex vision of the individual lives he inscribes along an arc of personal and historical reflections. For Levine, the passage of time answers to and goes by many names. In this long poem, as these sonnets, snapshots and shifting temporalities of "Naming" are shuffled and laid out across these pages, Levine shows he remains the most astonishing of all sleight-of-hand poets, revealing to us the face cards of women and men retrieved by memory, sung of and celebrated, and whose names again become urgent, human and everlasting. It is a kind of incantation and summoning; it is the resurrection allowed us by the poetry of a great poet.

RICHARD ROBBINS

"A Dozen Dawn Songs, Plus One"

I FIRST SAW PHILIP LEVINE READ his work in 1975 at Palomar Junior College in Southern California. At the center of the school's planetarium, he leaned against the concrete base supporting the huge spherical machine that would, at some other time, project the heavens and its movements on a high domed ceiling. Into that space he read his poems about the fighter Baby Villon, a pig that dies with ferocity, the snows and riots of Detroit, the tramontana of Spain, the ghosts of 1933. The light that evening came not from pinpricks of white on a dark ceiling but from the majesty and music of Levine's made universe.

In the foreword to *The Last Shift*, Levine's last book of his own making, Edward Hirsch touches on some of that universe. He remarks on the poet's long career by observing that Levine's poetry "began in rage, ripened toward elegy, and culminated in celebration." The statement makes a lot of sense, as long as one also allows that all three impulses can and do appear in any collection from any period. Hirsch acknowledges as much about *The Last Shift*, although it is certainly the case that the poems in this final book celebrate their subjects more than anything else. Even the cosmos Levine argued with his entire life for its silence, its indifference, gets its due in "I Was Married on the Fiftieth Birthday of Pablo Neruda." The life of the poet of love rhymes and with the love of another poet yet to come into his own.

"A Dozen Dawn Songs, Plus One" is the primary long poem of *The Last Shift*.

Its first focus is the lives spent on the midnight shift, the soul-feeling of those coming off a dark night of work, released to a lit world. At first the pieces reminded me of the morning songs of William Carlos Williams, who wrote similarly visionary fragments after exhausting all-nighters at the hospital. Levine's thirteen sections and a coda—the thirteen sections ranging from seven to fourteen lines, mostly with three- or four-beat lines—build beyond a sharply drawn focus, though, to include public and private moments in the lives of those forgotten to all but each other. The poem moves, linearly and metaphorically, not just from darkness to dawn but from anonymity to recognition, and finally to the last darkness and mystery. The long poem's clock is the clock of the day and the clock of a life. Its final celebration is the stupidity of youth standing beside a kind of stupidity about the other side of death.

Levine's first two songs establish us in the occasion. He begins with the imminent end of the midnight shift:

> Williams lights up
> and says, "It's on the way," but
> I can't hear him over the overhead
> cranes. I don't look up
> because up is not sunlight . . .
> Up is the flat steel
> ceiling from midnight till now.

This is a familiar beginning for a Levine poem: in the moment, a person at work, no relief coming from the traditional direction of heaven. The second song captures the reprieve of shift's end, where the speaker recovers his freedom temporarily:

> we punch out
> and leave the place to our betters,
> the day-shift jokers who think
> they're in for fun. It's still Monday
> 2,000 miles and fifty years
> later

In fewer than seventeen lines, the speaker establishes his occasion, a specific moment in a day like every other working person's day, *and* splits the clock in two. It is 1951, and it is also a time outside of that time. From this moment so early in the poem, the reader has permission to experience both the immersive experience of the 1951 speaker recording, mostly in present tense, a Monday that is all Mondays, as well as a speaker listening to himself talk from a distant future which is also far removed in space from the location of the poem. Levine takes advantage of this split in the third song to break any predictable point of view as well. Even though we are, for the moment, moving through the early hours of a day, we are not just following a man:

> A warm breeze from
> nowhere and even the rats scent
> the first perfumes of what's
> to come . . .

                              Surrender
         nothing and never, their motto.

         And in the fourth song, a river:
                                        it just runs
                 at its own sweet will its whole

         blue-brown length toward five burned
         lakes and seven seas.

In the first four songs, then, Levine accomplishes what he often does in his
long poems: He uses familiar techniques of his shorter lyrics to establish place
and time and an implied narrative structure but then finds a way to break any
expectation we have in favor of something more improvisational.

    The fifth song returns us to the clocked-out shift-workers, but here they are
"owls, puffing out / our spent breath into the pure air / of 1951." The poem
now exists in some protean atmosphere where things can become other things,
where men can become birds. It's a thought impossible to imagine inside the
tedium of the late shift, but now in the sixth song, released to the light, the
speaker can say

                         if I were reliable and hardy
            and had wings I'd pick
            about the piss-speckled snow
            with the sparrows.

    And in the seventh song, quoted below in its entirety, there are more spar-
rows, except here Levine must manage the trick, as he does in all of his poetry,
of rendering the things of this world as they are, in their simple dignity, as well
as their part, simultaneously and often unknowingly, in an emerging vision:

                              Ragged
            flights swarm the upper branches
            of the elms only to abandon
            their roosts and wheel
            across the sky they've wiped
            clean, back and forth, back
            and forth they wipe until
            no clouds or divine signs are left.
            Must be some tremor only they

                              213

can feel or hawk stink or hint
of human treachery.

It's worth noting here, halfway through the poem, where we have traveled: from being on the job to being off it, from a dark with stationary duties to a light one can walk around in, from being inside a diminished tired body to identifying beyond oneself—from two temporal perspectives—with a diminished, seemingly exhausted world. Even though we ostensibly are moving through a day, we are, despite the relative backgrounding of the older version of the speaker, moving through a life. What does it mean for the old man to remember, in present tense, the sparrows wiping the sky clean of their auguries? The sparrows may sense something, but the human mystery of it remains. The old man has no explanation.

Where another poet might have picked up on the end of the last song to push logically into more metaphysical territory, Levine zags in the next two songs, this time expanding the point of view beyond the last-shift speaker to those just waking. In the eighth song, it's the owner of a vacant lot who

> kicks off the covers and calls for
> sleep and dreams of her, the one
> he'll never know.

> And in the ninth song, women:
> Half of us are
> women. Think of that! Women,
> women alone rising from
> single beds meant for sleeping,
> women in pairs, women with men
> yearning to be free of us,
> the men they met last night
> or last century.

It's important, for the kaleidoscopic organization of this poem, to include those waking from sleep as well as those moving in the direction of it. Just as the solitary shift worker enters a light that includes the rats, the river, and the sparrows, and thereby expands the awareness of the poem, the poem expands further by opening into the lives of "day-shift jokers" in the preceding songs. In the eleventh song, the poem focuses on two more of them, Harvey and Mona:

214

> Don't she
> know it's Monday workday.
> The weekend—the last one, the
> one—is long gone and Harvey's
> got to have his coffee and his
> oatmeal and his lunch box packed
> just right, right now.

And the focus continues in the twelfth:

> Slam goes
> the outside door, while upstairs
> the teakettle sirens its answer . . .
> Then quiet, the actual quiet
> of public lives in private places.

The final two songs of the poem and its coda bring the fifty-years-later shift-worker to the fore. The tea kettle of the last song, singing out in 1951, triggers the musical retrospection of the twelfth song, quoted here in its entirety:

> There was music. Not
> the trite tunes of the blind stars
> circling unseen or the gnashed jazz
> the trolleys carved
> into the avenues or the bas-assed
> anthems of the airwaves—
> of John Lee, Baby Boy
> and Big Maceo—, not even
> the music of the immortals,
> Bird, Diz, Pres, music of bone
> and breast, and breath, music
> never heard before. Or again.

All through the poem, Levine manipulates our expectations about where the poem is going, even what it's about. He violates chronology here, he switches point of view there. It's worth pointing out the obvious, though, that Levine is all along manipulating tone as well, and thereby the felt gravity of the piece. Just as the first half of the poem ends with the intensely lyrical seventh song about the sparrows and their auguries, this twelfth song is a stunning lyrical answer to the more prosaic scenes of Harvey and Mona. The poem has

215

left 1951, and with the full force of the older speaker's age, perspective, and understanding it acknowledges that even the art that survives that time is no match to the music "of bone, and breast, and breath" none of us will ever hear again. If we had wondered where the poem was going, or what is was about, we can witness now the scattered parts of this poem beginning to come together, in what will result in two kinds of ending.

One, in the thirteenth song, is a kind of recovery operation of what is lost, the prospects of which the speaker has just undercut:

<blockquote>

West

through Toledo, on past Flat Rock
going north. The sign is gone. Leo's
prewar '39 Chevy four-door
doing its dance routine: a little slide,
a little hold, a little slide on
black ice . . .
But maybe it's not a return at all:
The sign's gone, the one
that said "Heaven Ahead" (or was it
Wyandotte?). Sunup behind us,
last night dissolving in the brine
of light. Coming home one
last time, yes we are!
</blockquote>

In this baker's dozen of songs, there is something too perfect about this ending: The long day has become the long life. Young man and old man have become one. A drive back to home, remembered from the speaker's youth, is transformed into the aged speaker's drive back home from across time and distance. But we have already been alerted that the music can never be recovered, that the sign to Heaven is gone, despite the apparent enthusiasm of the last two lines. So what the last full song leaves us with is an enthusiasm for what is clearly uncertain, for a darkness that will surely come, but at least not one on the last shift.

Lest we celebrate too much at those last two lines, or wonder about their tone, the coda follows quickly and directly, a second kind of ending:

<blockquote>

Oh

to be young and strong and dumb
again in Michigan!
</blockquote>

Does Levine feel the need to undercut any kind of cheer at the end of the thirteenth song with the apparent sarcasm of the coda? We might ask ourselves what's so cheerful about coming to the end of a life with little certainly and in a posture that embraces a new darkness? The silence of the "blind stars" has spoken, after all. The sign to Heaven is gone. Nothing after this point is written. How to reconcile the two ways the poem moves us toward the silence after its words?

Levine's long-poem strategy, here and elsewhere, requires first a patience with both content and form. As I said earlier, the poem begins like many of his shorter pieces, in a narrative moment focused on a solitary character, but this long poem expands its scope and ambition by gathering other humans, animals, and the earth to it, by confounding an easy chronological development, by enriching its repertoire with both witness and meditation, by muting lyricism for the most part in order to give the piece sustainability over the long haul. The poem does no "irritable reaching after fact and reason," in the words of Keats, even though, as readers, we can nonetheless see in retrospect the poem guided by a fundamental belief in mortal things—"bone/and breast, and breath"—over a silent God and a universe that promises nothing. The improvisational nature of this last long poem, the zigging and zagging that is both restraint and rumination, creates a reading experience different from the felt simultaneity of the short lyric by allowing readers to steep longer in the poem's concerns. If the resolution for a sustained, multivalent experience like this is not one thing, but two side-by-side—well, then, the long-poem structure Levine has created for this moment has brought us to a place where they can co-exist.

In the end, I would propose that the two endings mentioned above actually reinforce each other by virtue of their close juxtaposition. The first is a kind of cheer in the face of mystery, a signing on to a new shift. The second is less sarcasm and more straight-ahead truth: It might be preferable to be "young and strong and dumb / again in Michigan" than to be old and weak and knowing right here. But here is where the speaker is. His "music of bone / and breast, and breath" is disappearing, and the last three lines of the poem, cast in the language of a backward-looking sentimentality, in fact defeat it. For its weight and for its sense, his last long poem could have been the last poem of the book.

That place was reserved for the title poem of *The Last Shift*, however, which ends in synch with the one I've been discussing:

> These places where I had lived
> all the days of my life were giving up
> their hold on me and not a moment too soon.

The last time I saw Philip Levine read his poems was in my hometown in Minnesota in 2010. At the craft talk earlier in the afternoon, someone asked innocently why anyone would want to write poems these days. Perhaps the person was thinking of how little poems are read, or how little poems are paid. Phil answered, "For the glory!"—at which point people laughed, thinking they had just witnessed the famous Levine sarcasm. But then they stopped when they realized he was serious. There was nothing left to be said. Having gotten us to a point where we could be surprised twice by something he said, in a matter of mere seconds, he had us right where he wanted.

CONTRIBUTORS

CHRISTOPHER BUCKLEY has edited: *A Condition of the Spirit: The Life and Work of Larry Levis*, with Alexander Long (Eastern Washington University Press, 2004); *Homage to Vallejo* (Greenhouse Review Press, 2006); and *Bear Flag Republic: Prose Poems and Poetics from California*, with Gary Young (Greenhouse Review Press, 2008). With David Oliveira and M.L. Williams he is editor of *How Much Earth: The Fresno Poets* (Roundhouse Press, 2001), and he has edited *On the Poetry of Philip Levine: Stranger to Nothing* (University of Michigan Press, 1991), and *First Light: A Festschrift for Philip Levine on His 85ᵗʰ Birthday*, 2013. He coedited, with Christopher Howell, *Aspects of Robinson: Homage to Weldon Kees* (The Backwaters Press, 2011) and, again with Gary Young, published *One for the Money: the Sentence as a Poetic Form* (Lynx House Press, 2012). With Jon Veinberg, he edited *Messenger to the Stars: A Luis Omar Salinas New Selected Poems & Reader* (Ash Tree Poetry, 2014). His most recent book of poetry is *Agnostic* (Lynx House Press, 2019). *Naming the Lost: The Fresno Poets—Interviews and Essays* is forthcoming from Stephen F. Austin State University Press.

KEVIN CLARK'S *Self-Portrait with Expletives* won the Pleiades Press contest, and his first book of poems, *In the Evening of No Warning*, earned a grant from the Academy of American Poets. Kevin's recent chapbook *The Wanting* won the Five Oaks Press contest. His poetry appears in *The Georgia Review, The Southern Review, Ploughshares, Prairie Schooner, Iowa Review, Gulf Coast*, and *Crazyhorse*. A regular critic for *The Georgia Review*, he's also published in *The Southern Review, Papers on Language and Literature*, and *Contemporary Literary Criticism*. He teaches at the Rainier Writing Workshop. A new book of poems, *The Consecrations*, is due soon from Stephen F. Austin State University Press.

KELLY CHERRY is the author of twenty-seven books. She and her husband live near the bottom of Virginia. She holds two titles at the University of Wisconsin-Madison but prefers the weather in Virginia.

KATE DANIELS is the author of six volumes of poetry, editor of Muriel Rukeyser's *Out of Silence: Selected Poems*, and has written and presented on the poetry of Philip Levine for many years. She is the Edwin Mims Professor of English and Director of Creative Writing at Vanderbilt University where she also teaches in the Medicine, Health, and Society program. Her most recent book is *In the Months of My Son's Recovery* (Louisiana State University Press, 2019).

GLOVER DAVIS is Professor Emeritus of Creative Writing at San Diego State University, where he taught after studying with Philip Levine at Fresno State and graduating from the Iowa Writers Workshop. His books of poetry are *Bandaging Bread, August Fires, Legend, Separate Lives, Spring Drive*, and *My Cap of Darkness*. Davis is currently finishing *Academy of Dreams: New and Selected Poems*. Davis' work has appeared in *The Southern Review, Poetry, Yale Review, Crazy Horse, Prairie Schooner,* and *The New England Review.*

PETER EVERWINE was one of the most accomplished and valued poets and translators writing in the United States. His estimable career included the Lamont Poetry Prize, a senior Lecturer Fulbright award for the University of Haifa, Israel, fellowships from the National Endowment for the Arts and Guggenheim Foundation, and an American Academy of Arts and Letters Award in Literature. Recent collections include a translation, *The Countries We Live In: Selected Poems Natan Zach 1955-1979* (Tavern Books, 2011); *Listening Long and Late* (University of Pittsburgh Press, 2013); and *Pulling the Invisible but Heavy Cart: Last Poems* (Stephen F. Austin State University Press, 2019). He taught at Fresno State/CSU Fresno for over thirty years. He died in late October of 2018 in Fresno.

KATHY FAGAN'S fifth book is *Sycamore* (Milkweed, 2017), a finalist for the 2018 Kingsley Tufts Award. Recent work has appeared in *Poetry, Tin House,* and *The Nation.* Fagan directs the MFA Program at Ohio State in Columbus, Ohio, where she also serves as series co-editor for the OSU Press/The Journal Wheeler Poetry Prize.

JAMES HARMS is the author of nine books and four chapbooks of poetry including, most recently, *Rowing with Wings* (Carnegie Mellon University Press, 2017). He's received three Pushcart Prizes and an NEA Fellowship, among other distinctions.

CHRISTOPHER HOWELL'S twelfth book of poems, *The Grief of a Happy Life,* was recently released by the University of Washington Press, also publisher of *Dreamless and Possible: Poems New & Selected* (2010). Another recent volume, *Love's Last Number* (2017), was published by Milkweed Editions. He teaches in the MFA program at Eastern Washington University.

RICHARD JACKSON is the author of fifteen books of poems most recently *Broken Horizons* (Press 53, 2018); *Traversings,* with Robert Vivian (Anchor and Plume, 2016), and the forthcoming *Take Five,* as well as four chapbook adaptations from Pavese and other Italian poets. His ten other books include translations, anthologies, and criticism, and his poems appear in seventeen languages. He has received Guggenheim, NEA, NEH, and two Witter-Bynner fellowships, a Prairie Schooner Reader's Choice Award, the *Crazyhorse* prize, and he is the winner of five Pushcart Prizes and has appeared in *Best American Poems '97* as well as many other anthologies, and has been awarded the Order of Freedom Medal for literary and humanitarian work in the Balkans by the President of Slovenia.

MARK JARMAN is the author of many collections of poetry, most recently, *The Heronry* (Sarabande Books, 2017). Paul Dry Books published a collection of his essays on poetry, Dailiness, in early 2020.

CHRISTINE KITANO is the author of two collections of poetry, *Sky Country* (BOA Editions) and *Birds of Paradise* (Lynx House Press). She co-authored *Who You: The Issei*, a collection of oral histories about the first generation of Japanese immigrants to settle in Hawai'i. She is currently co-editing *They Rise Like a Wave: An Anthology of Asian American Women Poets* which is forthcoming from Blue Oak Press. She teaches at Ithaca College and in the MFA Program for Writers at Warren Wilson College.

DORIANNE LAUX is the author of *What We Carry* (1994), a finalist for the National Book Critics Circle Award; *Smoke* (2000); *Facts About the Moon* (2005), winner of the Oregon Book Award and also a finalist for the Lenore Marshall Poetry Prize; *The Book of Men* (2011), which was awarded the Paterson Prize; and *Only As the Day Is Long: New and Selected* (2020) which was a finalist for the Pulitzer Prize. She has received fellowships from the Guggenheim Foundation and the National Endowment for the Arts, and has been a Pushcart Prize winner. Laux has taught creative writing at the University of Oregon, Pacific University, and North Carolina State University. She is the co-author, with Kim Addonizio, of *The Poet's Companion: A Guide to the Pleasures of Writing Poetry* (1997).

ALEXANDER LONG'S fourth book of poems is *On Distance* (Stephen F. Austin State University Press, 2018). Poems and essays appear in *AGNI, APR, American Journal of Poetry, Blackbird, Callaloo, Miramar,* and *Valparaiso Poetry Review.* An Associate Professor of English at John Jay College, CUNY, he's completing a literary biography of Larry Levis.

SUZANNE LUMMIS was a 2018/19 COLA (City of Los Angeles) fellow, a prestigious endowment from the Cultural Affairs Department to create a new body of work. She writes about film noir, with essays in *The Los Angeles Review of Books, Malpais Review,* and an extended Q & A exchange with David Lehman on the subject appearing on *The Best American Poetry Blog.* Poetry.la produces her web series on film noir and the poem noir, *They Write by Night.* At CSU Fresno, she studied with Philip Levine.

PAUL MARIANI is the author of twenty books, including biographies of William Carlos Williams, John Berryman, Robert Lowell, Hart Crane, Gerard Manley Hopkins, and Wallace Stevens. He has published eight volumes of poetry, most recently *Ordinary Time* and *Epitaphs for the Journey.* He has also written two memoirs, *Thirty Days* and *The Mystery of It All: The Vocation of Poetry in the Twilight of Modernism.* His awards include fellowships from the Guggenheim Foundation, the NEA and NEH. He is the recipient of the John Ciardi Award for Lifetime Achievement in Poetry and the Flannery O'Connor Lifetime Achievement Award. His poetry has appeared in *Poetry, The Agni Review, The New England Review, The Hudson Review, Tri-Quarterly, The Massachusetts Review,* and *The New Criterion.*

DEREK MCKOWN'S poems, essays, and reviews have been published in many noted journals and anthologies, including *Packinghouse Review, Miramar, Quarterly West, Sentence, Bear Flag Republic: Prose Poems and Poetics from California, Aspects of Robinson: Homage to Weldon Kees,* and *A Condition of the Spirit: The Life and Work of Larry Levis.* His book of poetry is *Arrows in Hand* (Greenhouse Review Press, 2008). He has taught creative writing and literature at several universities and colleges in California, Texas, and New York over the past twenty years, and presently teaches in the Writing and English Departments at Ithaca College in Ithaca, NY.

RICHARD ROBBINS has published six books of poems, most recently *Body Turn to Rain: New & Selected Poems* (Lynx House Press, 2017). He has received awards from The Loft, the Minnesota State Arts Board, the National Endowment for the Arts, and the Poetry Society of America. From 1986 - 2014, Robbins directed the Good Thunder Reading Series at Minnesota State University Mankato, where he continues to direct the creative writing program.

DAVID ST. JOHN has been honored with the Rome Fellowship and the Award in Literature from the American Academy and Institute of Arts and Letters, the O.B. Hardison Prize for teaching and poetic achievement from the Folger Shakespeare Library, and the George Drury Smith Lifetime Achievement Award from Beyond Baroque. He is the author of twelve collections of poetry: *Study for the World's Body* (1994), which was nominated for the National Book Award, and more recently the *The Auroras* (2012), *The Window* (2014), and *The Last Troubadour: Selected and New Poems* (2017). St. John is also the author of a volume of essays, interviews and reviews entitled *Where the Angels Come Toward Us* (1995) and is coeditor of *American Hybrid: A Norton Anthology of New Poetry* (2009). He lives in Venice Beach, California.

M.L. WILLIAMS is the author of the chapbook *Other Medicines* and co-editor of *How Much Earth: The Fresno Poets.* He co-emcees the Poetry corner of the *Los Angeles Times* Festival of Books and teaches creative writing and contemporary literature at Valdosta State University in Georgia. His book *Game* will be published by What Books Press in Fall 2021.

GARY YOUNG'S most recent books are *Precious Mirror,* translations from the Japanese (White Pine Press, 2018) and *That's What I Thought,* which won the Lexi Rudnitsky Editor's Choice Award (Persea Books, 2018). His book *No Other Life* won the William Carlos Williams Award, and in 2009 he received the Shelley Memorial Award from the Poetry Society of America. Young teaches creative writing and directs the Cowell Press at the University of California Santa Cruz.